Andrew M. Gre[eley] P9-DGX-977

Director,
Center for the Study of American Pluralism
at the National Opinion Research Center,
The University of Chicago

Academic Advisor in Sociology
Peter H. Rossi
Johns Hopkins University

The Denominational Society

A Sociological Approach to Religion in America

Scott, Foresman and Company
Glenview, Illinois   *London*

Preface

This is a book about American religion. Although it is an exercise in
the sociology of religion, it does not pretend to be a comprehensive
textbook on the sociology of religion. Such comprehensive textbooks
of varying quality exist, but I am sure that I have neither the tempera-
ment nor the inclination to enter another competitor to the list of such
books. This volume is, rather, a sociological book about American
religion. It is a book written from a definite perspective, and those
sociological writings on the subject of American religion which do not
fit in with this perspective will not be considered.

Nor is the book a comprehensive compilation of source material
about American religion. Such source material is available in a wide
variety of different places and a new compilation of it might be definitely in order, but if this is to be done, someone else will have to
do it. There will be some history and the data will be pieced together
in what the author hopes is not too much of a patchwork fabric—a
fabric designed to clothe a very definite morphology of American
religion.

This volume, then, is neither a source book nor a textbook, but
an *interpretation*—an attempt to order some of the most fascinating
data that can be observed in the American religious scene. Whether
my perspective and my interpretation can qualify to be categorized
as a "model" (to use the currently fashionable terms), or perhaps
even better, as a "theory" (*Deo adjuvante*) will be for others to
judge. It is a perspective and interpretation which enables me to
understand somewhat better the rich complexity of American religious behavior. If it helps others to order this complexity, or even
stimulates them to develop their own perspective and their own interpretation, so much the better.

It is primarily a volume for students. If any book at all is going
to be put in the hands of young people as they begin a course in the

sociology of religion, I should like to think that it is one that will challenge them, and the best way of challenging them is to present them with an interpretation that may anger them, affront them, infuriate them, enlighten them, and above all, make them think. Information, they can get elsewhere; I would much prefer that they will want to argue while they are reading this volume, for I suspect arguing with the teacher is the best part of the educational experience.

I would also hope the volume might be of interest to the now almost mythical "general reader" who is curious about religion in American society and wishes that someone would try to explain to him whether there is any rhyme or reason in American religious behavior. Perhaps for some readers this book will play the same important part in developing their own religious thinking that Will Herberg's *Protestant, Catholic, and Jew* [1] did for me almost a decade and a half ago. If it does, then I shall be delighted indeed.

Finally, I am encouraged to think that the book could also be of some use to religious leaders, lay and clerical, in American society, many of whom are all ready to pontificate about what sociologists say without having gone through the perhaps unpleasant task of actually reading what sociologists have written. I fear that these readers will probably find more in the present volume to infuriate them than will students, the general reader, or even social science scholars, however. But then any Irishman who writes a book that doesn't infuriate people is bound to be disappointed.

My intellectual debt to Clifford Geertz is immense. His way of viewing American religion has shaped my way both professionally and personally. My colleagues at the National Opinion Research Center through the years have provided many helpful insights, particularly Peter H. Rossi, James A. Davis, and Norman Bradburn. Nella Seifert, Virginia Quinn, and Julie Antelman have seen the typing through many difficult and parlous days. My students in the sociology of religion class which I have taught intermittently at the University of Chicago have provided me with many stimulating ideas. But just as I expect to claim credit for whatever strength this book has, so I will take full responsibility for all its weaknesses.

ANDREW M. GREELEY

---

[1] Will Herberg, *Protestant, Catholic, and Jew* (Garden City, N.Y.: Doubleday & Company, Inc., 1955).

Table of Contents

Introduction   1

Chapter 1   The Nature of Religion   5

In Search of a Definition   5
Man and the Sacred   10
Styles of Religion   18
Dimensions of Religion   21
Summary   28

Chapter 2   The Origins and Functions of Religion   30

Functionalism: a Sense of Belonging   31
A Source of Meaning   38
The Comfort Theory   63
Summary   69

Chapter 3   Religion as an Organization   71

Definitions of Sect and Church   71
Institutional Religion   79
Summary   85

Chapter 4   The Present Condition
of American Religion   86

Some Comments on Statistics   86
The Basic Facts   89
Religion and Social Class   93
Religious Beliefs   94
The Overview of the Denominational Society   102
Summary   107

Chapter 5   Religion as an Ethnic Phenomenon   108

Ethnicity Defined   109
The Ethnic Role of the Churches   115
Catholic Ethnic Groups   119
Summary   125

Chapter 6 The Secularization Myth 127

Secularization Defined 128
Theories of Secularization 132
A Look at the Data 136
Religion and Youth 142
Secularity and Religiousness 151
Summary *154*

Chapter 7 The Civil Religion 156

The Religion of Americanism 156
Civic Religion Evaluated 167
"The Times of Trial" 170
Summary *173*

Chapter 8 Diversity Within Unity 175

Protestants 175
Catholics 186
Jews 194
Summary *203*

Chapter 9 Religion, Prejudice, and Conflict 205

Religious Attitudes Correlate with Prejudice 206
Sources of Friction 213
Jews Versus Catholics 223
Summary *226*

Chapter 10 Growing Up Religious 227

A Pattern of Values 227
Identifying One's Place in Society 231
Must One be a Martyr to be Religious? 233
Summary *234*

Chapter 11 Theories and Predictions 236

Apostasy 237
Intermarriage 244
Ecumenism 247
The Relationship Between Meaning and Belonging 248
The Future of Religion 249
Summary *251*

Bibliography 255

Index 259

Tables

1 American Denominations 89
2 Continuities in Religious Beliefs and Behavior 95
3 Belief in God 98
4 Belief in the Divinity of Jesus 100
5 Additional Beliefs about Jesus 101
6 Selected Attributes of Catholic Ethnic Groups in U.S. 121
7 Selected Attributes of Catholic Ethnic Groups in U.S.
   —High-school Graduates of Third or Later Generation Only 124
8 Continuities in Religious Beliefs and Behavior 137
9 Changes in Religious Beliefs and Behavior 139
10 Changing Attitudes Among Catholics 140
11 Trends in Attitudinal Change Among Catholics by Age and Education 140
12 Religious Attitudes of Young People 143
13 Religious Affiliation of Arts and Sciences Graduate Students in Top Twelve Universities 145
14 Church Attendance of Graduate Students by Religion (Original Religion) 146
15 Church Attendance by Religion by Field 147
16 Religion and Attitudes Toward Academia 148
17 Religious Catholics and Attitudes Toward Academia 149
18 Level of Religious Observance by Generation, Descent, and Parents' Level of Home Observances 201
19 Church Attendance and Prejudice Among Faculty Members of a Midwestern University 207
20 Prejudice and Religious Orientation 209
21 Attitudes of Jews and Catholics Toward Each Other, 1952 and 1965 225
22 Net and Gross Loss for Major American Religious Groups 238
23 Sources of Conversions for Protestants and Catholics 238
24 Character of Protestant Leavers (1961 and 1968) and Returners (1968) 239
25 Characteristics of Catholic Leavers 240
26 Characteristics of Jewish Returners 241
27 The Joint Effects of Parental Relations and the Personality Predisposition Index on Apostasy in Each Religious Group 243
28 Denominational Intermarriage 245

Introduction

In this volume we will contend that denominationalism is a central characteristic of American religion, and that one cannot understand American religion unless one understands the complex relationships between the denominations and the larger social structures. The United States is a denominational society—indeed, one of the four denominational societies in the Western world. By the denominational society we intend to describe a religious form found only in Canada, the United States, Holland, and Switzerland—that is to say, a relationship between religion and society which is characterized neither by an established church [1] nor protesting sect. Rather, in the United States religion and the rest of society relate to each other through multiple quasi-equal ecclesiastical organizations which are not a halfway house between a sect and the Church but actually a social organizational adjustment to the fact of religious pluralism. Indeed, we will go further and contend that in the absence of understanding the denominations, one cannot understand America society, either.

This attempt at understanding will proceed from a sociological perspective and will attempt to integrate into a social-structural viewpoint some of the findings of history and psychology, as well as the pertinent observations of social criticism—an activity which has always been popular when American religion was the object of the criticism. In the early chapters we will concentrate on the relevance of the literature generally included under the heading Sociology of Religion for coping with the American religious phenomena; and we will conclude that religion provides not merely meaning in the lives of its

---

[1] We use "established" here in the broadest possible sense—that is to say—a nation with a basically one-religion society. Catholicism may not be established in the legal sense in France and yet it is, from the sociological viewpoint, *the* French church.

practitioners but also a sense of belonging, factors which go far toward explaining the role and the power of the denomination. Religion is indeed, as the sociological theorist would tell us, a meaning-giving cultural system, but the religious denomination is also a belonging-providing ethnic group,[2] to use that term in a broad sense.

Therefore, in our model of American religion, we view the denomination as the point of intersection of meaning and belonging functions in a society where an urban industrial social order emerged in a society that had no established church. We will further suggest, therefore, that the failure of the established churches in Europe to hold the urban masses is in part due to the very fact that their establishment made it impossible for them to play the belonging role of the ethnic group at a time when the need for belonging became acute. We will further suggest that the idea advanced by Lipset and Glock [3] and others, that a Western nation going through the industrial revolution either has radical political parties or working-class religious sects as a response to deprivation, is but a specification of a wider phenomenon. In the disorganization, personal and social, that occurs as a part of the pilgrimage from the peasant communalism to the industrial city, man attempted and still attempts to compensate for the deprivation he endures and for the absence of the social support and the intimacy of the village by evolving quasi-*Gemeinschaft* [4] institutions—the nationality group, the lower-class religious sect, the radical political party and, in the United States and Canada, the denomination. The deprivation involved need not (and here we go beyond Glock and Lipset) be economic; it can be social and human.

The model of a denominational society is advanced to improve our understanding and not to provide a causal explanation. Interrelationships between denominationalism and social structure in the United States are too complex to be explained by simple causal links. The model of the denominational society is a way of ordering and

---

[2] As we shall make clear in a later section of this work, ethnic group here is being used in a broader sense than a mere nationality group; Max Weber's favorite description of the role of ethnic groups will be of particular importance to us in subsequent chapters.

[3] Seymour Martin Lipset and Charles Y. Glock—both men and their writings will be referred to in considerable detail in later chapters.

[4] *Gemeinschaft* society is one in which human living is guided in part by traditional, sacred, and ascriptive norms of behavior. *Gesellschaft* society, on the other hand, is marked by achievement, universality, rationality, and secularity. The typical *Gemeinschaft* relationship is with one's cousin or one's brother; the typical *Gesellschaft* relationship is one with the man who drives the bus on which one rides to work. The former is personal and informal; the latter is impersonal and quite formal. A typical *Gemeinschaft* community is the peasant village in which our ancestors were born; a typical *Gesellschaft* community is New York City or Los Angeles.

viewing the complex phenomena of American religion. It exists at a rather low level of abstraction though one suspects that high levels of abstraction are either not possible or very useful. Whether this model could be dignified with a title of social theory or not depends on how one chooses to define social theory. It is very much to be feared that the categories and analysis used in this book will be far too concrete and probably far too clear to satisfy the rigorous demands of contemporary sociological theorists. However, the model will provide what much sociological theory does not seem to provide—testable hypotheses.

We are suggesting, therefore, that religion in America takes the denominational structure for the following reasons:

1. The religiously pluralistic origins of the original colonies made impossible the appearance of an established church.

2. The deprivation, social disorganization, and anomie of the immigration from Europe to America and from peasant village to industrial metropolis created a "belonging vacuum" which converted religious denominations from being merely meaning-giving agencies to becoming also providers of belonging. Christian religions in particular have had strong theoretical tendencies to become providers of "community" for the relatively undifferentiated *Gemeinschaft* society. In such a society membership in the Church was the same as membership in the society. There the community-providing function of religion was neither possible nor necessary. American denominations emerged as quasi-*Gemeinschaft* groups precisely because at the same time in history the religious pluralism in the United States made a distinction between membership in a society and membership in a church possible and the industrial revolutions made quasi-*Gemeinschaft* groups such as the American denominations necessary.

Whether someone who himself is, to use the modern term, a religionist, is better qualified to write about religion or not seems to be a question that can never be solved. He who is inside religion has some advantages over him who is outside. But, in any case, the reader who wishes to be alert to biases should be warned that the present writer is, in fact, a member of an American denomination—indeed, one which claims to be the oldest of the Christian denominations. More than that, he is a religious functionary in this denomination, though not (popular misunderstanding to the contrary) a Jesuit. However, although the writer is a Catholic priest, let it be noted that he is also a profoundly skeptical and at times even a cynical one and, as his writing will probably make clear, a profound disbeliever in "party lines," be they to the left, to the right, or in the center.

The first three chapters of the book will attempt to describe the tools of the sociology of religion which are particularly relevant to the model we are trying to build. The remaining chapters will look at the present condition of American religion and attempt to explain the meaning of religious phenomena to be observed in our society. The last two chapters will summarize our model, the penultimate by describing the process of "growing up religious," and the final one, by specifying somewhat formally the testable hypotheses which we might derive from our theory and by submitting two such hypotheses to actual tests.

Chapter 1

The Nature of Religion

In this chapter we will attempt to define religion from the sociological viewpoint and then to define religion's correlate, "the sacred." We will conclude with an elaboration of styles and dimensions of religious behavior, so that in the very beginning of our attempt to understand American religion we will be prepared with the knowledge that religion is an immensely differentiated kind of human behavior.

In Search of a Definition

One cannot even approach the question of defining religion without becoming involved in controversy. There are almost as many definitions of religion as there are authors, though in recent years two categories of definitions seem to have developed; the basic difference between the two categories depends on whether the definer wishes to include a transcendental or supernatural object as part of the definition. The question is complicated by the related controversy of whether religion is universal or not. If you postulate some sort of supernatural object as part of religion, then clearly some men do not have a religion, and herein would be included not merely agnostics and atheists in modern Western society, but also followers of many of the forms of Buddhism in Eastern civilizations. On the other hand, if religion is merely man's "ultimate concern," as Paul Tillich suggests, then every man is to some extent religious because every man has ultimate concerns in some fashion or another.

Professor J. Paul Williams follows this latter viewpoint in defining religion:

Religiousness is a mental quality which modifies certain aspects of the life of individuals (and through individuals of groups); this quality must have each of the following characteristics in some degree:

a belief-attitude that the Ultimate for man exists (however it may be conceived) and that certain aspects of life derive from the Ultimate;

a belief-attitude that the derivation (from the Ultimate) of these aspects of life is beyond empirical demonstration;

a belief-attitude that these aspects of life are of supreme importance (at least potentially) for the concern of the individual (and perhaps of groups and/or all men).[1]

Under such a definition may be included not only the traditional religions, but also such variant forms of value systems as communism, socialism, Nazism, liberal humanism, and those elements with agnostic orientations within Unitarianism, Ethical Culture, Quakerism, and other quasi-Protestant groups in American society. A number of modern writers are in agreement with Williams such as Horace Kallen, Thomas Luckmann, and Milton Yinger.

However, other writers are inclined to a more traditional view of religion and require some notion of "the transcendental," "the supernatural," or "the sacred" as part of their definition of religion. The most elaborate implication of such a definition has been enunciated by Professor Talcott Parsons:

A religion we will define as a set of beliefs, practices, and institutions which men have evolved in various societies, so far as they can be understood, as responses to those aspects of their life and situation which are believed not in the empirical-instrumental sense to be rationally understandable and/or controllable, and to which they attach a significance which includes some kind of reference to the relevant actions and events to man's conception of the existence of a "supernatural" order which is conceived and felt to have a fundamental bearing on man's position in the universe and the values which give meaning to his fate as an individual and his relations to his fellows.

Defined in this way a religion or religious system will include at a minimum: (1) a more or less integrated set of beliefs concerning entities which are "supernatural," sacred, or as Durkheim

---

[1] J. Paul Williams, "The Nature of Religion," *Journal for the Scientific Study of Religion*, 2 (Fall 1962): 8. Reprinted by permission of the author and the Society for the Scientific Study of Religion.

said, "set apart" from the ordinary objects and events of utilitarian or instrumental significance for human affairs and interests, on his relation to which the meaning of man's life is fundamentally dependent; (2) a system of symbols, objects, acts, persons, empirical and nonempirical, which have the quality of sacredness and in relation to which men express the emotional states relevant to the religious sphere, in short, a system of expressive symbols; (3) a set of more or less definitely prescribed activities which are interpreted as important and often obligatory in the light of the beliefs involved, but which from the point of view of the instrumental interests of daily life are "useless" in that they do not "accomplish anything." These activities will usually be prescribed for different types of occasions, forbidden on others and may be differentiated for different statuses in the social group; (4) to some degree a sense that "we" who share common beliefs of this character, and participate in what is felt to be an integrated system of such activities, constitute a "collectivity"— a group which by virtue of that fact is bound together in what Durkheim called a "moral community"; finally, (5) a sense that man's relation to the supernatural world is in some way intimately connected with his moral values, with the nature of the goals he is called upon to live for, and the rules of conduct he is expected to comply with. The sharing of these common moral values as well as more specifically "religious" beliefs and practices will be constitutive of the moral community spoken of above.[2]

Emile Durkheim and William James, from days gone by, and Clifford Geertz, Charles Glock, and Louis Schneider, among others of the contemporary observers of religion, seem to postulate some sort of element of the sacred as part of an essential definition of religion. Professor Glock, for example, resolves the problems as follows:

1) Value orientations are those institutionalized systems of beliefs, values, symbols and practices that are concerned with the solution of questions of ultimate meaning. Such orientations are a universal feature of human societies and are mutually exclusive.

2) Value orientations may have a supernatural referent (religious perspectives), or they may not (humanist perspectives).

3) Both alternative forms are on the same level of abstraction

[2] Talcott Parsons: "Sociology and Social Psychology" in *Religious Perspectives in College Teaching* by Hoxie N. Fairchild, et al. Copyright © 1952 The Ronald Press Company, New York.

and are functionally equivalent, although they may have some-
what different consequences for other societal institutions.[3]

The controversy over whether religion requires a sacred or transcendental or supernatural object in a definition is not trivial at the
beginning of a study of American religion. There are a number of
value systems of considerable importance in American society which
do not postulate the existence of a God or, indeed, any transcendental
elements. The convinced communist, or Unitarian, or secular humanist, or even "hippie" is very likely to have a creed, a code, and a cult
of his own, complete with myths and dogmas and ritual observances.
The UNICEF Christmas card, the quotation from *The New Republic*
or I. F. Stone, faith in progress through science, belief in the con-
spiracies of the Establishment, devotion to the American Civil Liber-
ties Union and the American Association of University Professors,
grave suspicion of Irish politicians (or Texas ones), idolization of
"the workers" or "the blacks" or "the intellectual"—all of these, at
least to some devotees, have a strong religious aura about them, particularly for those secular humanists who have come from strong religious family backgrounds against which they have rebelled.

The civil religion (or American Way of Life religion) which
Robert Bellah describes (and which we will examine in detail in
Chapter 7) is so vague and deistic that if one insists on the transcendental as an essential of religion it may be problematic whether it can
be called a religion. However, one need not agree with any or all of
the above-mentioned values to observe that in many instances they do
seem to assume the cloak of religion.

It will help us to understand the implications of this controversy
about the definition of religion if we pause to reflect that only in contemporary society has the problem arisen, for only in the modern
world has it been possible for there to be overarching systems of explanation which are not precisely the same as the religion that society
professes. This is not to say that at other points in history there were
not individuals whose value systems differed sharply from the official
religion of society but only that the value systems of the overwhelming majority of human beings were intimately identified with religion.
However, in the contemporary world, as Thomas Luckmann has
shown (in a book we shall discuss later on), organized religion represents only one of the value systems competing in the open marketplace for popular attention.

The reader must judge for himself which definition he finds

[3] Charles Y. Glock and Rodney Stark, *Religion and Society in Tension*, ©
1965 by Rand McNally & Company, Chicago, pp. 11–12. Reprinted by permission
of Rand McNally College Publishing Company, Chicago.

preferable. If he chooses the traditional definition, then he would exclude from consideration of American religion a number of groups which play a role in the lives of their members quite similar to that which the organized churches play in the lives of their members. If, on the other hand, he chooses the newer definition, he seems to exclude the important element of the sacred or of "the totally other" from his definition of religion.

It is possible that a compromise between the two can be found. One might argue that man has a tendency to sacralize his ultimate systems of value. Even if one excludes the possibility of a transcendent or a supernatural, one nonetheless is very likely to treat one's system of ultimate explanation with a great deal of jealous reverence and respect and to be highly incensed when someone else calls the system of explanation to question or behaves contrary to it. It is precisely this tendency to sacralize one's ultimate concern that might well explain the many quasi-religious phenomena to be observed in organizations which officially proclaim their non- or even anti-religiousness. The communist, for example, may vehemently deny the existence of a "totally other" and yet treat his communism and its prophets, its dogmas, its code, and its ritual with as much respect as does the devout Christian approach his religion. This may not quite make communism a "totally other" for its members, but it certainly does suggest that the transcendent may be lurking in places where one would least expect to find it.

A definition which seems to take into account this "straining toward the sacred" is furnished by Clifford Geertz:

> . . . *a* religion *is:*
>
> *(1) a system of symbols which acts to*
>
> *(2) establish powerful, pervasive, and long-lasting moods and motivations in men by*
>
> *(3) formulating conceptions of a general order of existence and*
>
> *(4) clothing these conceptions with such an aura of factuality that*
>
> *(5) the moods and motivations seem uniquely realistic.*[4]

Religion, then, may not necessarily explicitly speak of transcendence or the sacred, but it does provide conceptions of a general order of existence and makes the moods and motivations resulting from

---

[4] Clifford Geertz, "Religion as a Cultural System," in *Anthropological Approaches to the Study of Religion,* ed. Michael Banton (New York: Praeger Publishers, Inc., 1966), p. 4. Reprinted with permission of the Association of Social Anthropologists.

such conceptions seem uniquely realistic. One need only add that for most Americans in most societies at most times this uniquely realistic dimension of religion implies the "totally other," the transcendent, the sacred.

Man and the Sacred

Leaving aside, therefore, the question of whether man necessarily sacralizes his ultimate concern, and whether therefore there must be a sacred dimension in the life of every man, we must turn to the question of the sacred, for under all definitions discussed in the previous section, where there is the sacred, there is also religion.

We use the word sacred so frequently in our conversation and so loosely that it is difficult to say precisely what it is. We are quite clear that some things are sacred—the Roman Catholic Mass, the speaking of tongues at a Pentecostal meeting, the hearthfire of the family in the Roman Republic, the rite of passage for an adolescent in a primitive tribe. We are also quite conscious that many other things are not sacred, at least not for most people—turning on the ignition key in a car, opening a book, dialing a number on the telephone, walking across the street. Unfortunately, there are a number of phenomena which are not so easily categorized—the funeral of John Kennedy, the celebration of Memorial Day and the Fourth of July, described so astutely by Lloyd Warner in his *Yankee City* [5] series, the singing of the national anthem before an athletic contest, and the recitation of the Lord's Prayer by the Green Bay Packers after they have disposed of yet another hapless foe.

The sacred clearly is something which leads us to behave with reverence and respect—something out of the ordinary, something apart from the mundane experience of everyday life—though just as clearly, not everything that is extraordinary is sacred and what is sacred for one man need not be sacred for another, even if they share a common religious faith. Thus, some Catholics felt that Pope Paul vi's visit to New York and the United Nations was a highly sacred event while others no less devout in their Catholicism were hardly moved by the Papal visitation.

Under such circumstances, we will not be able to evolve a definition of the sacred that will tell us precisely where the line between the sacred and its opposite, the profane, can be drawn, but we can at

[5] W. Lloyd Warner, ed., *Yankee City* (New Haven, Conn.: Yale University Press, 1963).

least listen to some of the voices who have attempted to describe sacredness so as to get a "feel" of what it really is. A category of thought and response so basic to human life probably cannot be defined in any other way.

In the third lecture of his classic, *The Varieties of Religious Experience,* William James has a collection of superb descriptions of man's encounter with "the other."

> *I remember the night, and almost the very spot on the hilltop, where my soul opened out, as it were, into the Infinite, and there was a rushing together of the two worlds, the inner and the outer. It was deep calling unto deep—the deep that my own struggle had opened up within being answered by the unfathomable deep without, reaching beyond the stars. I stood alone with Him who had made me, and all the beauty of the world, and love, and sorrow, and even temptation. I did not seek Him, but felt the perfect unison of my spirit with His. The ordinary sense of things around me faded. For the moment nothing but an ineffable joy and exaltation remained. It is impossible fully to describe the experience. It was like the effect of some great orchestra when all the separate notes have melted into one swelling harmony that leaves the listener conscious of nothing save that his soul is being wafted upwards, and almost bursting with its own emotion. The perfect stillness of the night was thrilled by a more solemn silence. The darkness held a presence that was all the more felt because it was not seen. I could not any more have doubted that He was there than that I was. Indeed, I felt myself to be, if possible, the less real of the two.*[6]

After reading such a paragraph, one is reminded of Duke Ellington's definition of rhythm: "If you got it you don't need a definition, and if you haven't got it no definition will help." Ecstatic experiences of the sort just described don't happen to everybody, and even minor religious ecstasies are anything but universal. However, one can take it as pretty well established that some form of contact with the sacred, in a very much diminished fashion, perhaps, occurs for most men at most times in human history.

Are there other kinds of ecstasy besides the sacred? My colleague, Philip Ennis, suggests that there may be. He quotes:

> *Mannheim: "It is that achieving from time to time a certain distance from his own situation and from the world is one of*

[6] William James, *The Varieties of Religious Experience* (New York: The New American Library, Inc., 1961), p. 67.

the fundamental traits of man as a truly human being"; Weber ". . . a state of possession, not action, and the individual is not a tool but a vessel *of the divine"; and Freud: "A peculiar feeling . . . of something limitless, unbounded, something 'oceanic . . .' "—have all described the ecstatic experience even though admitting that they did not fully understand it.*[7]

With an exercise of wit that is not particularly common in sociology, Ennis suggests that a machine might be built which could produce the ecstatic experience of man's "being outside himself":

In principle it is quite easy to make an ecstasy machine. You build, in an empty lot, a high circular fence with a small door. Inside the fence, there is either a deep well that goes down to nowhere or a high ladder that goes up to nowhere. The direction is a matter of taste. Then you let people in a few at a time—you can't let everyone in because someone has to watch the store. Before you let them down into the well or up onto the ladder, you tie a rope around their waist to make sure you can get them back. Since the capacity for ecstasy varies among individuals, as does their height and weight, people can climb down or up as far as they like to find their level of ecstatic satisfaction.

This, in essence, is the architectural mode of the cathedral, the theatre, the lover's couch and the bottle. For separately and in various combinations, the institutions of religion, the arts, of love, and finally alcohol and other drugs have all been charged at one point or another in history with the mission of being the vehicle of legitimate ecstatic transcendence.

These are not the only forms containing ecstatic behavior, of course. Three others might be mentioned briefly; first is the political community itself, with the symbols and actuality of state power as the core ecstatic object. Second is the world of rational mastery, the institutions of science and industry, in short, work. *Even though work in the everyday world appears the very antithesis of the state of ecstasy, there are interesting modulations between the two that conceivably could be effective for some people. Finally, there is insanity and psychosis. This path to transcendence has enjoyed a recent vogue, but it seems too disorderly for the fastidious and too irreversible for many to emulate.*[8]

[7] Philip Ennis, "Ecstasy and Everyday Life," *Journal for the Scientific Study of Religion*, 6 (No. 1 (Spring 1967): 42. Reprinted with permission of the author and the Society for the Scientific Study of Religion.
[8] Ibid., p. 43.

Thus, there are many phenomena that can occur in man's life which can take him outside himself, giving him the feeling of being released from the bonds of limitation, matter, and mortality, and putting him in touch with the transcendent. By no means are all of them religious, though there does seem to be a tendency to equate many of them with religion—for example, the frequent use of religious terms in describing the effects of the hallucinogenic drugs. However, if not all ecstatic experiences are religious, some of them are; and men who have experienced the ecstasy of art or of love (much less alcohol) describe them as though there are similarities in the various experiences.

Perhaps the classic description of man's reaction to that which he perceives as sacred comes from the German philosopher and theologian Rudolf Otto in his famous *Das Heilige*. In describing phenomenologically man's behavior toward the sacred, Otto says that there is first of all a feeling of terror in the face of the sacred, terror in the face of the awe-inspiring majesty and the fascinating mystery which results from man's contact with what Otto describes as the numinous —an experience of the revelation of an aspect of divine power. The numinous appears as something "wholly other," something basically and totally different from man and before which he feels, as Abraham did before the Lord, that he is nothing "but dust and ashes." [9]

That the sacred is the "totally other" which inspires both dread and fascination is also the conclusion of sociologist Emile Durkheim. He sees man dividing reality into two worlds, the world of the sacred and the world of the profane:

> *This heterogeneity is even so complete that it frequently degenerates into a veritable antagonism. The two worlds are not only conceived of as separate, but as even hostile and jealous rivals of each other. . . . The sacred thing is* par excellence *that which the profane should not touch and cannot touch with impunity. . . . Sacred things are those which interdictions protect and isolate; profane things, those to which these interdictions are applied and which must remain at a distance from the first. Religious beliefs are the representations which express the nature of sacred things and the relations which they sustain, either with each other or with profane things.*[10]

[9] Rudolf Otto, *Idea of the Holy*, 2nd ed., trans. J. W. Harvey (New York: Oxford University Press, Inc., 1950).

[10] Reprinted with permission of The Macmillan Company and George Allen & Unwin Ltd. from *The Elementary Forms of Religious Life* by Emile Durkheim. Copyright 1915 by Allen & Unwin, Ltd. First Free Press Paperback edition, 1963.

Thus, for Durkheim religion itself is the very act of separating the sacred from the profane. As we shall see, man makes this distinction, in Durkheim's view, precisely because he is awed by the tremendous and fascinating power of society.

The most careful students of the sacred at the present time are a group of scholars who used to be called comparative religionists and are now called historians of religion. These men, of whom perhaps the most famous is Mircea Eliade, have attempted to find common patterns of religious behavior running through all, or almost all, of the religious systems man has devised for himself. For Eliade the sacred is "the manifestation of something of a wholly different order, a reality that does not belong to our world, in objects that are an integral part of our natural 'profane' world." [11] There are, for example, two kinds of space—the ordinary, everyday space in which ordinary, everyday events take place and "sacred space," that which man experiences as a manifestation of divinity. But more than this, "sacred space" is the real space and other space receives its reality from the sacral space. "In the homogeneous and infinite expanse, in which no point of reference is possible and hence no *orientation* can be established, the hierophany reveals absolute fixed point, a center." [12] Eliade goes on to say:

> So it is clear to what a degree the discovery—that is, the revelation—of a sacred space possesses existential value for religious man; for nothing can begin, nothing can be done, without a previous orientation—and any orientation implies acquiring a fixed point. It is for this reason that religious man has always sought to fix his abode at the "center of the world." If the world is to be lived in, it must be founded—and no world can come to birth in the chaos of the homogeneity and relativity of profane space. The discovery or projection of a fixed point—the center —is equivalent to the creation of the world; and we shall soon give some examples that will unmistakably show the cosmogonic value of the ritual orientation and construction of sacred space.
>
> For profane experience, on the contrary, space is homogeneous and neutral; no break qualitatively differentiates the various parts of its mass. Geometrical space can be cut and delimited in any direction; but no qualitative differentiation and, hence, no orientation are given by virtue of its inherent structure. We need only remember how a classical geometrician defines space. Nat-

---

[11] Mircea Eliade, *The Sacred and the Profane* (New York: Harcourt Brace Jovanovich, Inc., 1959), p. 11. Used by permission of Rowohlt Verlag. © 1957 by Rowohlt Taschenbuch Verlag GmbH, Hamburg.

[12] Ibid., pp. 20–21.

urally, we must not confuse the concept *of homogeneous and neutral geometrical space with the* experience *of profane space, which is in direct contrast to the experience of sacred space and which alone concerns our investigation.*[13]

The sacred, then, according to Eliade, is experienced by religious man as the "totally other" breaking in to ordinary experience and giving order and meaning to them. Just as sacred space (ground for worship or a temple or merely a tabooed area) gives meaning to ordinary space, so there are sacred times which give meaning to ordinary times and sacred rights which give meaning to ordinary behavior. Eliade and his colleagues find that in most human religions there are certain key manifestations of the sacred—the sky, the sun, the moon, water, stones, earth, fertility, and trees, or on occasion, simply a tree. The explanation of these nearly universal patterns is not always the same. Some writers lean to a version of Jung's collective unconsciousness; others speak of the structure of the human personality; and still others speak of "the patterns of man's reaction to existential situation." We probably do not know at present enough about cross-cultural psychology to explain, for example, why in most religions water has both the birth and death sacred symbolism, but the fact remains that it does, and that sacred water bringing life and death apparently enables religious man to explain the tremendous power that water exercises in human life.

If one tries to collect the strands of thought from Otto, Ennis, Durkheim, and Eliade, one can say at a minimum that man's behavior in relationship to the sacred is a form of being impressed with the extraordinary; for whatever else the sacred is, it is not ordinary, and however else man behaves toward it, he does not take it lightly. Clifford Geertz tells the story of a rather pedestrian manifestation of the extraordinary:

When a peculiarly shaped, rather large toadstool grew up in a carpenter's house in the short space of a few days (or, some said, a few hours), people came from miles around to see it, and everyone had some sort of explanation—some animist, some animatist, some not quite either—for it. Yet it would be hard to argue that the toadstool had any social value in Radcliffe-Brown's sense, . . . or that it was connected in any way with anything which did and for which it could have been standing proxy, like the Andaman cicada. Toadstools play about the same role in Javanese life as they do in ours, and in the ordinary course of things Javanese have about as much interest in them as we do. It was

[13] Ibid., pp. 204–205.

*just that this one was "odd," "strange," "uncanny"—aneh. And
the odd, strange, and uncanny simply must be accounted for.
Or, again, the conviction must be sustained that it could be accounted for. One does not shrug off a toadstool which grows five
times as fast as a toadstool has any right to grow. In the broadest
sense, the "strange" toadstool did have implications, and critical
ones, for those who heard about it. It threatened their most general ability to understand the world, raised the uncomfortable
question of whether the beliefs which they held about nature
were workable, the standards of truth they used valid.*[14]

Geertz's toadstool in itself may not be quite sacred, but at least
it was such a challenge to his Javanese friends that they had to fall
back on their religion to find an explanation for it. One can, of course,
say that religion is necessary to explain everything extraordinary that
happens, but there are certain kinds of extraordinariness which for
most men thus far in human history religion has been the appropriate
answer.

As one reads through the literature of the sacred, it begins to become clear that there are two kinds of extraordinariness in particular
which seem to produce reactions that traditionally have been called
religious. One is that kind of phenomenon which simultaneously imposes upon man a demand for explanation and also provides him with
an explanation. The second is that sort of phenomenon which both
imposes on man and provides him with a sense of being profoundly
related to his fellowmen. Sacredness, then, relates to man's experience
of the need for meaning and the need for belonging, as well as the
fulfillment of these needs. Not all meaning and all belonging, of course,
excite sacred attitudes and behavior, but more precisely those which
in some fashion or other fall into the area of the ultimate can be expected to produce in men reverence and awe for something that is outside themselves and belongs to the "totally other."

One can think of many examples of both aspects of the sacred.
Geertz's toadstool was so out of the ordinary that it demanded an explanation lest it disrupt man's conviction about the order of nature.
Kennedy's funeral was a means of reaffirming faith in American society. The fertility rites of the nature religions which Eliade discusses
at great length were designed as an intermediate step between the
annual planting, cultivating, and harvesting of crops and the sacred
realities which this process reflected. The God word "Ford" in Huxley's book, *Brave New World,* is a wonderful invention to indicate the
evocation of a mystical response in a technological society.

[14] Geertz, op. cit., p. 16.

Similarly, the worship owed by a Roman at the time of the Republic to his ancestors and, in fact, the organization of much of the society around the principles of this worship was an affirmation of man's unity with his family and his people. The rites of passage in primitive (and some not so primitive) religions which mark major points in the life cycle—birth, adolescence, marriage, maturity—thus reassure man at critical times in his life that he is indeed part of something larger than himself. The civil religion of American society described by Robert Bellah (to which we will turn later) based on such national demigods as George Washington and Abraham Lincoln, such national myths as the Civil War, such national feasts as Memorial Day, the Fourth of July, and Thanksgiving, reaffirm the basic unity of American society. Man wants to know "why" and "with whom." The sacred represents the ultimate responses to these questions.

It hardly need be affirmed that the two questions are very closely connected. As Thomas Luckmann (to whom we will turn later, also) says, the tradition of Weber which describes religion generally as meaning and the tradition of Durkheim which describes religion generally as belonging, can easily be harmonized. Man learns his interpretation of reality through social interaction. He is able to explain the apparently disordered phenomena around him precisely insofar as he is integrated into a culture which transmits to him as part of his socialization process a series of propositions and attitudes which enable him to interpret life. Similarly, it is the sharing of explanations and interpretations which provide the common bonds of unity and enables man to unite himself with his fellowmen. Over most human history religion has provided meaning and belonging simultaneously. Religious men would not have seen much point in a distinction. However, as we shall observe later in this book, these two aspects of religion have been divorced in the modern urban industrial world and there has been a strong tendency by those who try to analyze religion to emphasize one aspect or the other. Most recently in the United States, it seems that the social scientists choosing Weber over Durkheim have emphasized the meaning dimension of religion, while the religious critics have emphasized the belonging dimension of American religion, a dimension which, by the way, they distinctly dislike. We will contend that only by giving serious consideration to both elements of religion are we able to understand why America has become a denominational society.

We can now address ourselves once again to the question of whether all men are religious, defining religious as relating in some fashion or other explicitly to the sacred. We can say, first of all, that most men in most societies have been more or less religious. Some anthropologists such as Geertz suggest that there has been too much emphasis on the "more" and not enough on the "less," and that unbelief and skepticism are by no means modern phenomena. He even goes so far as to suggest that some day a book might be called *Faith and Hypocrisy in the Primitive World.*

The degree to which men are religious, one supposes among other things, is also the need created by their physiological and psychological systems for explicit affirmation of meaning and fellowship. He who for one reason or another does not need explicitly or consciously to affirm "the relatively modest dogma that God is not mad" (Geertz's phrase) and the relatively modest ethic that one's fellowman can generally be trusted, will not be religious. Whether such a superior being, modeled something after the existentialist heroes of Sartre or Camus, staring bravely in the face of meaninglessness and loneliness, is superior or inferior to the religious man is a question which is beyond the scope of this volume.

Styles of Religion

There are a vast number of possibilities available to man to respond to the "totally other," but the choices he makes from the available repertoire of responses are not likely to be random, but rather will fit into some pattern which results from his heredity and environment, from his biology, his physiology, his psychology, his sociology, and his culture; these patterns or styles of religious behavior are different in each one of us, but there are enough similarities in large groups of us that we can speak of certain common religious styles. Perhaps the most impressive effort of elaboration of these styles is to be found in Max Weber's *Sociology of Religion.* He describes at great length the different kinds of religion which appeal to the scholar, to the merchant, to the warrior, to the landed aristocrat, to the slave. We ourselves are quite well aware that in American society a religion with which a Boston Brahman feels comfortable will hardly be satisfactory to a sharecropper in Mississippi or even, for that matter, to a wealthy industrialist in Mississippi; and a divinity student at the University of Chicago will have a different religion than does his grandmother (at least in most circumstances, though nowadays one can never be sure).

An extremely important distinction that we shall use later on in this book is between folk and elite styles of religion. Gustav Mensching points out that a number of things happened to human religion in the millennium before the birth of Christ; the old nature and folk religions based on a local community and profoundly integrated in the food-producing processes were replaced in China, India, Greece, and the Near East by the world religions. There were four elements in this change, according to Mensching:

1. It is the individual, not the group, that is the focus of the new religion.
2. Man no longer felt himself born into a divine relationship, but found himself in a "condition of nonsalvation."
3. Religion was denationalized as man became the object of salvation.
4. A universal religion required spreading the word of salvation to others.[15]

Mensching then goes on to point out that the world religions evolve a complicated theology, moral system, and cultic practice; but he also observes that this high religion is not always satisfactory to the masses. These latter are moved more by the subconscious than by the conscious, more by the unusual and fantastic than by the logical and rational, more by the traditional than by the intellectual, more by the magical than the mystical, and more by the demigod than by the saint. Therefore they select certain propositions, imperatives, and practices from the high religion, rearrange them to suit their own needs, and combine them with the folk traditions of more primitive religions to produce their own particular synthesis of the world religion and the nature religion which it succeeded. The remoteness of a single god made the common man want mediators who would intercede in times of distress. To fill this need, a panoply of saints, who might intercede with God, accumulated in the Catholic Church. Similarly in the Islamic religion, High Islam with its seemingly inaccessible God does not appeal to the masses.[16]

Folk religion is remarkably durable. The banshees of Ireland, the residual witchcraft to be found in England, fertility symbols on farmhouses and taxicab drivers' key chains in Italy, the maypole, the Christmas tree, the divining rod, are all signs that folk religion has survived and still prospers in the Christian world. And Mensching points out that Mazdaism, Buddhism, and Islam have spawned many varieties of folk religion. One might even go so far as to suggest that some of the newer religions, such as Marxism, also seem to have produced their own folk aberrations.

---

[15] Gustav Mensching, "Religion and the Holy," trans. Louis Schneider in *Religion, Culture, and Society,* ed. Louis Schneider (New York: John Wiley & Sons, Inc., 1964).
[16] Ibid.

It must be remembered, therefore, that the tendency for the folk to evolve their own versions of the elite religious traditions is a powerful one; conversely, there is an equally powerful tendency for the elite to denounce the folk for so doing. Students of American religion will not be surprised to find many such denunciations, nor will they be surprised to find that most of the denouncers show little or no sympathetic understanding of why folk versions of elite religions emerge.

In another important distinction Gordon Allport differentiates between extrinsic (or instrumental) and intrinsic religion. In Allport's words:

> . . . *while there are several varieties of extrinsic religious orientation, we may say they all point to a type of religion that is strictly utilitarian: useful for the self in granting safety, social standing, solace, and endorsement for one's chosen way of life. . . . By contrast, the intrinsic form of the religious sentiment regards faith as a supreme value in its own right. It is oriented toward a unification of being, takes seriously the commandment of brotherhood, and strives to transcend all self-centered needs.*[17]

Allport observes that the extrinsic orientation "provides a continual soil for all forms of prejudice, whether racial, national, political, or religious." With the intrinsic religion, "Dogma is tempered with humility" and "religion is no longer limited to single sentiments of self-interest."[18] As we shall see later, this distinction of religious styles is extremely important in wrestling with the knotty question of religion and prejudice and also in evaluating the possibilities of ecumenism.

Another distinction of religious styles is between the demonic in religion and what we shall call (for lack of a better name) the nondemonic. Religion is considered to be suprarational—that is to say it deals with realities which transcend man's ordinary mental processes. But man can of course behave either rationally or irrationally in coping with religious phenomena. He may evolve splendid theological systems whose complexity and fertility are tributes to the skills of the human intellect; or he may engage in behavior which is not at all rational. But within the nonrational ultimates of religion there are both the demonic and the nondemonic. The nondemonic is that in which man is generally in control of what he is doing (for example, the contemplative—lost in prayer but still quite conscious of what he is contemplating). The demonic is that in which man has to some

---

[17] Gordon W. Allport, "The Religious Context of Prejudice," *Journal for the Scientific Study of Religion,* 5 (Fall 1966): 455. Reprinted by permission of the Society for the Scientific Study of Religion.
[18] Ibid., p. 455.

greater or lesser extent lost control of himself. This is simply another way of saying that religion can frequently be for man an occasion of what sociologists call collective behavior. The religious man, as an individual or as a member of the collectivity, may go berserk or run amok—to use two words which are precisely religious in their origins. Because of religion he may try to destroy society, he may succeed in destroying his fellowmen, including sometimes his friends and neighbors, and also destroy himself. The millenarian religious movements which have appeared in the West for a thousand years or more are beyond the scope of this volume. It is worth noting that those movements (based on the notion that the end of the world is about to come and the thousand-year reign of Christ and the saints predicted in the Book of Revelation is at hand) has provided an immensely useful outlet for man's destructive urges. Norman Cohn's classic work, *The Pursuit of the Millennium,*[19] shows how madly destructive of others and of himself man can become when he is caught in a certain kind of religious fervor. Religion is clearly not the only kind of collective madness, but since religion by definition deals with experiences that take man outside himself, it seems to have certain built-in strains toward the demonic and the destructive. As Cardinal Newman put it, "Men will die for a dogma who will not even stir for a conclusion."

Dimensions of Religion

Within a context of more or less permanent religious inclinations, man's religious behavior encompasses immense variety and diversity. In this section we intend to provide eight continua which constitute useful models for viewing and interpreting religious change. They are theology, ritual, liturgy, organization, minister or clergy, piety, ethics, and world view. The models are essentially dialectic as we oppose liberal and conservative, Simple Church and High Church among other polarities. There are no philosophical assumptions behind these models. It is not the author's intention to insist that all movement is circular, that nothing is new under the sun, and that, for example, the new surge of the nonrational in religious liturgy is the same as the nonrational of the past. But there is some cyclic motion in human affairs and even if one cannot describe adequately, much less demonstrate their existence, cyclic models still provide us with a very useful framework with which to view and order social reality.

[19] Norman Cohn, *The Pursuit of the Millennium* (New York: Oxford University Press, Inc., 1957).

In *theology* there is a strain between the desire to maintain religious revelation or religious doctrine in its original pristine state and a desire to present that doctrine in such a way that it is meaningful for the world in which the theologian and his contemporaries live. The first tendency is generally called orthodox, the second, liberal or modernistic. Some popular theologians seem to assume that modernism is an invention of the twentieth century—or at least of the late nineteenth. In fact, however, it is well to remember that St. Thomas Aquinas was condemned for being far too modern and that his books were burned at Oxford University shortly after his death on the grounds that he was so advanced that he must be considered heretical.

Catholic theology was closed from counterreformation by the Second Vatican Council—not in the sense that there was no important theologizing done, but that no major changes occurred in either the style or the substance of the theology. But Protestant theology has been much more open and flexible. In the early twentieth century the liberals were in fashion and dominated most of the theological schools and seminaries in the country. But from the late 1920's until the 1950's, the influence of the great German theologian, Karl Barth, was extremely strong and Barth's version of neoorthodoxy was popular. However, in the 1950's, particularly under the influence of Paul Tillich and Rudolf Bultmann, more modernistic theology launched a counterattack as Tillich tried to interpret the Christian tradition in existentialist categories and Bultmann tried to demythologize the scripture in order that it might be intelligible for scientific man. The death-of-God theologians in the early and middle 1960's and other forms of radical or atheist theologies represented more advanced liberalism. Toward the end of the 1960's the new popularity of eschatology and the theology of hope may represent an orthodox resurgence.

It is obvious enough that the shift from one end of the continuum to the other can be rather rapid in Protestant theology, with perhaps fifteen or twenty years at the most being the length of a theological generation. In Catholicism one can anticipate that now that the Vatican Council has opened the way to much more freewheeling and innovative theologizing, there will be shifts in theological emphases at least as rapid as occur in the Protestant churches. As a matter of fact, one might argue that since Catholic theologians feel that they have four hundred and fifty years to make up for, their theological fashions will change even more rapidly.

The point to be made is that the claim of any theological writer or school to have brought theological dialectic to an end must be, as Mark Twain said of the report of his death, "premature." Given that man simultaneously wishes to preserve his doctrine pure and un-sullied and at the same time wishes to make it relevant to the prob-lems which he finds, there is no reason to believe that shifts back and forth along the orthodox-liberal continuum will stop. As a matter of fact at the present time it is likely that Protestant theology is mov-ing in another neoorthodox direction and one can anticipate that Catholic theology will also begin such a movement.

There are two continua that are useful for viewing *ritual* and *liturgy*. The first is the Simple Church versus the High Church and the second is Dionysian versus Apollonian.

Simple Church liturgy is simple, informal, casual. It takes place in plain churches or in parlors or basements. It usually involves a small group of people, little in the way of elaborate art, and is short and to the point. It represents a belief that God should be worshiped plainly, since elaborate ceremonial merely creates an artificial barrier that God does not need and man should not want. High Church ritual, on the other hand, is based on the concept that whatever is being done for the Deity should be done with a maximum of human effort. Hence High Church liturgy takes place in elaborate churches with complex ceremonial, highly stylized patterns of action, a great deal of emphasis on artistic perfection, and frequently for as long as is humanly possible.

Apollonian liturgy argues that, since man is after all basically rational, his dialogue with the Almighty should be basically rational —sober, moderate, with a bare hint of emotion. Such liturgy is classic and exercises a tight restraint on outburst and display. Even if display is elaborate, it still is careful to maintain precise and classic forms in its elaborateness.

The Dionysian dimension on the other hand stresses the fact that man is more than rational, more than intellect; he has dimensions of his personality which are both infrarational and superrational, both mystical and orgiastic. Dionysian liturgy, therefore, emphasizes the nonrational, the ecstatic, the emotional in man's prayer, arguing that man can only come in contact with the Deity if he transcends the sedate rationality of his everyday life.

Examples of the four possibilities that these two continua pro-vide should illustrate what the definitions mean:

1) Simple Church and Dionysian. Here the best example that comes to mind is Pentecostalism—both Protestant and now more recently Catholic. The direct intervention of the Spirit, particularly when the emotions have been excited in such a fashion as to be open to them, combined with a simple, plain, and matter-of-fact approach

to prayer produce a liturgy which enables those who follow it to avoid elaborateness and at the same time give free vent to their emotions.

2) Simple Church Apollonian. Here there are many examples, principally in the ordinary Sunday liturgies of the more traditional Protestant denominations, Methodists, Congregationalists, Presbyterians, and Low Church Anglicans. The services are relatively plain and simple and at the same time sober, restrained, and dignified. Even the hymns, which do make room for some emotional display, are still quite sedate and restrained, at least compared to the vigor and enthusiasm of a Pentecostal or even Negro Baptist prayer meeting.

3) High Church Dionysian. A liturgy that is at the same time elaborate, artistic, stylized, and ecstatic, emotional, and nonrational is hard to find in the Western Christian experience. A Coptic mass, a Javanese dance, or even the Nazi ritual in a sports stadium at Nuremberg serve, however, as evidence that these two sets of characteristics can be combined.

4) High Church Apollonian. A liturgy that is dignified, rational, and restrained, while at the same time elaborate, artistic, and stylized is not hard to find. One need only look at the traditional Latin Mass in the Roman liturgy, particularly at the Solemn High Mass, to find what may be the best possible example.

Trends in the Simple Church-High Church continuum are somewhat hard to define at present. There is a tendency in Catholicism to go from High Church to Simple Church liturgy, while some large Protestant denominations tended in the opposite direction at least until recently. However, there is little doubt as to what is happening in the Dionysian-Apollonian continuum. In keeping with the violent revolt against scientific rationalism manifested by the psychedelic world, liturgy, both Protestant and Catholic, is tending at present to be more and more nonrational and emotional, not to say ecstatic, and on occasion even orgiastic.

The principal continuum in the area of church *organization* can be represented by church and sect. The church responds to man's instinct to make his religion as universal and as comprehensive as possible. The church responds to man's instinct that his religion should be as comprehensive as possible, cover as much of the earth as possible, and include as many men as possible. If this is to take place, of course, the church must be elaborate and have a complicated structure and an established hierarchy in order that some sort of unity can be preserved. The sect, on the other hand, represents the human tendency to keep one's religion as authentic as possible. If religion is to be authentic and meaningful, if it is to reflect the spirit of its founders, it must necessarily be small in numbers, because once just anybody is permitted into a religion, the original purity and authenticity is diluted and eventually lost. The sect represents a small band of true believers living in itself and for itself and disregarding the rest of the world, save to pray either for its salvation or damnation. The church, on the other hand, represents the people of God on earth, extensive enough to include all men within its boundaries, and tolerant enough not to expect perfection of most men at once. It is a mistake to think of the church and the sect as separate entities, as many sociologists do. Rather, they are separate tendencies that exist within almost any major religious denomination, some of whose members stress the organizational and the institutional, while others stress the interpersonal and the communal. In American society it is pretty hard for a small community to avoid becoming organized. As soon as the first mimeograph machine is bought the process of institutionalization begins. (Perhaps it is currently more accurate to date the organization from the rental of its first Xerox machine.)

While even those religions whose ideology is antistructure become organized nonetheless the present trend is toward the sect end of the dichotomy. Just as the Dionysian emphasis on the liturgy is the church's response to the new concern for the nonrational, so the trend toward sects in church organization responds to man's new quest for meaningful relationships in small groups. The so-called underground church, both Protestant and Catholic, is the religious version of the search for meaningful relationships to be found in such secular manifestations as T-groups and encounter groups.

There is also a continuum of emphasis on what is desired from a religious *minister*. From one point of view he is expected to be a man *of* God. He should be separate and apart from his fellowmen, more holy than they, more given over to the things of God than they. Such an emphasis we can call monastic and in its extreme manifestation would take the whole man out of ordinary interaction with others and put him down in the desert, or at least in an isolated monastery where together with his fellows he would practice the strictest sort of poverty, chastity, and obedience if he were a Catholic. In more modern forms the minister would indeed live in the world, but in a culture all his own and from which he would depart only on highly specific occasions to perform certain highly specified functions for his flock. That kind of behavior was characteristic of the Catholic clergy until recently and is described ably by the Reverend Eugene Kennedy as clerical culture.

On the other hand, it is also felt that the minister should be a *man* of God, and here the emphasis is on his humanity, on his closeness to his fellowmen, his involvement in the human condition, his sympathy with human suffering because he has undergone human problems just as have the members of his flock. Perhaps the best symbolic difference between the two emphases is the question of celibacy, for the unmarried cleric is considered a man apart and the married cleric very much a man in the midst of the community. This is not to say, of course, that the unmarried clergy cannot be deeply involved with his people's problems or that the married clergyman cannot also be a mystic. However, celibacy does represent, at least in its traditional explanation, the monastic dimension of the clerical role, while the married clergyman represents the secular and inner-worldly emphasis. The tendency at present is to emphasize very strongly the secular dimensions of the clerical role, though there are a few signs on the horizon, no bigger, as the Scripture says, than the size of a man's hand, to indicate that the monastic may be returning. Surely in the world of psychedelia we already see considerable mo-nastic emphasis in dieting, contemplation, and mysticism, and it is not totally out of the question to expect that there may be reverbera-tions of this in the clerical life.

The monastic secular continuum in the role of the clergy is but a reflection of the continuum between the incarnational and the eschatological in the area of religious *piety*. The incarnational ap-proach stresses the fact that man works out his salvation by being in and of the world. He is to redeem the world, or at least transform it, and his ordinary, everyday activities have a redemptive and trans-forming value. It is not necessary for him to depart from the world to be religious; indeed, every action he takes in the course of the day—from brushing his teeth to sleeping with his wife—can be religious if it is done out of religious motivation, or at least in a religious context. It is argued that the world, while imperfect, is not evil and that it is the vocation of the believer to redeem it.

On the other hand, in the eschatological emphasis, it is thought that man's home is not in this world; this world is a vale of tears which man must bear with until he can journey to his heavenly home. His mission, therefore, is to be as independent of this world as pos-sible and to detach himself whenever he can from its compelling obligations so that he may reflect on the glories that are to come. He is afraid of becoming too much involved in the cares and worries of this world because if he does his mind may be taken off the transcendent and eternal things and overwhelmed with the unimpor-tant and mundane concerns of everyday life.

The major emphasis at the present time in Christian piety is, of course, incarnational, one might even say incarnational with a vengeance. Nonetheless, there are signs in the world beyond the churches that modern man is beginning to believe that the world might be too much with us, and the hippie who advises us to tune out so that we can turn on, to leave behind the world of the "squares" so that we might see things the way they "really are," is surely giving an eschatological message.

Ethics, which in the Christian tradition tend to be identified with or closely related to religion, also can move from one emphasis to its opposite, from the systematic to the situational. Systematic ethics emphasize the fact that there are, after all, certain fixed principles of good and evil to which every religious man must be committed and from which religion cannot condone any exceptions— murder, lying, adultery are wrong, and that is all there is to it; there are no circumstances that will justify such behavior. In the systematic approach to ethics, therefore, the requirements of the ethical life can be deduced generally from a priori and theoretical systems, even though at times it may be somewhat difficult to apply systematic answers to concrete problems.

On the other hand, the situational approach stresses that moral decisions are in the final analysis made by individuals in highly concrete situations for which ethical systems may provide guidelines but not specific and concrete solutions. Murder may be wrong at all times, but is it murder to kill in self-defense or in a just war, or to execute a criminal? Lying is wrong, but what about protecting a secret that one has no right to reveal? Adulterous thoughts are wrong but what about a doctor whose responsibility it is to perform a physical examination on an extraordinarily attractive woman? One must not, therefore, take the escape of thinking that textbooks or theoretical systems can be the ultimate guide to morality. Each man must fashion his own morality for himself in the concrete set of circumstances in which he finds himself.

Systematic ethics are in bad repute presently in all the churches except the Catholic, and even here many more progressive Catholic theologians are extremely sympathetic to the general approach of the situationists. Earlier we noted that there was some sign of the eschatological and the monastic returning, but if systematic ethical systems are in the process of being reconstructed, no one has yet let the secret out.

Finally, there are different emphases in the religious *world view.* The pessimistic religionist can see nothing but sin, persecution, suffering, evil, and hardship. His viewpoint was summarized by the late Gustave Weigel (who in most of his moments was anything but a pessimist), when he said, "All things human, given enough time, go badly." On the other hand, the optimist is willing to stress that God does draw straight with crooked lines and that out of evil can come good. In the modern age, the optimist, having read Teilhard de Chardin, tends to be an evolutionist and sees the "big picture" while the pessimist concentrates on the "present situation." It is practically impossible to say whether pessimism or optimism, the big picture or the present situation dominate today's religious thinking and behavior, probably because they are more related to personality than to sociological variables.

Summary

The sacred, then, is the raw material out of which religion is constructed. It represents those kinds of phenomena which man, for one reason or another, sets aside as being different from the ordinary phenomena of his life. To the outsider the stones, the trees, areas of land, or buildings, or behavior may seem sometimes strange and unusual and sometimes no different from anything else; but to the believer they represent the point at which the "totally other" interjects itself into his life to give an order and purpose and meaning to life; they reaffirm the unity between his life and the other lives he perceives around him. Not everything that man perceives as extraordinary becomes sacred, but when the extraordinary touches on ultimate meaning or ultimate belonging, on the answers to the basic questions and the relationships which constitute the basic fellowship, man is so impressed by their importance that he treats them as though they were very different from anything else that happens in his life. Religion is nothing more than a set of symbols—doctrinal, moral, ritual, and organizational—that man has evolved for organizing his relationship with the sacred. Not all men are very religious, but most men in the course of history seem to have been religious on occasion, and even he who proudly argues that he is not religious and does not need religion, may find himself, without realizing it, sacralizing the events in his life. Even though meaning and belonging seem to be the essential elements in religion, there are various frequently unrelated dimensions of man's religious behavior and many different styles according to which man selects the components of his own religion. We see that theology can be orthodox or modernistic liturgy, Simple Church or High Church, Dionysian or Apollonian; the denominational organization can emphasize either the church or the sect; the clergy can be monastic or secular; piety either incarnational or eschatological; ethics either systematic or situational; and the world view either gloomy or hopeful.

Whether there will always be religion or not remains to be seen; there always has been, and there are no convincing data that the predictions of its demise being heard today will be any more accurate than those that have been repeated for the last several hundred years. Emile Durkheim, as stout and devout an agnostic as the world has ever seen, concluded his researches with the observation that there could not be a society without a religion. In any event, if there is such a society presently existing, it is most assuredly not present-day America.

Chapter 2

The Origins and
Functions of Religion

The sociologist attempts not only to describe social behavior as it is but, insofar as he can, to explain it. The approach in the previous chapter was essentially phenomenological. We observed that man is involved with the sacred, which provides him with both explanation and fellowship; and we discussed the extent of this involvement, its intensity, and its various styles. However, we did not raise the question of how religion came to be, nor the question of what the social science traditions have had to say about religion. Actually, these two questions develop into the same. For the two centuries or so that social science in one form or another has been in operation, scholars have tried to explain how religion got started; having failed at that, they then turned to analyze the relationship between religion and society—the functions of religion. A quick survey of this history running from Tylor to Glock is part of the ritual required in any book on the sociology of religion. This ritual procedure is not merely to affirm the unity of social scientists, one with another, but also to affirm that the insights and controversies in the history of the anthropology and sociology of religion provide us with extremely useful tools—indeed, essential tools—for understanding American religion.

Because it is necessary to put some sort of order into a presentation such as this, we have arranged our comments around three strains we find in the social scientific discussion of religion: (1) the functionalist followers of Durkheim, concerned essentially with religion as a source of social integration; (2) the disciples of Max Weber (particularly Talcott Parsons and his students), concerned primarily with the meaning-providing role of religion in contradistinction to Karl Marx; (3) the deprivationists like Sigmund Freud who see religion as a source of comfort in response to the deprivation and suffering that society inflicts upon certain groups. It is valid to say that the first group sees religion as essentially an integrator of society, the second as a purveyor of meaning and explanation, and the third as a response to suffering and discontent.

We will, then, in this chapter consider the three overlapping attempts at explaining religion (the functionalists, the Weberians, and the third group which we will subsume under the title "social comfort theorists"). We will then give a clue to the direction in which we are going by suggesting that a combination of Durkheim and Weber, of the "belonging" and "meaning" explanation of religion, provides us with an extremely useful tool for understanding American religion.

Functionalism: A Sense of Belonging

Evolution versus Function

The early social analysts of religion were concerned with explaining it away in the terms of the neat Darwinian world in which they lived. Religion was a holdover from the superstitious past which the human race would unquestionably dispense with in the course of its further evolution. In E. B. Tylor's classic description of how religious evolution occurred, man deduced from the experience of his dreams that he had a spiritual soul of some sort. This soul survived after death as a separate spirit which existed as a ghost; other spirits were to be found in the various forces of nature. Indeed, all things were animated by such spirits; hence, the religion of such pan-spirituality was called animism. In the next step man conceived of some spirits which were neither ghosts nor animating forces but gods existing to some extent independently of matter. The last phase was an evolution to the notion of many gods with one chief, then to a chief god who was all-powerful, and finally to monotheism. The path of the evolution was clear: from dreams to a monotheistic god, and then from Judaism to Christianity. Other writers such as James G. Frazer viewed the evolution beginning not with primitive magic because many primitive peoples had a magic but did not have deities; magic was universal and belief in God was not. Frazer considered myths, cults, rites to be the foci of the evolution of religion. Still other writers such as Lucien Lévy-Bruhl postulated some kind of prerational mentality for primitive man which enabled him to take seriously the myths and superstitions which constituted his religion.[1]

For all their evolutionary elegance, none of these theories have been able to survive, mostly because the anthropological data on which they were based were not sufficient to support them. The surveys of primitive tribes which provided the raw data for these writers were by contemporary standards grossly inadequate. More careful anthropological research has demolished the evidence on which the evolutionists built their theories. Furthermore, later anthropologists also concluded that there was no reason to think that the so-called primitive tribes of today represented varying stages of the evolutionary process from which the main part of the human race had proceeded on its way toward Victorian England. The Australian aborigine or the Congolese pygmy, for example, might be the most primitive people in the world, but that does not at all mean that they would be primitive in a sense comparable to that, say, of the human race when it was emerging from the caves. Such later anthropologists concluded that since there was no one there to take notes or to administer questionnaires, one cannot really say how religion got started, and attempts to do so are likely to be futile. Therefore, after Emile Durkheim thoroughly and devastatingly refuted the evolutionists, social scientists have generally assumed that religion is virtually everywhere and is likely to survive for a long time to come. This has not led very many of them to become religionists, but it has induced them to devote their efforts to trying to understand the relationship between religion and society rather than to explain the origin, growth, and, presumably, decline of religion.

Durkheim himself solved the question of the relationship between religion and society in a profoundly radical way. To Durkheim's mind society *is* religion, or at least society is that sacred object to which man turns and devotes himself through religion.

> Its [religion's] primary object is not to give men a representation of the physical world; for if that were its essential task, we could not understand how it has been able to survive, for, on this side, it is scarcely more than a fabric of errors. Before all, it is a system of ideas with which the individuals represent to themselves the society of which they are members, and the obscure but intimate relations which they have with it.[2]

[1] A bibliographical note: For a sampling of the ideas of the above-mentioned authors see E. B. Tylor, *Primitive Culture*, 1871; James G. Frazer, *The Golden Bough*, first published in 1890 with various revisions through 1936; Lucien Lévy-Bruhl, *Primitive Mentality*, trans. Lillian A. Clare, 1923.

[2] Durkheim, op. cit., p. 225.

And later:

> . . . *the sacred principle is nothing more nor less than society transfigured and personified, . . . the individual gets from society the best part of himself, all that gives him a distinct character and a special place among other beings, his intellectual and moral culture. If we should withdraw from men their language, sciences, arts and moral beliefs, they would drop to the rank of animals. So the characteristic attributes of human nature come from society. But on the other hand, society exists and lives only in and through individuals. If the idea of society were extinguished in individual minds and the beliefs, traditions and aspirations of the group were no longer felt and shared by the individuals, society would die. . . . We now see the real reason why the gods cannot do without their worshippers any more than these can do without their gods; it is because society, of which the gods are only a symbolic expression, cannot do without individuals any more than these can do without society.*[3]

The experience of the sacred, therefore, is man's experience of the pressures which society brings upon him, and also of the support which society provides for him, and particularly of that support which man perceives in the "effervescence" of "collective representations" —that is to say, those public ritual activities by which society affirms its existence and its unity. In Durkheim's words:

> *Religious forces are therefore human forces, moral forces. It is true that since collective sentiments can become conscious of themselves only by fixing themselves upon external objects, they have not been able to take form without adopting some of their characteristics from other things; they have come to mix themselves with the life of the material world, and then have considered themselves capable of explaining what passes there. But when they are considered only from this point of view and in this role, only their most superficial aspect is seen. In reality, the essential elements of which these collective sentiments are made have been borrowed by the understanding. It ordinarily seems that they should have a human character only when they are conceived under human forms; but even the most impersonal and the most anonymous are nothing else than objectified sentiments.*[4]

[3] Ibid., p. 347.
[4] Ibid., p. 419.

Religion, then, is society worshipping itself in order that it may focus its energies toward the idealization of itself.

The formation of the ideal world is therefore not an irreducible fact which escapes science; it depends upon conditions which observation can touch; it is a natural product of social life. For a society to become conscious of itself and maintain at the necessary degree of intensity the sentiments which it thus attains, it must assemble and concentrate itself. Now this concentration brings about an exaltation of the mental life which takes form in a group of ideal conceptions where is portrayed the new life thus awakened; they correspond to this new set of physical forces which is added to those which we have at our disposition for the daily tasks of existence. A society can neither create itself nor recreate itself without at the same time creating an ideal. This creation is not a sort of work of supererogation for it, by which it would complete itself, being already formed; it is the act by which it is periodically made and remade. Therefore when some oppose the ideal society to the real society, like two antagonists which would lead us in opposite directions, they materialize and oppose abstractions. The ideal society is not outside of the real society; it is a part of it. Far from being divided between them as between two poles which mutually repel each other, we cannot hold to one without holding to the other. For a society is not made up merely of the mass of individuals who compose it, the ground which they occupy, the things which they use and the movements which they perform, but above all of the idea which it forms of itself.[5]

The anthropological data on the Australian aborigines on which Durkheim based his theory has been to some extent superseded by more accurate information, and later scholars have called into question many, if not most, of Durkheim's propositions. Nonetheless, he has had a profound influence on the study of religion, and deservedly so, for his theory, albeit overstated, represents a brilliant insight into the intimate relationship between man's belonging to a society and his accepting that society's view of the nature of reality. Religion may not be society; it may not even, as some of the later revisionists point out, hold society together all the time, but it is intimately connected with social unity.

After Durkheim the most important commentator on religion and society was the Polish-English anthropologist Bronislaw Malinowski.

[5] Ibid., p. 422.

His work, done in the South Pacific while serving foreign duty during the First World War, was a classic combination of field work and theory. Malinowski effectively questioned many of Durkheim's assumptions: "The great collective effervescence during periods of concentration" could not, in Malinowski's view be the cause of religious phenomena, since there are all kinds of effervescence—"the lover near his sweetheart, the daring adventurer conquering his fears in the face of real danger, the hunter at grips with a wild animal, the craftsman achieving a masterpiece"—wherever effervescence occurs there is not, necessarily, religion. Even in primitive societies there are many nonreligious effervescent acts. Therefore, Malinowski concludes, "The *collective* and the *religious,* though impinging on each other, are by no means coextensive. . . ." [6]

Malinowski then goes on to show precisely what he feels is the real relationship between religion and society. He illustrates by analyzing religious rituals at the time of death.

> *These acts are directed against the overwhelming fear, against the corroding doubt, from which the savage is no more free than the civilized man. These acts confirm his hope that there is a hereafter, that it is not worse than present life; indeed, better. All the ritual expresses that belief, that emotional attitude which the dying man requires, which is the greatest comfort he can have in his supreme conflict.* [7]

Besides mobilizing social support for man at times of crisis, religion also helps society cope with the fact of death after a man dies.

> *After death, though the main actor has made his exit, the tragedy is not at an end. There are the bereaved ones, and these, savage or civilized, suffer alike, and are thrown into a dangerous mental chaos. We have given an analysis of this already, and found that, torn between fear and piety, reverence and horror, love and disgust, they are in a state of mind which might lead to mental disintegration. Out of this, religion lifts the individual by what could be called spiritual co-operation in the sacred mortuary rites. We have seen that in these rites there is expressed the dogma of continuity after death, as well as the moral attitude towards the departed. The corpse, and with it the person of the dead one, is a potential object of horror as well as*

---

[6] Bronislaw Malinowski, "Magic, Science, and Religion," in *Science, Religion, and Reality,* ed. Joseph Needham (New York: The Macmillan Company, 1925), pp. 55–56. Reprinted by permission of The Society for Promoting Christian Knowledge.

[7] Ibid., p. 57.

of tender love. Religion confirms the second part of this double attitude by making the dead body into an object of sacred duties. The bond of union between the recently dead and the survivors is maintained, a fact of immense importance for the continuity of culture and for the safe keeping of tradition. In all this we see that the whole community carries out the biddings of religious tradition, but that these are again enacted for the benefit of a few individuals only, the bereaved ones, that they arise from a personal conflict and are a solution of this conflict. It must also be remembered that what the survivor goes through on such an occasion prepares him for his own death. The belief in immortality, which he has lived through and practiced in the case of his mother or father, makes him realize more clearly his own future life.[8]

Malinowski goes on to say that religion holds society together. It is not the same thing as society, but it maintains the unity of society:

. . . public performance of religious dogma is indispensable for the maintenance of morals in primitive communities. Every article of faith, as we have seen, wields a moral influence. Now morals, in order to be active at all, must be universal. The endurance of social ties, the mutuality of services and obligations, the possibility of co-operation, are based in any society on the fact that every member knows what is expected of him; that, in short, there is a universal standard of conduct. No rule of morals can work unless it is anticipated and unless it can be counted upon. In primitive societies, where law, as enforced by judgments and penalties, is almost completely absent, the automatic, self-acting moral rule is of the greatest importance for forming the very foundations of primitive organization and culture. This is possible only in a society where there is no private teaching of morals, no personal codes of conduct and honor, no ethical schools, no differences of moral opinion. The teaching of morals must be open, public, and universal.[9]

Religion is "the very cement of social fabric." "Its function is to hold society together in face of the stress and strains brought to it by disasters and threats that are both internal and external." [10]

Malinowski also effectively distinguished between magic and religion by an observation that has become classic in the history of

[8] Ibid., p. 58.
[9] Ibid., p. 63.
[10] Ibid., p. 82.

social science. He noted that the Trobriand Islanders did not perform magic rites when they were fishing in the lagoon but did perform them when they went fishing on the high seas outside the lagoon. According to Malinowski, the reason for this was that in the lagoon one was dealing with known and controllable forces; it was a safe, comfortable, and well-understood place to work, and nothing out of the ordinary was likely to happen. Therefore, magic was not required. But when one ventured into the open sea, one was entering into the perils of the unknown; and so one turned to magic as a kind of insurance that one would be able to cope with it. Magic, therefore, was an attempt to allay the anxiety that man faces when confronted with the unknown. But it is not the same as religion. Magic has practical goals—that is to say, goals that are perceived as practical by those who perform them. Religion, on the other hand, produces emotions such as reverence for tradition, harmony with environment, courage and confidence in sorrow, accommodation with the prospect of death; these are not immediately and obviously practical. The magic ritual performed to prevent death in childbirth is quite different from the religious ritual which celebrates the birth of the child. The former has a definite practical purpose that is known to all, while the latter merely expresses the feelings of all concerned. Magic is immediately practical and utilitarian, religion looks to more remote goals and indirectly and unintentionally to the preservation of society.

In a historic controversy with Malinowski, the British anthropologist A. R. Radcliffe-Brown suggested an alternate explanation for the behavior of the Trobriand Islanders. The ritual does not exist among the Andaman Islanders to allay anxiety but to in fact cause anxiety, and the psychological effect of the rite is to create a sense of insecurity or danger. Whether rituals cause anxiety or allay it is a debate which need not detain us, though it does seem in social science circles that Malinowski has rather the better of the argument. For all practical purposes, however, we may be content with observing that some rituals seem to create anxiety in some people while other rituals allay anxieties in other people.

But this point on whether rituals contribute to the integration of a given personality or not brings us to the next phase in the development of the so-called functional approach to the study of religion and society. For several decades after Malinowski and Durkheim, almost all research in the sociology and anthropology of religion was concerned with showing how religion served to integrate society. However it became more and more clear that religion wasn't always an effective and integrating agent. Some elements of religion can contribute to social integration while other elements can contribute to social disintegration. Furthermore, religion can appear to be holding society together at one level while at another level its latent function is disintegrative. Finally, Robert Merton raised the question of what happens to a society that has two religions.

Since Merton formulated the problems of what has now come to be called naïve functionalism, there has been much more sophistication about the explanation of religion as the integrating force (or at least *an* integrating force) in society. Religion plays integrating roles sometimes, and other times it does not. Clearly, though, one of religion's essential functions is to provide a value system which, held in common by many men, can serve as the cement for social relationships.

Clifford Geertz in a remarkable article on a funeral in Java shows how a rite which was intended to be integrative, to console the family, and to pull it together again after the disaster of death, actually became disintegrative and caused more disturbance and trouble than it eliminated. Geertz's explanation demonstrates how religion can shift from being an integrator to being a source of disturbance. The religion or cultural system of the Javanese family was essentially rural, but the social system in which they lived was urban. The cultural system was integrative in a rural social setting; but faced with the realities of the city, it was incapable of exercising the function it formerly had. Therefore, Geertz suggests that at least one of the times when religion is disintegrative is when there is a lag between cultural and social structure, or to use nonsociological words between the propositions and rituals of faith and the social realities in which the people live.[11]

A Source of Meaning

Marx versus Weber

There are few literate Americans who do not know at least vaguely that Karl Marx was an economic determinist who thought that the organization of the means of production shaped all the other struc-

---

[11] Bibliographical note: Representative examples of the thought of the above-mentioned authors A. R. Radcliffe-Brown, Robert Merton, and Clifford Geertz may be found in *Religion, Culture and Society,* ed. Louis Schneider (New York: John Wiley & Sons, Inc., 1964).

tures of society. They are also aware that Marx viewed religion in particular as the product of the working of economic forces; that religion justified whatever class happened to own and control the means of production at any given time. Religion was the "opiate of the masses" because it served as a sacral justification for the tyrannization of the subject class by the ruling class.

The popular belief is that Max Weber attempted to refute Marx by proving that far from being shaped by the economic structure, religion can, at least on occasion, shape it. Proof of this theory supposedly lay in Weber's demonstration that the Protestant ethic caused modern capitalism. In whatever part of the hereafter Herr Professor Weber presently resides, he must be shaking his head in dismay. A man who all his life resolutely refused to engage in monistic thinking has his work interpreted as meaning something that he explicitly said it did not mean. Perhaps the fate of Weber's theory of the Protestant ethic is the fate of every man who refuses to settle for simple answers and insists on seeing both sides of the question.

He did not reject Marx completely. On the contrary, he found the Marxist interpretation of history extremely useful. What he did reject was the notion that the direction of causality ran entirely in one direction; that the economy shaped the rest of society without being shaped in return; and that a belief system was structured by society without society in its turn being structured by a belief system. Weber was not a religious determinist. He was, rather, a believer in pluralistic interaction; he argued the not particularly outrageous position that religion and society influence each other.

For we are merely attempting to clarify the part which religious forces have played in forming the developing web of our specifically worldly modern culture, in the complex interaction of innumerable different historical factors. We are thus inquiring only to what extent certain characteristic features of this culture can be imputed to the influence of the Reformation. . . .

On the other hand, now, we have no intention whatever of maintaining such a foolish and doctrinaire thesis as that the spirit of capitalism (in the provisional sense of the term explained above) could only have arisen as the result of certain effects of the Reformation, or even that capitalism as an economic system is a creation of the Reformation. In itself, the fact that certain important forms of capitalistic business organization are known to be considerably older than the Reformation is a sufficient refutation of such a claim. On the contrary, we only wish to ascertain *whether and to what extent religious forces have taken part in the qualitative and the quantitative expansion of that spirit over the world.*[12]

The problem he attempted to solve was much more modest.

> *Now, how could activity, which was at best ethically tolerated, turn into a calling in the sense of Benjamin Franklin? The fact to be explained historically is that in the most highly capitalistic center of that time, in Florence of the fourteenth and fifteenth centuries, the money and capital market of all the great political powers, this attitude was considered ethically unjustifiable, or at best to be tolerated. But in the backwoods small bourgeois circumstances of Pennsylvania in the eighteenth century, where business threatened for simple lack of money to fall back into barter, where there was hardly a sign of large enterprise, for only the earliest beginnings of banking were to be found, the same thing was considered the essence of moral conduct, even commanded in the name of duty.* To speak here of a reflection of material conditions in the ideal superstructure would be patent nonsense. *What was the background of ideas which would account for the sort of activity apparently directed toward profit alone as a calling to which the individual feels himself to have an ethical obligation? For it was this idea which gave the way of the new entrepreneur its ethical foundation and justification.*[13]

We propose to spend a number of pages on the detailed examination of the Weberian theory, both because it is the most influential antecedent of contemporary sociological theorizing about the nature of religion and society and also because it is a classic example of the caution with which a sociological thinker ought to approach the complex issue of the relationship between religion and society.

It was part of the agony of Weber's life that he lived when it very much looked like the development of history was proving Marx correct. Mills and Gerth [14] remark that as he grew older Weber was more and more inclined to accept economic determinism, but he nevertheless stubbornly held to a liberal conviction that ideas did have consequence. Thus at the end of his life he wrote: "Not ideas,

---

[12] Reprinted by permission of Charles Scribner's Sons and George Allen & Unwin Ltd. from *The Protestant Ethic and the Spirit of Capitalism* by Max Weber, translated by Talcott Parsons.

[13] Ibid., pp. 74–75.

[14] C. Wright Mills and H. H. Gerth (trans.), *From Max Weber: Essays in Sociology* (New York: Oxford University Press, Inc., 1958), p. 63.

but material and ideal interests directly govern man's conduct. Yet very frequently the 'world images' which have been created by 'ideas' have, like switchmen, determined the tracks along which action has been pushed by the dynamic of interests." [15] It is against the world view expressed by this remark that we must understand Weber's thinking on religion and the development of capitalism.

The Protestant Ethic and the Spirit of Capitalism

Weber begins his preliminary investigation by noting indisputable facts: the Protestant sections of Germany are more industrialized than the Catholic sections, Protestants are more likely to be among the industrial millionaires than Catholics, Protestants are more likely to attend the kind of schools which would equip them for business enterprise than Catholics. He asks what kind of historical processes could be responsible for this situation, and suggests that there may be something in Protestant belief which would incline Protestants to the kinds of activity which are essential for capitalistic success.

Before attempting a direct historical analysis, Weber tries to establish exactly what the spirit of capitalism is. As an illustration of the typical capitalists he adduces that model American pioneer, Benjamin Franklin. For "Poor Richard" the making of money was an end in itself:

> . . . *the* summum bonum *of this ethic, the earning of more and more money, combined with the strict avoidance of all spontaneous enjoyment of life, is* . . . *thought of so purely as an end in itself, that from the point of view of the happiness of, or utility to, the single individual, it appears entirely transcendental.* . . . *Man is dominated by the making of money, by acquisition as the ultimate purpose of his life. Economic acquisition is no longer subordinated to man as the means for satisfaction of his material needs.* . . . *If we thus ask, why should "money be made out of men," Benjamin Franklin himself, although he was a colorless deist, answers in his autobiography with a quotation from the Bible which his strict Calvinistic father drummed into him time and again in his youth: "Seest thou a man diligent in business? He shall stand before kings." The earning of money within the economic order is thus done legally, the result and the expression of virtue and proficiency in a calling; and this virtue and proficiency are, as it is now not difficult to see, the real Alpha and the Omega of Franklin's ethic.* . . .[16]

[15] Ibid., p. 64.
[16] Weber, *The Protestant Ethic and the Spirit of Capitalism,* op. cit., p. 53.

Thus for Weber the capitalist spirit is not merely the desire to make money—a desire which has marked man wherever he has lived—but rather turning the making of money into a vocation which of itself justifies human existence. Capitalism is not merely the rationalized pursuit of profit, for this was present in the greedy and well-organized economy of Renaissance Florence; yet the Florentines lacked the spirit of capitalism because they did not justify their operations as a vocation. On the other hand, the spirit of capitalism could and did exist in the Pennsylvania of Benjamin Franklin despite the minimal capitalistic organization of the economy there. Nor is the capitalistic spirit to be equated with rationalism; the rationalism of the Enlightenment was rife in Catholic countries and yet gave rise to little in the way of capitalistic development. The spirit of capitalism is, rather, the rationalization of economic life in terms of one's God-given vocation.

Turning to his historical investigation, Weber first considers the possible influence of Lutheranism on the development of capitalism. He concludes that there is little in Luther's teaching or the attitude of his church to justify the capitalist spirit. However, he suggests that Luther's use of the German word *Beruf* in his translation of the Bible and his teaching on the nature of a "calling," while certainly in keeping with the traditional approach, opened the way to further development of this notion by the Calvinists.

In Chapter Four of *The Protestant Ethic* Weber turns to the essential point of his thesis. He maintains that the Calvinist notion of an absolute predestination, which is manifested by the performance of good works, is at the heart of the justification of capitalist activity. In common with the monks of the Middle Ages, the Calvinist is expected to prove his worth by an ascetic life (or more precisely to prove a conviction of his worth as one of the saved). But unlike the monk his asceticism is not to be otherworldly asceticism, which is separated from the events of everyday life, but rather an innerworldly asceticism which demands a meticulous attention to the affairs of everyday life as a proof of one's predestination.

> But in the course of its development Calvinism added something positive . . . the idea of proving one's faith in worldly activity. Therein it gave the broader groups of religiously inclined people a positive incentive to asceticism. By founding its ethic in the doctrine of predestination, it substituted for the spiritual aristocracy of monks outside of and above the world the spiritual aristocracy of the predestined saints of God within the world.[17]

[17] Ibid., p. 121.

Weber continues to investigate the relations of other forms of Protestantism to the capitalist ethic. He finds that pietism insofar as it had a Calvinist bent would not be uncomfortable with the capitalist spirit; but, since it was somewhat more interested in human emotions, it lacked the drive which orthodox Calvinism was capable of instilling in its adherents. With perhaps some irony he comments:

> *We . . . can point out . . . that the virtues favored by Pietism were more those on the one hand of the faithful official, clerk, laborer, or domestic worker, and on the other of the predominantly patriarchal employer with a pius condescension. Calvinism, in comparison, appears to be more closely related to the hard legalism and the active enterprise of bourgeois-capitalistic entrepreneurs.*[18]

Weber concludes this key chapter by noting that the Baptist sects were able to carry the doctrine of Calvin one step further. For the orthodox Calvinists there was still a church organization of one kind or another (and in Geneva, a most efficient organization). But in the Baptist groups the emphasis on an invisible church and the reception of salvation removed active church participation as one of the manifestations of salvation and enabled the capitalists to identify his worldly vocation almost completely with his conviction of salvation.

In the last chapter of *The Protestant Ethic* Weber turns to a detailed consideration of the maxims of the worldly asceticism. Richard Baxter is cited as the exemplar of the Puritan approach to a vocation, that is, the complete relinquishment of all forms of pleasure and amusement in favor of hard, continuous physical or mental labor. Labor is an approved ascetic technique and a defense against "all those temptations which Puritanism united under the name of the unclean life, whose role for it was by no means small." [19] But labor is more than just an ascetic technique. "Unwillingness to work is symptomatic of the lack of grace." [20]

The penultimate paragraphs of Weber's classic contain a summary of the work and a caustic comment on the effects of the spirit of capitalism in modern life and on the ironic destruction of asceticism by the capitalism which it helped to create.

> *The puritan wanted to work in a calling; we are forced to do so. For when asceticism was carried out of monastic cells into everyday life, and began to dominate worldly morality, it did its part in building the tremendous cosmos of the modern eco-*

[18] Ibid., p. 139.
[19] Ibid., p. 158.
[20] Ibid., p. 159.

nomic order. This order is now bound to the technical and economic conditions of machine production which today determine the lives of all the individuals who are born into this mechanism, not only those directly concerned with economic acquisition, with irresistible force. Perhaps it will so determine them until the last ton of fossilized coal is burnt. In Baxter's view the care for external goods should only lie on the shoulders of the "saint like a light cloak which can be thrown aside at any moment." But fate decreed that the cloak should become an iron cage.

Since asceticism undertook to remodel the world and to work out its ideas in the world, material goods have gained an increasing and finally an inexorable power over the lives of men as at no previous period in history. Today the spirit of religious asceticism—whether, finally, who knows?—has escaped from the cage. But victorious capitalism, since it rests on mechanical foundations no longer needs its support. The rosy blush of its laughing heir, the Enlightenment, seems also to be irretrievably fading, and the idea of duty in one's calling prowls about in our lives like the ghost of dead religious beliefs. Where the fulfillment of the calling cannot be directly related to the highest spiritual and cultural values, or when, on the other hand, it need not be felt strongly as economic compulsion, the individual generally abandons the attempt to justify it at all. In the field of its highest development, in the United States, the pursuit of wealth, stripped of its religious and ethical meaning, tends to become associated with purely mundane passions which often actually give it the character of sport.[21]

It is to the United States that Weber looks in "The Protestant Sects and the Spirit of Capitalism," a brief essay which well might be thought of as an appendix to *The Protestant Ethic*. However, it was an America still very much involved in the religious justification of work that aroused Weber's interest in this article. He had noted from several things he had observed during his trip to America that church membership seemed to be required of anyone who wished to be a respected member of the business community. He traces the development of the sects which seemed popular in the United States and suggests that church membership is required not so much as a sign of salvation but rather as a guarantee that one can be expected to observe the ethical norms required for business operation. If a man does not belong to a church and does not thereby testify to his

[21] Ibid., pp. 181–182.

dedication to the principles on which capitalist enterprise must depend, how can other business men trust him? It is unthinkable that a church member, no matter how "sharp" he might be in his business practices, might do anything which goes against the ethical code on which money capitalism depends. For if he would violate this code (and get caught), he would no longer be an approved member of the church; he would become a social outcast.

Religions of the East

The Protestant Ethic was intended by its author to be little more than an introductory sketch in a long and ambitious investigation of the relationship between rationalism and capitalism. In three volumes of minute historical, sociological, and legal investigations of Asian culture, Weber is really asking one basic question: Why did not modern capitalism arise in the Orient when many of the inventions necessary for it had been developed, or at least suspected, before they became known in the West and when in China there was a rationalistic culture and in India a considerable development of asceticism?

Weber observes that the level of rationalization a religion represents depends on two yardsticks: "One is the degree to which religion has divested itself of magic; the other is the degree to which it has systematically unified the relations between God and the world and therewith its own ethical relationship to the world." [22]

The religion of China has achieved some success on the former norm. Confucianism rejects magic, in principle at least. However, the strict rationality of orthodox Confucianism was limited to the bureaucratic literati who did not much care whether the people they governed engaged in some harmless magic; and Taoism, the second religion of China, was much more heavily involved in magical practices.

It is on the second norm of rationalization that the religions of China must be reckoned failures from the viewpoint of the capitalist spirit. To the Confucianist the world is the best of all possible worlds and human nature is basically good. Tension between man and the world must be reduced to an absolute minimum. The only kind of salvation to be sought is from a barbaric lack of education. There is

---

[22] Reprinted with permission of The Macmillan Company from *The Religion of China* by Max Weber. Copyright by The Free Press, a Corporation, 1951.

in these religions little sense of "sin" and even less sense of the need for an asceticism by which man is to dominate the world.

> *Chinese ethics developed its strongest motives in the circle of naturally grown, personalist associations. . . . This contrasts sharply with the Puritan ethic which amounts to an objectification of man's duties as a creature of God. The religious duty of the pious Chinese, in contrast, enjoined him to develop himself within the organically given personal relations.*[23]

Weber goes on to point out that the Protestant ethic had succeeded in destroying the fetters which bound the individual to the family, while the Chinese religion on the other hand tied man ever more closely to his responsibilities to the extended family. Confucianism demanded that man adjust to the world and the human relations processes around him. To Calvinism: "Men are equally wicked and fail ethically; the world is a vessel of sin; and there can be no adjustment in creatural wickedness in the face of the Lord. Adjustment to 'vanity fair' would be a sign of rejection; self-perfection in the sense of Confucianism would be idolatrous blasphemy." [24]

None of this implies that the Chinese was not interested in making money. He certainly was. "In conjunction with the tremendous density of population in China, a calculating mentality and self-sufficient frugality of unexampled intensity developed under the influence of a worldly-minded utilitarianism and belief in the value of wealth as a means of moral perfection." [25] But despite such greed the Chinese never developed a rational method or organized enterprise, no truly rational organization of money and finance and law, no system of commercial correspondence or bookkeeping or accounting.

> *The Chinese lacked the central, religiously determined and rational method of life which came from within and which was characteristic of the classical Puritan. For the latter, economic success was not an ultimate goal or end in itself but a means of proving oneself. . . . The Puritan was taught to suppress the petty acquisitiveness which distinguishes the conduct of the Chinese shopkeeper. Alien to the Confucian was the peculiar confinement and repression of natural impulse which was brought about by strictly volitional and ethical rationalization and ingrained in the Puritan.*[26]

[23] Ibid., p. 227.
[24] Ibid., p. 238.
[25] Ibid., p. 242.
[26] Ibid., p. 243.

The Puritan in other words worked because it was his mission in life to work. The Confucian worked so that he might acquire wealth and devote his time to leisure pursuits, especially the study of literary classics. To the Puritan such activity was an ungodly waste of time. It would be no exageration to say that the Puritan is an inner directed man and the Confucian an other directed man. For a Puritan the goal is production. For a Confucian the goal is consumption. For the Puritan the world is an evil place to be remade, for the Confucian it is a good place to be adjusted to and enjoyed. The Confucian was indeed an acquisitive rationalist, but he was not and could not become a capitalist in the sense that Ben Franklin and Richard Baxter were.

The religions of India were no more successful than those of China in eliminating magic from the belief of the masses; but where the Chinese were optimistic about the world and strove to adjust to it, the Indians were pessimistic and strove to escape from it. Both Puritanism and Indian religion (whether Hindu or Buddhist) were salvation religions; both prescribed an asceticism by which man was to wrestle with an essentially evil world. But the object of the asceticisms were vastly different. The Indian seeks not to control the world, to bring it under rational domination, but rather to understand it, to have a philosophical insight into its significance—or lack thereof. The Indian wants to obtain by an emptying of his worldly concerns a mystical experience. In the strictest sense of the word the Indian is a gnostic. Hence for him the Puritan notion that "for transitory deeds of transient beings on this earth 'eternal' punishment or rewards in the future could be assigned and indeed by power of the arrangement of a simultaneously all powerful and good God is for all genuine Asiatic thought absurd. . . ." [27]

The pursuit of wealth in India was considered by the literate classes to be barbaric.

> *The orthodox or heterodox Hinduistic or Buddhistic educated classes . . . found the true sphere of their interests quite outside the things of this world. This was in the search for mystical, timeless salvation of the soul and the escape from the senseless mechanicism of the "wheel" of existence.* [28]

For the lower classes the pursuit of wealth was permitted, but the influence of the religious ideals of the land were strong enough so

---

[27] Reprinted with permission of The Macmillan Company from *The Religion of India* by Max Weber. © by The Free Press, a Corporation, 1958.
[28] Ibid., p. 338.

that these classes would never become capitalists in Weber's definition of the term.

Thus, in neither China nor India did Weber find the prerequisites for the evolution of the capitalist spirit. His investigations of ancient Jewry reached no conclusion on this point, at least partly because these investigations were incomplete at the time of his death. The main theme of the finished sections of his study of Judaism is the development of the Jews as a pariah people—a guest people living among others and yet remaining separate from them. In his development of this theme Weber displays subtle virtuosity in describing the interrelations between religion and material culture, with religion now acting as a cause and now as an effect. Indeed, in many ways this volume is the most sophisticated of all Weber's work in the sociology of religion and should put to rest forever the charge that he tried to explain everything in terms of ideas to the detriment of the influence of material factors.

The clearest statement of Weber's ideas on the precise nature of the relationship between religion and society reexamined *The Protestant Ethic* in light of the years of research which had passed since its original publication. The most important fact about this essay is that now Weber puts capitalistic rationalism and its puritan ethic in perspective against the rationalizing tendency which had gone on in occidental civilization long before the Reformation. Only in the West, according to Weber, is there to be found a rational natural science; the rational historical scholarship, begun by Thucydides; the rational harmonious music based on the harmonic third; the rational use of the Gothic Vault as a means of distributing pressure and of roofing spaces of all forms; and the rational organization of the legal and political systems. Thus it is not surprising that in the West there should develop a rationalized economic system complete with the separation of business from the household, the systematic keeping of books, the separation of corporate from personal property, and above all, the rational organization of the labor force.

What Weber seems to be saying in this Introduction is that capitalism represents an economic manifestation of a factor which has been at work in occidental society for a long time. Protestantism did not cause this factor to work in the economic order; rather capitalism and Protestantism both are manifestations of the same factor and hence related through a common antecedent cause. The similarity between the two should not be surprising. It was inevitable that certain forms of Protestant rationalism should be so congruent with certain forms of capitalistic enterprise that the Protestant ethic would inevitably give considerable encouragement to capitalistic development and make possible its reaching toward its logical conclusions. We say "what Weber seems to be saying" because he does not say this in so many words. However, it is quite certain after a careful reading of this essay that Weber—perhaps because of the controversy the earlier edition had stirred up—was leaning over backward to insist that he did not claim that Calvinism had "caused" capitalism. He makes quite clear his position that capitalism can trace some of its causes to elements in the occidental spirit which long antedated the Reformation.

Weber's Method

Reinhard Bendix sums up Weber's methodology by saying that Weber believed that only concrete social facts existed and that therefore history must be concerned with investigating the cause of unique events. In Bendix' words Weber was

> led (1) to deny that collectivities exist; (2) to assert that all historical data are unique constellations of individual behavior patterns; (3) to conceive of historical data as receiving their organization through the historian; (4) to assign to the historian the task of establishing the causation of unique events; and, finally, (5) to conceive of sociology as a comparative study of meaningful individual behavior in all societies and throughout time.
>
> This comparative study would eventually result in a knowledge of the universal regularities of human conduct. These could be formulated in a system of ideal types which would encompass the historical range of these regularities and which would furnish the scientist with unambiguous conceptual tools.[29]

It is impossible for a social scientist to develop concepts which fit a given kind of conduct or a given form of domination in all instances and in all particulars. But since he must have such concepts, he must construct ideal types at the cost of simplifying the complexity of historical data and exaggerating their uniformities. Such ideal types are just as scientific in sociology as the model of economic man is in economics. They are not descriptions of reality but rather abstract models against which reality can be judged. They are not generalizations but conceptual tools. Thus Weber's theory of the relationship between Protestantism and capitalism would not, in his terms, be

---

[29] Reinhard Bendix, "Max Weber's Interpretation of Conduct and History," *American Journal of Sociology*, 2 (May 1946): 523. Copyright © 1946 by The University of Chicago Press.

taken as a generalization for describing exactly what happened in the early centuries of our era but rather as a concept, a model against which the events of those years in all their complexity could be examined. Weber did not deny pluralistic causation; quite the contrary, it was because of the fact of pluralistic causation that he found it necessary to insist on "atomistic isolation" of the ideal type method. One could not proceed scientifically, in Weber's view, unless one isolated one conceptual tool and analyzed all its implications. To try to describe the totality of pluralistic causation would be to run the risk of becoming bogged down in an unscientific morass of conflicting trends and countertrends. One had to abstract, but abstraction did not at all mean that one was insisting on just a single cause. It was the very multiplicity of causes which made abstraction inevitable.

One may, of course, disagree with Weber's approach to history and sociology. One can further say that the average reader of *The Protestant Ethic* could hardly be expected to know what the ideal type method is all about. One could maintain that Weber at times tends to contradict his own earlier statements—or at least to broaden them substantially—without admitting the change. One can claim that he occasionally allows himself to be carried away and to forget this ideal type method and thereby make statements which seem to be indicative of a monist causation approach. One can certainly criticize him for the obscurities of his style and for his failure to use his own tools the way they should have been used in a deeper and more nuanced investigation of Calvinism. All these criticisms have their validity, but they do not destroy the brilliance and ingenuity of Weber's insights. His exposition of these insights, whatever its defects, tremendously stimulated the study of the origins of capitalism, provided new understanding of its growth, and occasioned the development (unfortunately incomplete) of an imposing edifice of thought on the relationships between religion and society.

The Parsonians

It is not surprising that the sociology of religion of America's foremost social theorist, Talcott Parsons, has been greatly influenced by the writings of Max Weber. It was Parsons who translated *The Protestant Ethic and the Spirit of Capitalism* into English, and it was from Weber's viewpoint on the reciprocal relationship between religion and society that Parsons drew one of the major components of his own more generalized theory of the nature of the relationship between cognition and social action. For Parsons, like Weber, ideas do have consequence for action, and social action in its turn has a reciprocal impact on the formation of idea systems. Therefore, even though Parsons does not overlook religion's role as an integrator of society his major emphasis is on the meaning-providing function of religion. His insightful treatment of the meaning of denominationalism in American society emphasizes it as a source of personal meaning for the individual agent of social action rather than as a social community in which man may enjoy intimate relationships with his fellow believers. Parsons and his students have emphasized religion's role of enabling man to realize his own individual identity, but even here the emphasis seems to be on that identity over against the group rather than identity flowing from membership within the group. Parsons does not completely overlook the belonging dimension of religion, but his major theoretical concern is with the meaning dimension.

In Parsons' words:

> *From the psychological point of view, then, religion has its greatest relevance to the points of maximum strain and tension in human life as well as to positive affirmations of faith in life, often in the face of these strains. It is most deeply and intimately involved with the "emotional" problems of men, precisely as these are related to the higher levels of culture, to the problems to which in the widest sense man finds it most difficult to adjust.*[30]

Religion, then, is designed to cope with man's frustrations, particularly those frustrations which deal with disasters such as death or natural catastrophe or situations which produce feelings of uncertainty and insecurity. In Parsons' words:

> *Good fortune and suffering must always, to cultural man, be endowed with meaning. They cannot, except in limiting cases, be accepted as something that "just happens." Similarly it is impossible to live by moral standards and yet be wholly indifferent either to the extent of conformity with them or to the fate of conformists and violators respectively. It is necessarily disconcerting that to some degree "the good die young while the wicked flourish as the green bay tree."*[31]

Parsons described the relationship between the individual and religion in modern society thus:

> *. . . the principle of religious toleration inherent in the system of denominational pluralism, implies a great further extension of*

[30] Parsons, "Sociology and Social Psychology," in Fairchild, op. cit., pp. 298–299.
[31] Ibid., p. 296.

the institutionalization of Christian values, both inside and out-side the sphere of religious organization. At least it seems to me that this question poses a sharp alternative—either there is a sharp falling away so that, in tolerating each other, different denominations have become fellow condoners of an essentially evil situation or . . . they do in fact stand on a relatively high ethical plane so that whatever their dogmatic differences, there is no basis for drawing a drastic moral line of distinction which essentially says that the adherents of the other camp are in a moral sense not good people in a sense in which members of our own camp are. . . . This does not mean, however, that Christian ethics have become a matter of indifference in the society. It means rather that a differentiation between religious and secular spheres has gone farther than before and with it the extention of the individualistic principle inherent in Christianity to the point of the "privatizing" of formal, external religious commitment, as the Reformation made internal religious faith a matter for the individual alone.[32]

In Parsons' view, then, religion has become a private matter with a subsequent freeing of the individual conscience, because in the denominational society the principle of Christian trust has been institutionalized both in relationships with members of other religions and in the general value system of the society. That religion has now become a matter of free individual choice does not mean that it is unimportant. It merely means that it now has its impact on society indirectly and in two fashions: (1) through its shaping of the individual conscience, and (2) from the fact that most of the institutions of society do accept more or less the basic ethical principles of Christianity as norms for action. Parsons sees this changing manner in which religion exercises its basic function of providing meaning and explanation as being analogous to changes taking place in the family.

In this respect the religious group may be likened (up to a point) to the family. The family has lost many traditional functions and has become increasingly a sphere of private sentiments. There is, however, reason to believe that it is as important as ever to the maintenance of the main patterns of the society though operating with a minimum of direct outside control. Similarly, religion has become largely a private matter in which the individual associates with the group of his own choice and in this respect

[32] Reprinted with permission of The Macmillan Company from *Sociological Theory, Values & Sociocultural Change* edited by Edward A. Tiryakian. © by The Free Press of Glencoe, a Division of The Macmillan Company, 1963.

has lost many functions of previous religious organizational types. . . . we may note that the development of society has been such that it should not be operated without an upgrading of general levels of responsibility and competence, the acquisition and exercise of the latter of course implying a high degree of responsibility. . . . Responsibility has a double aspect. The first is the responsibility of the individual in that he cannot rely on a dependent relation to others, or to some authority, to absolve him of responsibility. . . . this is the aspect we have been referring to as his autonomy. . . . The other aspect is the responsibility for and to, responsibility for results and to other persons and to collectivities. Here the element of mutuality inherent in Christian ethics, subject to a commonly binding set of norms and values, is of central concern.

* * *

. . . because this human initiative has been more daring and has ventured into more new realms than ever before, greater demands are put on the human individual. He has more difficult problems, both technical and moral; he takes greater risks. Hence the possibility of failure and of the failure being his fault is at least as great as, if not greater than, it ever was.[33]

Modern religion, therefore, has endowed man with both independence and responsibility, while at the same time modern culture has provided him with a host of new and rather terrifying moral problems. Religion does not impose ready-made solutions to these problems through the forms of institutional social control it exercised in the past but rather through a heightened consciousness of both personal responsibility and moral reality. Clearly Parsons' view is right—we live in an age which is more moral rather than less:

There is a widespread view, particularly prevalent in religious circles, that our time is one of unprecedented moral collapse. In these circles it is alleged that modern social development has entailed a progressive decline of moral standards which is general throughout the population. This view is clearly incompatible with the general trend of the analysis we have been making. Its most plausible grain of truth is the one just indicated, that as new and more difficult problems emerge, such as those involved in the possibility of far more destructive war than ever before, we do not feel morally adequate to the challenge. But to say that because we face greater problems than our forefathers faced we

[33] Ibid., p. 67.

are doubtful of our capacity to handle them responsibly is quite a different thing from saying that, on the same levels of responsibility as those of our forefathers, we are in fact handling our problems on a much lower moral level.[34]

Parsons' contribution, then, to the theory of sociology of religion is to affirm, first of all, the importance of the system of religious ideas for human action; secondly, to point out that religion's function is essentially a providing of meaning for the extraordinary events of life, which meaning, however, quickly filters down to explain also life's ordinary events; and thirdly, suggests quite powerfully that because modern religion has provided man with greater moral initiative and responsibility and thus operates on society only indirectly, the meaning-providing role of religion is no less important than it was in the past.

Geertz

Parsons' brilliant student Clifford Geertz defines religion as "a system of symbols which acts to establish powerful, pervasive, and long-lasting moods and motivations in men by formulating conceptions of a general order of existence and clothing these conceptions with such an aura of factuality that the moods and motivations seem uniquely realistic." [35] Geertz thinks that man must be able to interpret disorganized and chaotic phenomena that impinge on his consciousness. He must have a system of meaning which can serve as a road map through his life. There are three points where chaos threatens to deprive man not merely of interpretations but indeed of interpretability. Meaning is required in times of bafflement, pain, and moral paradox—when man's analytic capacities or his powers of endurance or his moral insights are pushed to their limits. The strange, the painful, the unjust, all have to be explained or the world stops being interpretable. Religion is not the only meaning ssytem: common sense, science, ideology, aesthetics are others; but:

> *The religious perspective differs from the commonsensical in that, . . . it moves beyond the realities of everyday life to wider ones which correct and complete them. Its defining concern, moreover, is not action upon those wider realities but acceptance of them, faith in them. It differs from the scientific perspective in that it questions the realities of everyday life, not out of an*

[34] Ibid., p. 68.
[35] Geertz, op. cit., p. 2.

institutionalized scepticism which dissolves the world's firmness into a swirl of probabilist hypotheses, but in terms of what it considers wider, nonhypothetical truths. Rather than detachment, its watchword is commitment; rather than analysis, encounter. And it differs from art in that, instead of effecting a disengagement from the whole question of factuality, deliberately manufacturing an air of semblance and illusion, it deepens the concern with fact and seeks to create an aura of utter actuality.[36]

Religion, then, represents the "really real." Its meaning system is imbued with "persuasive authority" and is rendered "inviolable by the discordant revelations of secular experience." [37]

Geertz extends Parsons' meaning-providing role of religion to include the religious symbol system as embodied in ritual. "In a ritual, the world as lived and the world as imagined, fused under the agency of a single set of symbolic forms, turn out to be the same world." [38] Geertz, then, sees religion as man's attempt to idealize an ultimate meaning system to which he can turn through ritual in episodes of crisis. Ritual and religious symbol can extend the influence of the ultimate-meaning system throughout a man's and his society's existence.

Bellah

Robert Bellah is the other pupil of Parsons who has made a significant contribution to our thinking about the sociology of religion—particularly his concept of religious evolution. Religion for Bellah is "a set of symbolic forms and acts which relate man to the ultimate conditions of his existence." [39] This definition is quite in keeping with those of Parsons and Geertz. He views evolution as:

. . . a process of increasing differentiation and complexity of organization which endows the organism, social system or whatever the unit in question may be, with greater capacity to adapt to its environment so that it is in some sense more autonomous relative to its environment than were its less complex ancestors.[40]

Bellah makes more explicit than Parsons or Geertz the critical point, "religious symbolization relating man to the ultimate conditions of

[36] Ibid., p. 27.
[37] Ibid., p. 28.
[38] Ibid., p. 28.
[39] Robert N. Bellah, "Religious Evolution," *American Sociological Review*, 29 (June 1964): 359. Reprinted with permission of the publisher and the author.
[40] Ibid., p. 358.

existence is also involved in relating him to himself and to symbolizing his own identity." [41] In the process of religious evolution, then, not only does religion differentiate itself from the rest of the environment, it also enables man to differentiate himself more clearly from the world around him.

Bellah postulates five phases of religious evolution: primitive, archaic, historic, early modern, and modern.

> *Primitive* religious action *is characterized not . . . by worship, nor . . . by sacrifice, but by identification, "participation," act-ing-out. Just as the primitive symbol system is myth* par excel-lence, *so primitive religious action is ritual* par excellence. *In the ritual the participants become identified with the mythical beings they represent.*

* * *

> *In the archaic* religious symbol system *mythical beings are much more definitely characterized. Instead of being great para-digmatic figures with whom men in ritual identify but with whom they do not really interact, the mythical beings are more objec-tified, conceived as actively and sometimes willfully controlling the natural and human world, and as beings with whom men must deal in a definite and purposive way—in a word they have become gods.* [42]

In primitive religion there is little differentiation between religion and society, and man does not in his religious behavior sense himself as being distinct over against those to whom the behavior is directed. In archaic religion there is a step forward in that religion is now somewhat distinct from the rest of society, and man is relating to beings who do provide him with some sense of interacting with role opposites. But in the historic religions even more progress has oc-curred. Bellah says:

> *The identity diffusion characteristic of both primitive and archaic religions is radically challenged by the historic religious symboli-zation, which leads for the first time to a clearly structured con-ception of the self. Devaluation of the empirical world and the empirical self highlights the conception of a responsible self, a core self or a true self, deeper than the flux of everyday experi-ence, facing a reality over against itself, a reality which has a consistency belied by the fluctuations of mere sensory impres-sions. . . . the historic religions promise man for the first time that he can understand the fundamental structure of reality and*

41 Ibid., p. 362.
42 Ibid., pp. 363–364.

through salvation participate actively in it. The opportunity is far greater than before but so is the risk of failure.[43]

In his discussion of the next step, from the historic religions (what we have previously called the world religions) to early modern religion, Bellah restricts himself to the Protestant Reformation because it was the only reform movement that was successfully institutionalized.

What the Reformation did was in principle, with the usual reservations and mortgages to the past, break through the whole mediated system of salvation and declare salvation potentially available to any man no matter what his station or calling might be.[44]

He summarizes the evolution of the historic religions:

The historic religions discovered the self; the early modern religions found a doctrinal basis on which to accept the self in all its empirical ambiguity; modern religion is beginning to understand the laws of the self's own existence and so to help man take responsibility for his own fate.[45]

And so:

I see . . . the increasing acceptance of the notion that each individual must work out his own ultimate solutions and that the most the church can do is provide him a favorable environment for doing so, without imposing on him a prefabricated set of answers.[46]

There is, therefore, only an inchoate self in the archaic religions; a distinctive self in the historical religions; a moral, if empirically ambiguous self in the early modern religions; and, finally, a responsible and "existential" self in the modern religions. The increasing complexity of the differentiation of religion from society and the consequent increasing complexity of its relationship to society has been mirrored in the production through the religious symbols of an increasingly autonomous man—independent, responsible, ambiguous, moral, and yet still religious. For this modern man with his much more complex relationship to reality, a much more complex religious system is required. Bellah sees religious developments of our time not as secularization but as simply the emergence of this more complex religious posture.

[43] Ibid., p. 367.
[44] Ibid., pp. 368–369.
[45] Ibid., p. 372.
[46] Ibid., p. 373.

The Bellah theory is an impressive intellectual effort whose limitations and oversimplifications he is the first to admit. Using the tools of Parsons and Geertz, he has developed a theory of the relationship between religion and society which explains not only the present development of religious beliefs but also the nature of the relationship between the individual and his religion; he sees both phenomena as the present development of an ongoing pattern of differentiation. In our judgment, the principal weakness in the Bellah theory is that just as in the theories of Parsons and Geertz, it is extremely difficult to cope with religious organizations. They seem to these theorists to be merely institutions which pass on the meaning systems and which permit their individual members (souls, it often seems, as lonely and isolated as Søren Kierkegaard) to engage in the agonizing ambiguity of moral decision making. This does not seem to be what the denominations do in American society, or at least not the only thing they do.

Luckmann

Professor Thomas Luckmann might not be enthusiastic about being described as a Parsonian, particularly since he contends, quite correctly, that his theoretical interpretation of the relationship between religion and society goes considerably beyond that of Professor Parsons. Nonetheless, Luckmann is still writing in the Parsonian tradition. While he is considerably more concerned about the religious dimension of man's relationship to his fellow men, he still does not, at least in our judgment, seem to take into sufficient account the "community binding" or belonging function of religion.

Luckmann insists on the necessity of the distinction between organized religion and religion, observing that the appearance of religious organizations is a relatively recent human development, but that religion itself is inherent in the human experience of interacting with one's fellow men and becoming conscious of oneself.

According to Luckmann, man becomes conscious of himself as himself through the experience of interacting with his fellow men, and this sense of one's own distinction over against others forces man to construct interpretative schemes, the top layer of which—the ultimate interpretation—is religion.

> *Detachment from immediate experience originates in the confrontation with fellow men in the face-to-face situation. It leads to the individuation of consciousness and permits the construction of interpretive schemes, ultimately, of systems of meaning. Detachment from immediate experience finds its complement in*

the integration of past, present and future into a socially defined, morally relevant biography. This integration develops in continuous social relations and leads to the formation of conscience. The individuation of the two complementary aspects of Self occurs in social processes. The organism—in isolation nothing but a separate pole of "meaningless" subjective processes—becomes a Self by embarking with others upon the construction of an "objective" and moral universe of meaning. Thereby the organism transcends its biological nature.[47]

At the top of this interpretive scheme, which man is forced to when he realizes that he has transcended his biology, is a symbol system which refers to a domain of reality that is above and beyond the ordinary. This is labeled by Luckmann "the sacred cosmos":

The symbols which represent the reality of the sacred cosmos may be termed religious representations because they perform in a specific and concentrated way, the broad religious function of the world view as a whole. The world view in its totality was defined earlier as a universal and nonspecific social form of religion. Consequently, the configuration of religious representations that form a sacred universe *is to be defined as a* specific historical social form of religion.[48]

Luckmann then sees the development of specialized institutions which act as custodians of the ultimate layer of interpretation or the sacred cosmos. Man proceeds, therefore, from confrontation of others to consciousness of self, to need for an explanation, to an interpretive scheme, to a differentiated interpretive scheme with a specifically designed sacred cosmos, and then to social organizations which act as mediators of the sacred cosmos.

In modern society, however, Luckmann points out, the political, economic, and many of the social institutions provide their own meaning systems and do not require a religious interpretation. Therefore, modern religion tends to operate in the private sphere—that is to say, the sphere of family or of the "interstices" of society—the residual areas which do not fall under the domain of the self-providing meaning of the large corporate structures. Luckmann says:

The social form of religion emerging in modern industrial societies is characterized by the direct accessibility of the sacred

[47] Reprinted with permission of The Macmillan Company from *The Invisible Religion* by Thomas Luckmann. Copyright © by The Macmillan Company, 1967.

[48] Ibid., p. 61.

cosmos, more precisely, of an assortment of religious themes, which makes religion today essentially a phenomenon of the "private sphere." The emerging social form of religion thus differs significantly from older social forms of religion which were characterized either by the diffusion of the sacred cosmos through the institutional structure of society or through institutional specialization of religion.[49]

It will be noted that here one discovers the basic difference between Luckmann and the other Parsonians. Parsons, Bellah, and probably Geertz would contend that the secular institutions are influenced by religion both because these institutions have themselves internalized, at least in some fashion, the Christian ethical viewpoint and because individuals who operate within the systems have a world view which is shaped by their religion. Luckmann on the other hand finds that the norms and values within the secularist institutions are not religious but rational, that is to say, determined by the functional requirements of the given institution. Religion, now itself a distinct social institution, is capable of offering an official model of a meaning system, but cannot cope with the complexities of the other institutions to an extent sufficient to integrate their activities within its own official meaning system. What comes to exist, then, is really an assortment of ultimate meanings—the official religious one and a number of others produced by other institutions in society. The individual human being, then, is a consumer of religious schemes put together by himself—the meaning system composed of propositions from both the official religious model and the unofficial quasi-religious interpretive schemes:

In the absence of an "official" model the individual may select from a variety of themes of "ultimate" significance. The selection is based on consumer preference, which is determined by the social biography of the individual, and similar social biographies will result in similar choices. Given the assortment of religious representations available to potential consumers and given the absence of an "official" model it is possible, in principle, that the "autonomous" individual will not only select certain themes but will construct with them a well-articulated private system of "ultimate" significance. To the extent that some themes in the assortment of "ultimate" meanings are coalesced into something like a coherent model (such as "positive Christianity" and psychoanalysis), some individuals may internalize such models en bloc. Unless we postulate a high degree of reflection and conscious

49 Ibid., p. 103.

deliberation, however, it is more likely that individuals will legitimate the situation-bound (primarily emotional and affective) priorities arising in their "private spheres" by deriving, ad hoc, more or less appropriate rhetorical elements from the sacred cosmos. The assumption seems justified, therefore, that the prevalent individual systems of "ultimate" significance will consist of a loose and rather unstable hierarchy of "opinions" legitimating the affectively determined priorities of "private" life.[50]

Luckmann concludes by suggesting that there are five major themes in contemporary society which are to be found with a great deal of frequency in the interpretive schemes of modern man. The themes are individual autonomy, self-expression, self-realization, mobility ethos, sexuality, and familism. "Getting along with others," "adjustment," "a fair shake for all," "togetherness," are all American versions of these themes.

It is interesting to note that death does not appear even as a subordinate topic in the sacred cosmos of a modern industrial society. Nor are growing old and old age endowed with "sacred" significance. The "autonomous" individual is young and he never dies.[51]

Whereas Parsons and Bellah view modern man's autonomy as authentic and representative of man's increasing freedom from social institutions as well as a development of the differentiating process, Luckmann takes a much more pessimistic view. Man may feel he is autonomous, but actually he is not. Rather, it is the institution that has become autonomous.

The discrepancy between the subjective "autonomy" of the individual in modern society and the objective autonomy of the primary institutional domains strikes us as critical. The primary social institutions have "emigrated" from the sacred cosmos. Their functional rationality is not part of a system that could be of "ultimate" significance to the individuals in the society. This removes from the primary institutions much of the (potentially intolerant) human pathos that proved to be fateful all too often in human history. If the process could be viewed in isolation it could justifiably appear as an essential component in freeing social arrangements from primitive emotions. The increasing autonomy of the primary public institutions, however, has consequences for the relation of the individual to the social order—and

[50] Ibid., pp. 105–106.
[51] Ibid., p. 114.

thus, ultimately, to himself. Reviewing some of these conse-
quences one is equally justified in describing this process as a
process of dehumanization of the basic structural components of
the social order. The functional rationality of the primary social
institutions seems to reinforce the isolation of the individual from
his society, contributing thereby to the precariousness inherent
in all social orders. Autonomy of the primary institutions, "sub-
jective" autonomy and anomie *of the social order are dialectically*
related. At the very least it may be said that "subjective" auton-
omy and autonomy of the primary institutions, the two most
remarkable characteristics of modern industrial societies, are
genuinely ambivalent phenomena.

The new social form of religion emerges in the same global
transformation of society which leads to the autonomy of the
primary public institutions. The modern sacred cosmos legiti-
mates the retreat of the individual into the "private sphere" and
sanctifies his subjective "autonomy." Thus it inevitably reinforces
the autonomous functioning of the primary institutions. By be-
stowing a sacred quality upon the increasing subjectivity of human
existence it supports not only the secularization but also what
we called the dehumanization of the social structure. If this still
appears paradoxical we have failed in driving home the point of
this essay.[52]

Luckmann is not sure whether this new social form of religion is
good or bad.

While the new social form of religion supports dehumanization
of the social structure, it also "sacralizes" the (relative) relation
of human consciousness from the constraint of the latter. This
liberation represents a historically unprecedented opportunity for
the autonomy of personal life for "everybody." It also contains
a serious danger—of motivating mass withdrawal into the "pri-
vate sphere" while "Rome burns." On balance, is this good or
bad?[53]

Luckmann represents, at least at the present time, the most highly
developed theory of religion as a meaning-providing institution.
Whether his pessimistic view of the rationalization of modern society
is more accurate than that of Talcott Parsons may be debatable,
though it does seem safe to say that Luckmann is closer to Weber in
this respect than is Parsons. Luckmann's new social form of religion,

[52] Ibid., pp. 115–116.
[53] Ibid., p. 117.

that is to say, a religion which provides meaning for the private sphere of life assures man that he is autonomous in relationship to the public sphere (while in fact the public sphere has become autonomous from human control and from critical judgment by human values). It may not be much of a religion; indeed, it may be even more of an opiate for the people than Marx claimed. The issue probably still is in doubt. Man may well be able to recapture control of his organizations before they slip completely from his grasp. Man's religions, either the official ones or the folk ones, put together from the marketplace of interpretive schemes, may be able to evolve enough to provide man with values sophisticated enough to enable him to judge and to regulate the complex institutions in which he finds himself immersed. Parsons and Luckmann would both agree that the moral problems in the public sphere are extraordinarily complicated. Parsons' conviction that man's moral autonomy and concern lead him to infer that there is at least a possibility of moral response to the problems of complex organizations, in which, by the way, Parsons still sees many Christian values institutionalized. Luckmann, more skeptical about this moral autonomy and more pessimistic about moral concern, suspects that the values of the secular institutions are much more rational and functional than they are religious.

One pays his money and takes his choice. Suffice it to remark that one of the problems of resolving the issue between Luckmann and Parsons is that we suspect that at least as far as American society goes neither one of them has looked very carefully at the community-providing role of organized religion. It has not seemed to have occurred to either of them that the denomination (Parsons' term) or the religious institution (Luckmann's term) might, in fact, also be ethnic groups, and that as such they may have a far stronger influence on "the public sphere" than either Luckmann or Parsons realize.

The Comfort Theory

The third strain of thought about the sociology of religion which we wish to consider is that which sees religion as essentially providing comfort, serenity, and reassurance to those who are troubled or disturbed. Neither of the two previous traditions we have described is unaware of the "comfort factor" of religion. Parsons and his students see religion as providing meaning in the face of such disheartening and frustrating events as death. Durkheim and Malinowski of the anthropological school similarly point out how religious behavior reintegrates society when it is faced with the trauma of death. The comfort theory, proposed mainly by Charles Y. Glock and his associates, sees religion not so much as an overriding meaning system, though this function is not denied, but as essentially a conservative response to suffering and deprivation. Religion must, in their words, both comfort and challenge, but it seems to comfort far more than it challenges.

Glock and his associates make claim to being sons of Durkheim and Weber, and insofar as a comforting religion does contribute both to meaning and to social integration, one can concede that they are, though in fact they seem much closer to Sigmund Freud who viewed religion as "an illusion." [54] Religion according to Freud is a wish fulfillment born of the need to make tolerable the helplessness of man; and man's relationship to God is merely a reassertion of the infantile relationship with his parents. Since religion is a recapitulation of infantile dependency on parents, it must be put aside in the mature world, particularly since religion does not make man's existential helplessness and defencelessness go away.

Glock and his associates do not go nearly that far, but they do suggest:

> . . . *religious value systems characteristically sanction prevailing institutions, thus contributing to social stability and integration. . . . religion not only bids the deprived to accept their lot, but maintains that it is the just outcome of rules that are the best possible, indeed, in some instances divinely inspired.*[55]

Glock and Stark then proceed to suggest that religion and political radicalism are mutually exclusive:

> . . . *the greater the degree of radicalism, the greater the tendency for the movement to conflict with prevailing values, and hence with institutions and elites primarily concerned with maintaining these values. Although a radical movement may claim a purely political character, it is likely to engender opposition on religious grounds.*[56]

At one level the assertion of Glock and his colleagues is certainly unassailable, and the substantial number of statistical tables they adduce to show that Catholics in France are not Communists and Communists are not Catholics represent sociological findings which are scarcely original. Similarly, data from England suggesting that the

---

[54] For a complete articulation of Freud's theory see his *The Future of an Illusion,* trans. W. D. Robeson Scott (Garden City, N.Y.: Doubleday & Company, Inc., 1957).

[55] Glock and Stark, op. cit., p. 191.

[56] Ibid., p. 192.

more ideological members of the Labor Party score lower on measures of religious behavior do not cause us very much surprise. But the data hardly support their assertion that "Religious involvement and political radicalism . . . tend to be mutually exclusive commitments."[57] If 27 percent of the French socialists have received communion recently and 70 percent of them think that the existence of God is certain or at least probable, it is clear that religious commitment and political radicalism can coexist in a very substantial number of people, though perhaps not in so many people as political conservatism and religious commitment can coexist.

The relationship between religion and radicalism in a country such as France is a complex historical question, and in the context of that history it is very difficult to say whether people are radical because they are unreligious or unreligious because they are radical. The most that could be said on the basis of the data adduced by Glock and Stark is that there is some relationship between religion and social integration (since social integration can be considered a conservative tendency) but that this relationship is not terribly strong and it does not necessarily go in one direction; and it offers relatively low level explanations of either religion or political radicalism. Glock and his associates ignore (as they do in other works) the work of Gordon Allport who suggests that personalities with a dogmatic cognitive style will be attracted both to religious orthodoxy and political conservatism. If Allport is right, and there is every reason to believe that he is, then the relationship Glock and Stark claim to have found between religion and conservatism may be even less powerful than it appears, if not, indeed, spurious. Finally, one has the feeling in reading the Glock version of the deprivation theory that the comments of Merton and others about the social functions of religion have been completely overlooked. Religion can be functional in a society, but it can be dramatically dysfunctional. As we shall shortly see in discussing the work of Norman Cohn, religion can hold society together, or it can tear it apart. It can substitute for political radicalism, or it can facilitate political radicalism of the wildest most demonic sort. Religion may comfort, but it may also destroy.

Perhaps a more helpful way of putting the issue has been followed by Seymour Lipset. He suggests that with the lower class religious sects, radical political parties are alternative outlets for lower-class frustration. Lipset admits:

> *Such sects often drain off the discontent and frustration which*
> *would otherwise flow into channels of political extremism (but)*

[57] Ibid., p. 201.

*the point here is that rigid fundamentalism and dogmatism are
linked to the same underlying characteristics, attitudes and pre-
dispositions which find another outlet in allegiance to extremist
political movements.*[58]

The discontented and the frustrated, therefore, particularly when
they have narrow, dogmatic cognitive styles, have several different alternatives available to them. They may turn to "withdrawal" religious
sects which cut them off from political activity; they may engage in
activity with political extremist parties; or, thirdly, they may become
members of militantly political religious sects. The historical and social context very likely determines which of these three alternatives
they take.

In his comments on the "churches of the disinherited," Richard
Niebuhr describes one such form of religious comfort.

*An intellectually trained and liturgically minded clergy is rejected
in favor of lay leaders who serve the emotional needs of this religion more adequately and who, on the other hand, are not allied
by culture and interest with those ruling classes whose superior
manner of life is too obviously purchased at the expense of the
poor. . . .*

*Ethically as well as psychologically, such a religion bears a
distinct character. The salvation which it seeks and sets forth is
the salvation of the socially disinherited. Intellectual naivete and
practical need combine to create a marked propensity towards
millenarianism, with its promise of tangible goods, and of the
reveral of all present social systems and rank. . . .*

*Whenever Christianity has become the religion of the fortu-
nate and cultured and has grown philosophical, abstract, formal,
and ethically harmless in the process, the lower strata of society
find themselves religiously expatriated by a faith which neither
meets their psychological needs nor sets forth an appealing
ethical ideal. In such a situation the right leader finds little difficulty in launching a new movement which will, as a rule, give
rise to a new denomination.*[59]

Niebuhr notes that such a sect may become either religiously
conservative, as in the case of Methodism (John Wesley himself
lamented the fact that the sobriety and reliability of his moralistic fol-

[58] From *Political Man* by Seymour M. Lipset. Copyright © 1959, 1960 by
Seymour M. Lipset. Reprinted by permission of Doubleday & Company, Inc.
[59] R. Richard Niebuhr, *The Social Sources of Denominationalism* (Hamden,
Conn.: The Shoe String Press, 1954), pp. 30–32. Reprinted by permission of
Mrs. H. R. Niebuhr.

lowers would probably make them wealthy and thus undo precisely what Methodism was trying to do), or may become politically radical. Niebuhr's basic concern was with the conservative sect becoming a denomination, but there are other possibilities.

Norman Cohn is perhaps the most famous student of the millenarian religious movement, a movement which seems to appear wherever the salvationism of the Christian tradition has spread. According to Cohn:

> . . . *I propose to regard as "millenarian" any religious movement inspired by the fantasy of a salvation which is to be*
>
> *(a) collective, in the sense that it is to be enjoyed by the faithful as a group;*
>
> *(b) terrestrial, in the sense that it is to be realised on this earth and not in some otherworldly heaven;*
>
> *(c) imminent, in the sense that it is to come both soon and suddenly;*
>
> *(d) total, in the sense that it is utterly to transform life on earth, so that the new dispensation will be no mere improvement on the present but perfection itself;*
>
> *(e) accomplished by agencies which are consciously regarded as supernatural.*[60]

The various millenarian sects which have appeared would include the Ghost Dance among the Indians in North America, the Cargo Cults in Melanesia, and the various uprisings in the backlands of Brazil, some sects which have appeared in Spain and Italy, and, most especially, the fantastic millenarian sects which appeared in Flanders, Northern France, the Rhine Valley and Thuringia at the end of the Middle Ages and the beginning of the modern world, the most famous of which were the radical Anabaptists led by Thomas Muntzer in Thuringia and Jan Bockelson in Munster. Cohn's analysis of these groups represents one of the most fascinating chapters in the history of the sociology of religion and merits careful study.

The late medieval sects were not interested in withdrawing from society but rather in smashing the existing society and building one of their own, usually by force of arms. The New Jerusalems which were established by some of these leaders were places of political and sexual anarchy where preparation was allegedly being made for the beginning of the new creation, preparation which was

[60] Norman Cohn, "Medieval Millenarism: Its Bearing on the Comparative Study of Millenarian Movements." Reprinted by permission of Schocken Books Inc. from *Millennial Dreams in Action* ed. by Sylvia L. Thrupp.

furthered by the fact that the millenarian groups seemed consistently to be able to generate a high degree of military skill and a ruthless fierceness in battle. Cohn argues that such sects arise in the midst of politically unsettling circumstances. It is not merely, according to him, that there is suffering and deprivation but rather that the established order of things, if it has not already been destroyed, is seen to be under threat of destruction. Catastrophe and the fear of catastrophes, the failure of traditional authority to maintain social order, dramatic changes in the political, social, and economic environment—all of these seem to provide the raw material out of which millenarianism can arise. Indeed, Cohn points out that late medieval sects and the Anabaptists coexisted with much more secularly oriented political reform movements. In apparent agreement with Lipset, Cohn sees the political reformist movement and the antinomian millenarian sect as alternative responses to situations of tension or social disorganization. But it is important to note that for Cohn not just any kind of deprivation gives rise to religious movements; it is precisely that kind of deprivation, often moral rather than physical, that occurs at a time of rapid social change or apparent social disorganization:

> *It seems that there is in many, perhaps in all, human psyches a latent yearning for total salvation from suffering; and that that yearning is greatly intensified by any frustration or anxiety or humiliation which is unaccustomed and which cannot be tackled either by taking thought or by an institutionalized routine. Where a particular frustration or anxiety or humiliation of this nature is experienced at the same time and in the same area by a number of individuals, the result is a collective emotional agitation which is peculiar not only in its intensity but also in the boundlessness of its aims.*[61]

Cohn then goes on to argue that all that is required to turn this emotion into a millenarian sect is the appearance on the scene of the prophet who will lead the movement. But for our purposes, it is enough to establish that a religious response to deprivation need not at all be functional for social integration. Jan Bockelson was anything but the leader of a functional movement.

From the preceding paragraphs it will be clear to the reader that there is certainly a comfort element in religion, and that religion does enable man to respond to deprivations, sometimes by piously accepting them and sometimes by attempting to create a new

[61] Ibid., p. 42.

order in which the deprivations will be removed. In the absence of religion, a third alternative, a radical political movement, may arise. In Spain, for example, the political anarchists were strong precisely in those areas where in years gone by religiously radical political movements arose. However, it would be a serious mistake to assume that the staid comfort of upper middle-class American suburban churches represents the only style of religion relating to society. Religion does comfort men in the very broad sense that meaning and purpose surely make life more tolerable; but the meaning systems may also drive men to effort and sacrifice and suffering, which however "comforting" they may be intellectually and emotionally, can also be horrendously uncomfortable physically.

The comfort or deprivation theory does not rank nearly as importantly as the other two strains in thinking about the sociology of religion. Nonetheless, we think it has an extraordinarily important role to play in helping us to combine the meaning and belonging theories of religious behavior into some sort of theoretical explanation of religion in American society, but we shall turn to this question in a later chapter.

Summary

We have noted several times in the present chapter the three basic "explanations" of religion that we have described are not mutually exclusive. There is much overlapping in these traditions. Most of the Parsonians would claim to be "functionalists" of one sort or another, and to comfort deprivation is certainly one of the all-time functions of religion. Furthermore, Marx could easily be listed as a deprivationist; and Parsons and his students are not unconcerned with social integration, though their emphasis is on integration through the meaning which religion provides and much less through the fellowship it provides. Religion simultaneously provides belonging, meaning, and comfort—comfort because it does give meaning to the uninterpretable, and belonging because this shared explanation of the uninterpretable constitutes the basis for interaction. Religion further gives meaning precisely insofar as we are bound together in a society which helps to sustain us in times of trial and heartache. Finally, religion provides us with a society to which we may belong and from which we obtain both meaning and comfort in the midst of the uncertainties of life. But while these three different functions of religion overlap, they are not quite the same.

The work of Weber, Parsons, Luckmann, and Geertz represents the first emphasis; the work of Durkheim, Malinowsky, and the functionalists is characteristic of the second emphasis; and the work of Glock and Stark and Norman Cohn fit in with the third emphasis. But none of these emphases necessarily excludes the other two. Religion can provide both meaning and community, and, for most people probably does provide both—with the precise mix varying from person to person. Religion further does provide comfort in time of trial and does help to hold society together, but it also not infrequently helps to tear society apart. Religion is both an integrating and a disintegrating function. The various perspectives in this chapter all have their own utility. It would be a mistake for any serious student of religion to deprive himself of the insights that any one of the perspectives provides. The principal thesis of this book is that the relationship between the meaning and the belonging functions of American society are, to a considerable extent, responsible for the vigorous religious behavior in the United States and presumably also for the fact that religion does provide immense amounts of social comfort for the citizenry of this republic.

Chapter 3

Religion as an Organization

In this chapter we turn from explanations of why there is a religion to observations of what religion looks like in the contemporary world, and we discover that most manifestations of religion are organized and that the principal kind of organization in the United States is the denomination. We reject the notion that denomination is a compromise or halfway house between sect and church and argue that it is a unique and new social form of religion, and that the institutionalized denomination is not necessarily dysfunctional for religion's or our purposes.

Definitions of Sect and Church

It is easy when we consider the various theories of the sociology of religion, as we have in the previous chapter, to lose sight of what religion is in American society. We become so conscious of the function of religion as a means of belonging to society, as a provider of meaning, and as a comfort in time of deprivation, that it is possible for us to lose track of the empirical reality with which we are surrounded. American religion may very well provide meaning and social integration and comfort, but having said these things, we have by no means exhausted the existential reality that we are capable of observing, let us say, every Sunday morning. American religion is engaged in doing many things that can only remotely be connected to meaning, integration, or comfort. The vast system of Roman Catholic schools, for example, probably does provide some sort of explanation of the ultimate for many of the students; it may well contribute something to the social integration, at least to the Catholic community and, though heaven knows how, there may be times when it even provides some comfort for the deprived. But these three functions do not explain either how the school system came into existence or why despite many difficulties it continues to be popular with the overwhelming majority of American Catholics. Similarly, the ecumenical movement, the striking phenomenon of contemporary American religion, is very poorly understood if we see it simply as an attempt to evolve some sort of common American society. And the comfort and meaning functions seem quite irrelevant in any attempt to understand the ecumenic developments. We therefore must go beyond the theories discussed in the last chapter if we are going to be able to cope with the rich, varied, and complicated religious phenomena that are to be observed in the American republic.

It is safe to say that religion in America is organized—at least as organized as are any of the other major institutions in American society. The theorists we discussed in the previous chapter only occasionally advert to this fact of organization, and then, either, as in the case of Luckmann, to suggest that there is an important distinction between religion and church and that churches may decline but religion will not, or, as in the case of Parsons, to see the organizations as the purveyors of traditions which provide the individual with the moral and ideological resources that enable him to engage in social action. Both Luckmann and Parsons are right, of course, but while they tell the truth, they tell substantially less than the whole truth. The very fact that religion in this country is highly organized has a pervasive effect on the whole style and atmosphere of American religious behavior, particularly, as we shall suggest in this volume, because the fact of religious organization makes it possible for the churches to play a quasi-ethnic role in our denominational society.

Religious organizations are, from the point of view of the whole human history, relatively recent developments. Primitive and ancient civilized societies, of course, had their temple worship, their priestly castes, and their religious functionaries who lived either partially or totally off their religious activities. But the church as a distinct institution separated from and over against the other institutions of society such as state, economic enterprise, and family is, to a very large extent, a phenomenon of the Christian era and, interestingly enough, has even today affected the other world religions, such as Islam or Buddhism, substantially less than it has affected Christianity. Buddhism and Islam, as a matter of fact, seem to become organized churches only when Western influence has touched them and then, as in the Buddhist section in Vietnam, they often seem to become carbon copies of American denominations in many respects.

There is only one sociological theory (though many would concede that it is only a typology) concerned with religion as an organization—the famous distinction between church and sect. Unfortunately, this distinction, over which almost as much ink has been spilled as on the Protestant ethic hypothesis, is not very useful either for expanding our understanding of religion or providing us with testable research hypotheses, however attractive the dichotomy may at first seem.

The church-sect dichotomy first came into sociological use in the work of Max Weber and his pupil, Ernst Troeltsch. As Allan Eister points out, part of the problem of using the church-sect dichotomy is that there was a major difference in the way these two men used the concept. Weber was a sociologist and distinguished a sect from a church on the grounds that the former was an elective association of adults, exclusive in terms of some selective principle, belief, or practice, while the church was inclusive. For Troeltsch, a theologian primarily concerned with Christian ethics, the central characteristic of the church was its acceptance of the secular order. In Eister's words:

> By stressing the "accommodative" character of the church (and the non-accommodative character of the sect)—and by tying these to "compromise" (or non-compromise) of the Christian ethic, Troeltsch introduced what in effect is an open invitation, if not a demand, for subjective value-laden definitions. For what is "compromise" of an ethic to one believer—or even to a non-believer—is not compromise to another.[1]

Subjective definitions did evolve and so did numerous subclassifications. While Troeltsch implied that sects do grow into churches, his primary concern was not with the dynamic nature of the typology. However, the American social theologian, H. Richard Niebuhr, argued that a lower-class sectlike group would "move upward as its membership did, and if it did not become a church in the Troeltschian sense, would at least become a 'denomination.'" For Niebuhr, the denomination as it exists in American society representing a middle ground somewhere between church and sect is not a particularly

[1] Allan W. Eister, "Toward a Radical Critique of Church-Sect Typologizing," *Journal for the Scientific Study of Religion,* 6 (April 1967) 1: 87. Reprinted by permission of the author and the Society for the Scientific Study of Religion.

happy phenomenon, because identified as it is with social class or color or national origin, it stands as an obstacle to Christian unity.[2]

Howard Becker, the first full-fledged sociologist to use the church-sect typology in the United States, adds a fourth type, the cult, that is to say, the religious movement that has yet to develop a clearly defined social organizational structure.

J. Milton Yinger expanded the typology to six—the universal church, the ecclesia, the denomination, the established sect, the sect, and the cult. Yinger's definitions of the sect and the church are well worth quoting because they combine the variables usually used in the church-sect discussion:

> *The church as a type is a religious body which recognizes the strength of the secular world and, rather than either deserting the attempt to influence it or losing its position by contradicting the secular powers directly, accepts the main elements in the social structure as proximate goals. (As we shall see, some churches have defended an existing power arrangement not simply as a proximate good, but almost as though it were an absolute good.) It is built therefore on compromise; it is mobile and adaptive; "it dominates the world and is therefore dominated by the world." (Troeltsch) An individual is born into the church which claims universality, in contrast with the voluntary membership of a select group in the sect. The church supports the existing powers in peace and war. It ". . . utilizes the State and the ruling classes, and weaves these elements into her own life; she then becomes an integral part of the existing social order; from this standpoint, then, the Church both stabilizes and determines the social order; in so doing, however, she becomes dependent upon the upper classes, and upon their development." (Troeltsch)[3]*

Sect, on the other hand, according to Yinger:

> *. . . is a group that repudiates the compromises of the church, preferring "isolation to compromise"; in the Christian tradition it stresses literal obedience to the Synoptic Gospels. There is a small, voluntary membership, stressing individual perfection*

---

[2] We will argue later in this volume rather to the contrary, that were it not for denominationalism in American society American religion would be much weaker and ecumenism would be most improbable. We shall also suggest that for the foreseeable future ecumenism in American society will be denominational ecumenism.

[3] Reprinted with permission of The Macmillan Company from *Religion, Society and the Individual* by J. Milton Yinger. © by The Macmillan Company, 1957.

and asceticism, usually associated with the lower classes. It is either hostile or indifferent to the state, and opposes the ecclesiastical order. The sect is a lay religion, free from worldly authority, able therefore on one hand to forget the world in asceticism, or on the other to fight it in radicalism.[4]

Yinger distinguishes between the universal church and the ecclesia at the point that the universal church (for example, Catholicism in the Middle Ages) is able to incorporate within itself sectarian tendencies without schism (or at least with relatively infrequent sectarian schism). He also divides the sect into the established sect and the sect, the former showing a great deal more stability and organizational sophistication than the latter.

Bryan R. Wilson, in his study of various English sectarian organizations, described various sectarian tendencies.

The Conversionist *sects seek to alter men, and thereby to alter the world. . . . The* Adventist *sects predict drastic alteration of the world, and seek to prepare for (this event). . . . The Introversionists reject the world's values. The Gnostic sects accept (generally) the world's goals but seek (to achieve them by) new and esoteric ends.*[5]

The first is characteristic of "free will optimism," the second of "pessimistic determinism," and the fourth is characterized by "wishful mysticism." Wilson insists that even though elites may emerge within sects, such as the Christian Scientists or the Jehovah's Witnesses, it does not follow that the sect will automatically develop into a denomination. According to Wilson, the critical indicator of a denomination is ". . . whether the religious elite is specially trained and whether its function becomes that of a professional ministry." [6]

Clearly the jungle of types and definitions grows more complex; many of the articles in the church-sect literature consist of attempts either to redesign the typology or to develop a more comprehensive set of categories in order to cope with the problems posed by borderline religious organizations that apparently participate in some of the elements of two or more categories within the typology. Indeed, the present writer once reviewed for a scholarly journal an article proposing a sixty-four cell typology for religious groups based ultimately on the church-sect dichotomy. The typology was a sophisti-

---

[4] Ibid., p. 146.
[5] Bryan R. Wilson, "An Analysis of Sect Development," *American Sociological Review,* 24 (February 1959) 5–6. Reprinted with permission of the publisher and the author.
[6] Ibid., p. 10.

cated, intellectual exercise, though its usefulness in understanding American religion was not particularly obvious, especially since many of the cells in the typology were vacant due to the lamentable fact that man's religious ingenuity had not yet provided the kind of organization that would fit into the particular category. It was at that point that I began to suspect that not much good was going to come from the church-sect dichotomy, and none of the discussion since then has substantially affected such a conclusion.

The typology itself is attractive because two things are quite obvious: first of all, religious groups do grow, develop, and evolve. And secondly, charisma is, as Max Weber pointed out, routinized— that is to say, the fervor and the enthusiasm of the founder and his little band of followers is rather quickly spent.

However, the evolution of religious organizations does not necessarily proceed from cult to sect to the denomination to church (or from cult to sect to established sect to the denomination). Methodism was never a cult, and at least in the United States it probably never was a sect either. In American society any but the smallest religious groups very quickly develop an organizational structure of their own and therefore almost at once occupy a place somewhere between the sect and the denomination. Furthermore, the only predictor of how elaborate and bureaucratic the structure will become seems to be the size of the organization. Small religious groups do not need elaborate organizational structures and large ones do. If one wishes to say, therefore, that the sect is small and the denomination is large, one may, but such a distinction is hardly a very useful contribution to sociological theory.

Also, while it is clear that small groups of disciples around a charismatic leader do have a fervor and enthusiasm not to be found in later manifestations of the same religious group, it must be noted first that even among the intimate band of believers, the degree of enthusiasm (and the degree of alienation from the world) tends to vary rather dramatically and, secondly, that as soon as the organization once again reaches an appreciable size, the purity of enthusiasm and world rejection declines rapidly. (If the sectarians are millenarians bent on destroying the established social structure, the charismatic enthusiasm of the leader and his immediate bands of followers may persuade hesitant fellow travelers that the existing social structure must be destroyed, but the fellow travelers go along with such destruction reluctantly and with misgivings.)

Thus, it would seem that enthusiasm, world rejection, and organizational simplicity in American society are largely functions of such a simple variable as size. Some groups may maintain their enthusiasm and simplicity longer than others, either because of doctrinal vigor or because of the force of the personality of the founder and leader, but the tendency in the United States of almost any organization to publish a magazine or a newsletter, to select a full-time secretary, and to hold a national meeting is so strong that it is much to be feared that a religious group will embark on the road to denominationalism shortly after the first sermon is preached.

It would seem, therefore, that the church-sect dichotomy has only a rather low level of explanatory value which, according to Allan Eister, is no more than Max Weber intended it to have. Weber's ideal types are not meant to be research hypotheses.

> *The ideal type (is) a special kind of type resting upon a logic different from that of types and typologies as ordinarily conceived. The ideal type, as Weber fashioned it, was designed as an operation* verstehen—*to give an understanding "inside look" into the reasoning and motivations of "typical actors" in "typical situations" and, in this limited sense, an "explanation" for specific kinds of action.*[7]

Eister states further:

> *One wonders whether the major task of pushing forward a good theory and research on the processes of dynamics of religious movements (and their transformation under certain conditions, into "established" religious organizations) has not been sidetracked by fruitless argument over what constitutes "the sect" as distinguished from "the church" (or "the denomination"). It has certainly been almost hopelessly snarled by the frequent confusion of sect-to-Church "hypothesizing" with Church-sect "typologizing."*[8]

Thus, in the rather low level type of explanation with which Weber was concerned, church-sect is useful though not terribly relevant to understanding what happens in American society after the institutionalized phase begins (in our judgment it begins very early); but this typology ought not to be turned into a hypothesis about the kind of development which occurs in religious groups after the institutionalization phase has already begun. This author thinks Eister is quite right; the confusion between typologizing and hypothesizing has plagued the church-sect dichotomy to such an extent that it has become almost useless. Erich Goode says it well:

[7] Eister, op. cit., p. 87.
[8] Ibid., p. 85.

Too often because of a respectable ancestry, certain concepts and theories have been used, reused, and have been perpetuated long after their usefulness has come to an end. Church-sect is very much in danger of being in that position. As it stands to-day, it is a hodge-podge of definition and empirical correlates and empirical non-correlates. It has no power to explain or to elucidate.[9]

It therefore seems that the church-sect hypotheses (so-called) should be tossed into the ashcan, although it is very likely that the theories will survive, if only because those engaged in the sociology of religion feel the need for some sort of a special theory. It would be much more appropriate if the general theories of organizational sociology were to be applied to religious groups and that they be considered in the light of the same hypotheses that are used to study any other organization. Like all human organizations, religious ones have problems of growth, adaptation, innovation, efficiency and effectiveness. Those which might realistically be considered social movements can also be considered under the categories Professor Neil Smelser has advanced, that is, social movements as norm-oriented or value-oriented.[10] Eister indicates that the use of formal organizational theory or social movement theory would have the advantage of improving the articulation of theory and research in the sociology of religion as well as general sociology.

There is very little such research or theorizing. It seems to us that it would be more relevant to ask how religious organizations cope with their problems than to try to figure out whether a given organization is a church or sect, especially since it ought to be perfectly clear that after a certain size has been reached, almost any religious organization will contain within it both church and sect elements. However, only one study, Paul M. Harrison's *Authority and Power in the Free Church Tradition*,[11] can be said to have concerned itself with the questions of change, adaptation, and natural growth in a religious organization as an organization. Harrison faces the very interesting and difficult question of how a free church (such as the American Baptist), committed in principle to local autonomy, copes with the inevitable necessity of developing some kind of natural structure in a bureaucracy. Such research contributes not only to

[9] Erich Goode, "Some Critical Observations of the Church-Sect Dimension," *Journal for the Scientific Study of Religion*, 6, No. 1 (April 1967) 77.

[10] Neil S. Smelser, *Theory of Collective Behavior* (New York: The Macmillan Company, 1962).

[11] Paul M. Harrison, *Authority and Power in the Free Church Tradition* (Princeton, N.J.: Princeton University Press, 1959).

the understanding of religion as an organization, but also to the understanding of organizations as such. At this point, however, we can only lament the fact that a literature made up of books such as Harrison's does not exist. We note that while we will use the term denomination in developing our own theory of American religion, the church-sect typology is of little use in trying to cope with the complexities of the American religious scene. Indeed, it may be well at this point to emphasize the fact that in the rest of this volume, the term denomination will not be used to indicate some sort of half-way house between sect and church, but rather to describe a religious organization which emerges in a society which has no established church (official or unofficial) but permits and encourages the practice of religion by the various organized religious communities.

Institutional Religion

The question of institutionalization in religion is one that has been of great importance in the development of the sociology of religion in the United States. We noted before that the distinction between church and sect was relevant to the extent that it pointed out that otherworldliness and religious fervor and enthusiasm tended to wane after an organization reached a certain size. Complexity and differentiation inevitably occur and some sort of structure must be evolved to revive order, stability, and continuity. Roles and statuses must be defined, goals and means of achieving them must be indicated, and legitimating formulae must be devised. In Max Weber's terms, the charisma is routinized.

Now it should be no secret that Weber was profoundly pessimistic about the routinization of the charisma, as he was about most other things he observed in the modern world. When charisma was routinized it lost its fire and vigor. Weber saw this as representation in miniature of what was going on in the whole of Western society— the gradual rationalization, formalization, and bureaucratization of human life. His disciple, Roberto Michels, was equally pessimistic about the inevitability of the conversion of means into ends. The political parties he studied came into being to act as the bearers of revolutionary socialist faith and the leaders of equally revolutionary socialist movements. But with the passage of time, the party became rationalized and bureaucratized, and instead of serving as a means, it became an end in itself, devoting much of its concern to its presumed goals. Finally, the goals became little more than legitimating formulae which justified the existence of the organization. Troeltsch, similarly, was quite unhappy about the lack of committed social ethics in the Christian churches and lamented the fact that the sect, which had a valid and evangelistic ethic, was not able to be the unique form of Christianity.

One does well to realize that Weber, Michels, and Troeltsch (like Ferdinand Tonnies, on whom they all relied heavily) were profoundly pessimistic about the dramatic change from the feudal to the modern world they saw going on around them. Even though they maintained scholarly objectivity of a sort, there was not much doubt that they preferred *Gemeinschaft* society to *Gesellschaft*.

It is not our intention to defend either institutionalization or the modern world. Whether, in fact, institutionalization and *Gesellschaft* have made life less human or more human, may be difficult to answer, but modern man surely has more in the way of food and clothing, housing, medicine, education, and recreation than his ancestors had. Whether the large, rationalized, bureaucratized institutions that have made these material goods possible have deprived man of the community, social support, intimacy, or dignity that he had in *Gemeinschaft* society is not immediately evident, but there is a strong trend in contemporary research to suggest two things: (1) *Gemeinschaft* has managed to survive in the midst of a *Gesellschaft* society and may even be staging a strong comeback. (We will suggest later on in this volume that American religion plays a powerful quasi-*Gemeinschaft* role.) (2) Bureaucratic organizations may well be dehumanizing, and, indeed, bureaucracy may ultimately dehumanize man's life, but this is not a necessary development. The iron law of oligarchies is apparently repealable, and a bureaucracy can be not only efficient but also human and humane. As a matter of fact, Peter Blau has suggested repeatedly that contemporary research on social organizations would indicate that a humane and intelligent bureaucrat is likely to be a far more efficient one, particularly when he is dealing with a highly complex task. In this framework, the problem is not that modern life is being institutionalized but that, to the extent that institutions are depriving humans of freedom, dignity, and control of their own destinies, modern society is being unintelligently and inefficiently institutionalized.

We approach the literature on the institutionalization of the church (filled as it is with the usual implied or explicit call for the return to pristine enthusiasm and simplicity) with a great deal of skepticism. The classic statement of that literature is by Thomas O'Dea. O'Dea's article, "Dilemmas in Institutionalization," is an insightful and valuable commentary on the dangers inherent in institutionalization. It must be understood, however, that O'Dea's model for describing institutionalization is the Roman Catholic Church, with which he manifestly has a very strong love-hate relationship, and the model in which he compares the institutional religion is "the circle of disciples gathered about a charismatic leader." That even Roman Catholicism might be organized in a different fashion and that institutionalization could exist to foster many circles of disciples around the charismatic leader seems to have escaped O'Dea.

This digression is a prelude to suggesting that those who lament the institutionalization of the church on the grounds that it deprives religion of its fervor, are actually lamenting the fact that the church has been unintelligently and poorly institutionalized, and that an intelligent, humane religious institution may produce far more dedicated religionists than the tiny sect. For all its institutionalization (much of it incredibly incompetent) the Christian religion today surely has many more fervent members than it had when it was composed of a handful of men wandering through the hills of Galilee.

That there is a strong tendency for any sacred behavior to move from the ritual to the ritualistic can scarcely be denied, though there also seems to be built into the human religious organizations the possibility for a reverse journey. One of the objectives of the Reformation, for example, was to create a more meaningful form of worship for the common people, and one has recently witnessed the spectacle of the Roman Catholic Church engaging in a massive withdrawal from a highly ritualistic Latin liturgy and a return—in organized and institutional fashion—to the style of worship which frequently is so Simple Church as to be a scandal to Protestant liturgists.[12] The institutionalization of rituals is surely a danger, and it is probably true that organizations do not automatically generate countervailing forces.

Bureaucracies rarely commit suicide, and religious organizations have the distinct advantage that many of their rank and file members are committed to the goals of the organization, even if the bureaucracy does fall victim to the dilemma of mixed motivations. The history of Christianity can well be considered as a long series of confrontations between the religious enthusiast and the bureaucrat, with the enthusiast at times converting the bureaucrat (such as St. Francis' triumph over the Roman Curia of his time), or replacing the bureaucrat (the Benedictine reform of the eleventh and twelfth

---

[12] One Lutheran colleague remarked to me: "You people are trying to make in twenty-five years all the mistakes we made in four hundred and fifty."

centuries), or splitting away from the bureaucrat (the Reformation). The cry *Ecclesia semper reformada* ("The Church must always be reformed") is the cry of the enthusiast against the bureaucrat.[13] One need only look at the history of Christianity to see that as surely as a set of rules is evolved which encompasses the message in a formula, a group of enthusiasts will rise up to denounce the formula, even at some considerable risk that their own denunciation will itself become a formula.

We feel, on closer examination, that basically institutions provide a stable context for human activity and have certain countervailing mechanisms built into them which protect human vitality, creativity, and spontaneity; the "new," the "emergent," and the "coming-to-be" not only occur within institutions, but can, in fact, be promoted by the institution itself. Man's knowledge of the operation of institutions has become so sophisticated that some institutions have attempted with some success to build into their structures mechanisms for producing self-criticism and prophecy. That institutions can destroy vitality and spontaneity is true, but to argue that they necessarily must do so or even must necessarily tend to do so is in our judgment to take a very naïve view of human institutions. We do not wish to exaggerate the countervailing and self-correcting power of an institution built in part at least on the commitment of the rank and file membership (as well as some bureaucrats) to goals beyond the self-preservation of the organization. Clearly, sometimes this countervailing power does not work at all, and in other instances it is not powerful enough to accomplish innovation and reform. But just as clearly, sometimes it does work. Given the importance of religion in man's life and the depth of commitment that religion calls forth from some of its members, one is tempted to say that countervailing powers working against the harmful effects of institutionalization may be stronger in religious groups than elsewhere.

This lengthy discussion of the problems of institutionalization in religion is included in this volume because we do not wish to be accused of being unaware of the dangers and problems involved for religion when it becomes organized, particularly organized as it is in the denominations which constitute America's denominational society. We are fully aware of those dangers, but we are not prepared to

---

[13] One of the striking religious developments in modern times is that (at least in part because of increased understanding among all bureaucrats of the need for change if any organization is to prosper) many religious bureaucrats have in fact become enthusiasts. We witness the spectacle of bureaucrats prophesying to each other on the need for reform and on occasion joining common forces against the less reform-oriented rank and file.

accept the half-educated attitude which assumes that because a religious group can be described as institutionalized, it ceases to be authentically religious and can be written off as another secular organization masquerading as religion. To say that a religious group is institutionalized is not to settle the question but merely to define the problem.

Inevitability of institutionalization was insightfully described by "Pen-ultimate," the mysterious columnist of the *Christian Century:* [14]

The following press release issued by a conference on the Underground Church held in Acapulco, Mexico, seems to require a bit of interpretation for conventional-traditionalist Christians. Accordingly, we have appended explanatory footnotes.

"At this second annual meeting, the consensus was that we had finally succeeded in transcending institutional structures," said Protestant Minister Morris Maurice, co-spokesman for the Underground Church. He was interviewed along with Catholic priest Daniel O'Daniel in a penthouse suite atop the towering Mexicana Hotel. Together they cited some of the problems and gains of their burgeoning movement, which is based on rejection of conventional Christian norms and forms.

Explained Father O'Daniel: "We have become a more complex movement, and must get to know each other better. Therefore we are instituting a newsletter [1] which will go to all underground churches. We have a contact at each of the churches; he is the same person [2] who presides when these churches conduct an agape.[3] You see, it was getting so that we didn't know who was responsible at each location and we voted to select one representative. Because of the considerable confusion that has accompanied agapes held in high-rise apartments, we have asked each church to post helpers at the elevator doors." [4]

Maurice mentioned that some underground churches have moved so far in their repudiation of old-fashioned parish churches that they have been able to branch out. "We have stimulated the growth of avant-garde groups of men [5] and cadres of ladies [6] to carry the work into all the world. Because of rising expenses, we have also formed groups [7] to help bring in some nickels and dimes to support the newsletter and other activities —they will announce their means [8] soon."

O'Daniel reminded reporters that the Underground Church

was stimulating a new appreciation of the secular. Therefore this year's convention began by asking all local eruptions[9] of the movement to celebrate the birthdays of Albert Camus, Dietrich Bonhoeffer, Martin Luther King and Pope John XXIII[10] *with moments of reflection;[11] he urged groups to set aside extended periods of time to engage in such reflection[12] in order to help find viable alternatives to outmoded modes of piety and spirituality. Perhaps, one delegate suggested, some could make an annual trip to Haight-Ashbury.*[13]

A group of insurgents tried to obstruct the Acapulco meeting, but the Underground Church's originally constituted group[14] was able to prevail. Whereupon the insurgents[15] went to the basement of another hotel and held their own meetings, common meals and reflection group sessions. They also issued a statement to the press charging that the earlier-formed rebel movement[16] evidences no sign of self-renewal. Maurice and O'Daniel disagreed. Said the latter: "We feel that we have found a permanently viable noninstitutional structure for expressing the intentions of the church."

Footnote references given in above quotation are: [1] Diocesan press. [2] Bishop, priest. [3] Low mass. [4] Corps of ushers. [5] Knights of Columbus. [6] Sodality, Ladies Aid. [7] Stewardship committees. [8] Stewardship campaign. [9] Parishes, congregations. [10] Saints' days, church calendar. [11] Novenas. [12] The Forty Hours, thirty-day retreat. [13] Fatima. [14] The Establishment. [15] The underground church. [16] The power structure.

American religions are in a very institutionalized denominational form. There aren't many sects around and they don't remain sects very long. Nor is there any such thing as the established church. Religion in the United States seems definitively to be in the denominational format. Most Americans who are in any sense religious are religious within the context of the denominational society.

Summary

Religion, like any other form of human behavior, tends to get organized, and in the process of organization, something of the excitement, the spontaneity, the creativity, the innovative informality of the original religious thrust is lost. The sect church model describes the process of what Max Weber called the "routinization of charisma." But just because religion becomes institutional does not necessarily mean that it becomes institutionalized, and because it becomes organized it does not necessarily follow that it loses all vitality, for the same religious thoughts which originally generate a sect can recur within a church and, indeed, the large denominations in American society have many sectlike groups within them. While there is, then, a tendency for organized religion to lose its vitality, there also seems to be within organized religion a tendency to generate new critical groups which, if they do not restore vitality completely, at least prevent the denomination from atrophying.

Chapter 4

The Present Condition
of American Religion

In the three previous chapters we have developed the tools that are necessary for analyzing America's denominational society. With this chapter we turn to that society itself and begin by attempting an overview of the current condition of American religion, based first of all on available statistical material, and, secondly, on the present writer's own systematic impressions of some of the major currents that can be observed in the frantic outpouring of books and articles on American religion.

As St. Paul said of the Athenians, Americans are a very religious people. While more of them describe themselves as being religiously affiliated than are actual church members, still somewhere between a little less than two fifths and a little less than half (depending on which particular survey one credits) describe themselves as frequent or weekly church attenders; and most Americans endorse, more or less enthusiastically, traditional religious doctrines. To say that Americans are a religious people is not to say that they are devout (any more than St. Paul wished to imply the Athenians were devout). American religion is far from perfect and by the standards of religious ideals it is grossly imperfect. But just as it would be too simple to say that religion is prospering in the United States so, too, it would be too simple to say that religion is of no importance, or even of only minor importance in the country.

Some Comments on Statistics

It must be confessed, first of all, that the statistical data are not always of the highest quality. The general state of church statistics in America, based on the collections of data done by individual denominations, is abysmally bad. The survey research material on which we will depend in great part in this volume is accurate as far as it goes but, unfortunately, there are limits to what survey research can do. It is based on the rather broad assumption that an interviewer descending upon the house of a randomly selected American is able to learn through perhaps an hour of questions and answers significant and valuable information about the attitudes and behavior of the respondent. It further assumes that when a properly chosen random sample is assembled, the respondents interviewed will be representative of broad categories of the total American population. Both of these assumptions are taken for granted by most educated Americans, and only when sample survey findings violently conflict with one's own beliefs or prejudices are the assumptions questioned. It is perhaps unfortunate that more Americans do not understand the rationale behind these assumptions so that they could be more nuanced in their reactions to sample surveys.

The second assumption is easy to establish for those who are capable of understanding the complexities of probability mathematics. If the sample is properly random, then it can, within certain limits of confidence, be taken to represent accurately the larger population. The important question for the student of the survey is not does the sample work, but was the sampling in the particular survey well executed? Since most Americans cannot be expected to understand the methodology involved in sample surveys, they must rely on the integrity and competence of the national sampling organizations. They also, especially in a matter as newsworthy as religion apparently is, should learn to be quite skeptical about any poll which claims to have made startling or revolutionary discoveries about American religion.

The assumption that the interviewer can get at reality is a more difficult one to establish. What does the response to a question really mean? Does the question itself adequately measure the attitude or behavioral dimension in question? Is the respondent telling the truth? Even if he thinks he is telling the truth, will he behave according to that which he has said in his response? The answers to these questions are not particularly easy. Although those engaged in social research are constantly striving to improve their techniques, it must be understood that, at least in its present stage of development, survey research still must stand halfway between art and science. One can place a reasonable amount of trust in a questionnaire which has been carefully prepared by one of the major commercial or academic survey research organizations. It gets at *something* "out there" in reality, but it is still likely to be a rather crude and imperfect tool. One would be mistaken to reject out of hand the findings of survey research, but also one would be mistaken to think that there is no need for caution or reservation in accepting and interpreting the results of such research. It is a careful, systematic, and relatively economic way to measure certain rather broad aspects of behavior or attitudinal reality. It can collect information which is infinitely superior to personal impression or personal opinion. But the reader of any report from survey research on the sociology of religion must not think that the neat, orderly, statistical tables are any indication that human behavior has been precisely measured.

There are also special difficulties in the survey research approach to religion. The questions that survey research technology has so far devised to measure religious attitude and behavior seem to be frequently ill-suited for coping with the subtle nature of religious beliefs. When a respondent is asked, for example, whether he thinks God is a loving father or some kind of infinite power, it may well have occurred to him that the question really had no connection to his own notion of the nature of the Deity. Similarly, if he is asked to say whether the Bible is an inspired work of God or merely great literature, he could easily see the necessity for clarifying what he would mean by either answer. Both the professional theologian and the interested layman can easily criticize the wording of most questionnaires in the sociology of religion, but they will find it somewhat more difficult to rephrase the questions in such a way as to be confident that they have found a better format. Progress has been made in the last one and one-half decades, but the discipline is still in its infancy.

Secondly, there are particular problems in measuring the religious behavior of American Jews—problems which ought to lead us to have even more reservations about survey research reports on religious attitudes and behavior of Jews. The most important problem is that Jews are only 3 percent of the American population and even a fairly large national sample will have only a small proportion of Jewish respondents. In the later chapter on secularization our comments will be based on a sample of one hundred twenty-eight Jews, which is clearly a rather thin base from which to make broad generalizations. Further, the religious values and norms of the Jewish community differ radically from that of the gentile community. Those measures which would be important indicators of religiosity for gentiles would be considerably less important indicators for Jews, but since most religious surveys are primarily concerned with the 97 percent of the population which is gentile, the questionnaires usually have a strong gentile orientation about them, and hence are rather inadequate for tapping Jewish religiosity.

How seriously can one be expected to take the findings of religious survey research, then, in view of the qualifications and reservations which we have made in the previous paragraphs? The proper response is neither to reject survey research completely nor to accept it unreservedly. Like all survey research data, information on the sociology of religion based on survey research tells us something rather important, and tells it to us relatively inexpensively. Religious surveys give important hints, but they tell us considerably less than everything we need to know. The most appropriate stance, therefore, is tentative acceptance of the findings of competent survey research in the sociology of religion with the tentative emphasized and with the realization that even with all the survey research material on religion presently available to us, we have still far more unanswered questions than we have answered ones.

The first table in this chapter, however, deals with economic, social, and demographic information and merits considerably more confidence than do some of the subsequent tables which are devoted to religious attitudes and beliefs.

The Basic Facts

Even though we think quite correctly that America is a country with many religions, Table 1 shows that three religious denominations—

Table 1   American Denominations

Percent	Catholic	Baptist	Methodist	Lutheran	Presbyterian	Episcopalian	Jewish
Percent of population	25	21	14	7	6	3	3
Percent of college educated	17	10	20	20	34	45	44
Percent white	95	76	91	99	98	94	99
Percent professional and business	23	15	24	24	31	37	51
Percent living East and Midwest	78	33	53	76	56	50	90
Percent earning more than $7,000	47	26	42	49	60	64	69
Percent living in cities over 500,000	51	19	21	28	30	41	80
Percent weekly church attendance	68	37	34	43	36	31	22
Percent Democratic	56	55	40	34	28	27	64

Most of the data in this table are based on the United States census sample of 1957. Unfortunately, no adequate data have been collected since that time. The last two items are based on material collected by Bernard Lazerwitz.

the Catholics, the Baptists, and the Methodists—account for some three fifths of the total American population, and that if three more Christian religious groups—the Lutherans, the Presbyterians, and the Episcopalians—are added, three quarters of the total population is accounted for. Of the remaining one fourth, approximately 3 percent are Jews and the rest are in two residual categories—18 percent "other Protestant" and 3 percent "other or none." [1] Among the principal "splinter" groups that form the other 18 percent are the Congregational Church, the Disciples of Christ, the Christian Scientists, the "Christian Church," the Evangelical and Reformed Church, [2] the Mormons, the Seventh-Day Adventists, the Church of the Brethren, and the various Pentecostal bodies, such as the Pentecostal Assembly of the World, Incorporated; the Pentecostal Church of God of America, Incorporated; and the United Pentecostal Church.

It is to be noted that the four major Protestant denominations are split into a number of subgroups with sixteen Baptist bodies constituting the Baptist Church, four of them with membership of over one million, and the Southern Baptists, the largest of all, with membership approaching nine million. Similarly, there are five branches of the Methodist Church, several major branches of the Lutheran Church, of which the Lutheran Church in America, the American Lutheran Church, and the Lutheran Church Missouri Synod are the most important, and, finally, four principal divisions of the Presbyterian denomination. How important these divisions within the denominations are may vary from group to group. The Southern Baptists are much more likely to be fundamentalist in their theological approach than are some of the other Baptists, and the Missouri Synod Lutherans have traditionally been considered the conservative right wing of that denomination. Nonetheless, it is not unfair to lump these various subcategories under one denominational title and we will with an occasional exception treat the denominations as unitary bodies in this book, so the reader must keep in mind that there is considerable controversy within the denominations and even within the various subdivisions of the denominations.

The Roman Catholic denomination is technically one religious

---

[1] All the percentages described in this chapter represent church affiliation and do not have to do with church membership. The problem with the church membership variable is that membership means different things for different denominations; thus, for Protestants, as I understand it, church membership is a highly formal act. For Catholics there is practically no formality about it at all. One does not join a parish; one is simply part of a parish because one lives in the parish area.

[2] The Evangelical and Reformed Church and the Congregational Church have combined in the last decade in a new ecumenical body, the United Church of Christ.

body, though the Polish National Catholic Church of America represents a group that, while it is not in union with Rome or with the Roman Catholic Church in this country, nonetheless maintains a doctrine and cult which is very similar to that of the Roman Catholic Church. Furthermore, in some sense it is possible to say that the various nationality groups within Catholicism represent categories which can be compared to Protestant denominations. The principal groups are Polish, Irish, German, and French. We will return to the nationality subdivisions in Roman Catholicism in the chapter on the Roman Church.

It can be seen from Table 1 that there are considerable economic and geographic differences among the various religious denominations. Roman Catholicism as the largest denomination has now become respectably middle-class in its educational, occupational, and economic achievements. It tends to be concentrated in the northeastern and Middle Western sections of the country, particularly in large cities; its membership continues allegiance to the Democratic Party, and it can claim both organizational and devotional participation of an extraordinarily high proportion of its members, with more than two thirds of the Catholics in the country reporting weekly mass attendance.

The second largest group, the Baptists, are different from Catholics. One quarter of them are Negro; their educational, occupational, and economic achievements are the lowest of any of the major denominations; they are concentrated largely in the South, outside the Northeastern and Middle Western sections of the country, and are not to be found in appreciable numbers in large cities. On the other hand they are almost as likely to be Democrats as the Catholics, have a moderately high rate of church attendance, and comprise a similar percentage of the total population. The relationships between the Catholics and the Baptists, both organizationally and personally, tend to be marked by caution and reserve. At present there are no data available on interaction between Baptists and Catholics, but it seems safe to say that there is not much of either for at least these two participants in the denominational society. Almost one half of American society, therefore, is made up of these two denominational groups which represent different religious styles and geographic locations. Denominational distance is still an extremely important reality.

The next largest denomination, the Methodists, have with some reason claimed to be in the middle of the mainstream of American religion. They are less concentrated in the South and the West than the Baptists, less concentrated in the large cities than Catholics, middle-class in their education, occupation, and income, and moderate in their church attendance and percentage of the total population. This social and demographic position on the median can also in some ways be extended to questions of doctrine, organization, and worship. That the Methodists are typically American is not surprising, because Methodism is essentially an American religion, even though Wesley and Whitefield were English and their religious movement began as a part of the established Church of England. Its major success was in colonial America, and even before the Revolutionary War they could easily have claimed to be a typically American religion.

The Lutherans are the largest of the three smaller mainstream Protestant denominations. They constitute only 7 percent of the total population and for the most part represent German and Scandinavian immigrant groups. In a number of respects they are quite similar to the Catholics who also are immigrant groups of about the same vintage in American society. In education, income, and occupation, the Lutherans are quite similar to the Catholics, and also Lutheran church attendance and affiliation are the highest for any of the major Protestant denominations. The principal differences between the Lutherans and the Catholics is that the former, while concentrated in the East and Middle West, are much less likely than Catholics to come from large cities and, perhaps as a result, much less likely to be Democrats, politically. The Presbyterians and the Episcopalians (together with the Congregationalists who were too few in number to include in Table 1) constitute the upper class of the American churches, with very high proportions of college-educated, business and professional, and well-to-do members. The geographic distribution of these two groups seems to be relatively uniform throughout the country, with the Episcopalians being more likely to be in large cities. The Presbyterians have even fewer Negro members, and are more likely to attend church every week.

The final denomination, the Jews, are the most well-to-do, the most occupationally successful, almost the best educated, and are concentrated in the large cities in the East and the Middle West. They are mostly Democratic and have a lower rate of church attendance than do any of the gentile denominations. They are the only non-Christian denomination of any size in American society; and because of their geographic distribution, their high educational attainment, and their economic and social success, they are able to have considerably more influence on American society than their sheer numbers would lead one to suspect. However, it should also be noted by anyone quick to jump to anti-Semitic conclusions, that almost exactly the same comment could be made of Episcopalians.

If one is to rank these seven denominations at all, one must be careful to do so on a number of different dimensions. The Presbyterians, the Episcopalians, and the Jews represent the upper social classes; the Lutherans, the Catholics, and the Methodists, the middle classes; and the Baptists, the lower classes. Geographically, the Catholics and the Jews and Lutherans are concentrated in the East and the Middle West, the Baptists in the South, and the other three groups are fairly evenly distributed across the country. The Jews, the Catholics and, to a lesser extent, the Episcopalians, are in the large metropolitan regions. The largest proportion of the blacks are in the Baptist church, with each of the other denominations claiming less than 10 percent black membership. The Jews, the Baptists, and the Catholics are most likely to be Democratic politically. The Catholics have the highest church attendance rate, the Lutherans have the second highest, the other Protestant groups are clustered rather tightly, and the Jews have the lowest church attendance. Together, these seven groups account for four fifths of the American population. It would be an oversimplification to say that the study of the denominational society can safely be limited to these seven denominations because some of the smaller and less typical denominations may be extremely revealing in what they tell about the larger society. Nonetheless, these seven groups do represent the overwhelming majority of Americans, and religion as it is practiced within these seven communities can be said in sum to constitute most of American religion.

Religion and Social Class

Most readers already know that the more education and the higher the socioeconomic status of a person, the more likely he is to be religious. Of the Protestants who did not go beyond grammar school, 33 percent attend church regularly, while 52 percent of the Protestant college graduates attend church regularly. Similarly, 53 percent of the grammar-school Catholics and 89 percent of the college-graduate Catholics attend church regularly. Similarly, Protestants in professions are twelve percentage points more likely to attend church regularly than unskilled Protestant workers, and Catholics in the professions are nineteen percentage points more likely than the unskilled Catholics to attend church regularly. This relationship between social class and religion is to be found in most countries in Western society. What is surprising in the United States is not the difference but the very high levels of religious practice among the working-class groups. Indeed, this high level in comparison with the working-class church attendance in almost every other Western industrial country may be said to be the central problem with which this book is concerned.

The reason for the relationship between religious behavior and social class in the Western society is not yet fully understood. It is argued that church attendance is expected of members of the middle class and is really part of their life style. However, Lazerwitz and others have established that church attendance and membership are not simply a fact of middle-class inclination to join organizations. Something more is at work. One might suggest that in the United States religion seems to be more of an opiate of the middle and upper classes than it is of the working classes. Another possible explanation is that the Protestant ethic, which contributes something, at least, to the coming and being of the spirit of capitalism, still must be honored to some extent by those classes which have profited. It is certainly said frequently enough that middle-class religion in American society merely confirms the middle class in their own self-satisfied complacency. But such explanations really do not seem to cope with the heart of the problem; and we must at the present state of our knowledge be content with saying that in the United States, as in other Western countries, it is those who have gained most from society that are most likely to be committed to religion.

Another point that must be observed on religion and social class is that there is little in Table 1 to lend substance to the notion that education takes modern man away from his religious faith. Indeed, one would think that the figures almost by themselves would have put the notion to rest that education, involving a basic knowledge of the principles of science, would lead to a decline of religion. Those who argue that such decline occurs would respond by saying that it is only among the very best educated that the problem of the conflict between science and religion arises. Such a comment is undoubtedly a valid one, but it constitutes a reflection on (1) the quality of most American college educations, and (2) an admission that the modern man, with whom the secular theologians are so concerned, could only have gone to a very limited number of colleges and graduate schools in the country and does not constitute a statistically significant part of the total population.

Religious Beliefs

Table 2 presents a very brief summary of religious behavior and practice of the main American denominations in all of the Christian de-

Table 2   Continuities in Religious Beliefs and Behavior

Continuities	Protestant	1965 Catholic	Jewish
Believing in God	99%	100%	75%
Believing Christ is God	73	88	—
Believing in Trinity	86	96	2
Believing in prayer	94	99	70
Praying three times a day or more	23	25	5
Believing in life after death	78	83	17
Believing in heaven	71	80	6
Active church member	75	90	62
N	(3088)	(1162)	(128)

This table is from data collected by Public Opinion Surveys, Inc. for *Catholic Digest*. Reprinted by permission of *Catholic Digest*.

nominations. The vast majority of adherents profess belief in God and the Divinity of Christ and the Trinity, in prayer, in life after death and heaven. Similarly, the overwhelming majority of gentiles, whatever the denomination, describe themselves as active church members.

Among American Jews, the pattern is rather different. Three fourths of them believe in God, 70 percent believe in prayer, and some three fifths are active church members. However, Jewish belief in life after death is quite small. As we shall see in a later chapter, these differences between Jews and gentiles are even greater than they might at first have seemed because gentile beliefs are relatively stable, whereas the Jewish doctrinal stance, as represented in the table, is the result of a rapid decline in the past fifteen years.

There seems to be, therefore, at least among gentile Americans in the religious mainstream, a general acceptance of the central doctrinal tenets of traditional religion in spite of the fact that 27 percent of the Protestants do not believe in the divinity of Christ and 17 percent of the Catholics do not believe in life after death. A number of writers are inclined to see this as a decline of orthodoxy from some previous higher level of religious participation. Glock and Stark even suggest that from the writings in the literature of a century ago it seems fairly safe to assume that there were higher levels of orthodoxy, though one wonders how the literature of a century ago would enable us to know what those who did not write and were not written about really thought on religious matters. Surely the eighteenth and nineteenth centuries did not lack atheists and agnostics or skillful literary proponents of heterodoxy. On the contrary, it seems quite feasible to argue that, given the beleaguered condition of Christianity for the last several centuries, the percentage of those still giving orthodox responses in our tables is remarkably high. It is another situation where given the fact that we lacked precise data in the past, the reader pays his money and takes his choice. We will be content with simply noting that there is no substantial evidence that the percentages subscribing to the doctrines represented in the accompanying tables were any different one hundred years ago. They may have been and they may not have been. The suggestion is made by many anthropologists that there is a good deal of unbelief in primitive societies.[3] We shall return to the theme of religious decline in a later chapter.

Charles Glock and his associates asked more detailed questions about religious beliefs in a study of church members in northern California.[4] Tables 3, 4, and 5 summarize some of their data. There are two different ways one can approach the data in these tables. One can say that even in the least orthodox of the denominations (Congregationalists), 75 percent believe in the existence of God and 68 percent in the divinity of Jesus. Or one can, as Glock and Stark do, observe that substantial elements of many of the religious groups will concede that their beliefs are mixed with some kinds of doubts, with doubts most likely to be found among the Congregationalists, Methodists, and Episcopalians and least likely among the Lutherans (Missouri Synod), the Catholics, the sects, and the Southern Baptists. On the basis of this data, Glock and Stark conclude that differences in the religious outlook of members of the various denominations in American society are both vast and profound, and that "It is clear that substantial changes of the kind called secularization have, indeed, taken place . . . for only a minority of members adhere to these beliefs." [5] Both of these statements may be true, but the difference between a certain faith and a probable faith seems to us, at least, to be sufficiently obscure as to make the Glock and Stark assertions dubious, at least on the basis of the data they advance. Little is really known about the psychology of religious belief, but that one is able to admit that one has doubts or that one's acceptance is not, psychologically speaking, based on absolutê certainty could well be a sign of religious strength and not of weakness; or, alternately, a sign of a different style of adhering to doctrinal propositions. He who has doubts and still believes may simply be more honest with himself than he who is unable to face the doubts which certainly seem to be inevitable in any man's religious commit-

---

[3] Clifford Geertz's suggested book title, *Faith and Hypocrisy in Primitive Society,* underlines the anthropologist's skepticism about the religious orthodoxy of primitives. It would lead one to suspect that there was probably a great deal of skepticism, doubt, and hesitancy in earlier ages of Christianity, too.

[4] Glock and Stark, op. cit.

[5] Ibid., p. 116.

ment. Whether the mixture of doubt and belief that characterizes particularly the Congregationalist, Methodist, and Episcopalian respondents in the Glock and Stark study represents a modern development either in its reality or in its open admission, is something we cannot say in the absence of data from the past. Lacking such trends from the past, one cannot reasonably project further trends in the future, and lacking more detailed knowledge of how man faces and solves his religious problems, we cannot say that faith based on a belief in God that concedes the possibility of doubts is necessarily a religious deterioration.

Nevertheless, Glock and Stark can on the basis of their data quite legitimately evolve a typology of the new denominationalism. In their first category they have "the liberals comprising the Congregationalists, the Methodists, and the Episcopalians . . . characterized by having a majority of members who reject firm belief in central tenets of Christian orthodoxy." [6] One can accept this statement as long as one is willing to interpret Glock and Stark's term "reject firm belief" as saying, in reality, "admit belief mixed with doubts," a distinction which seems to have escaped the two authors.

Their second group is the moderates, composed of the Disciples of Christ and the Presbyterians. At least as they are manifested in northern California, this group is less secularized than the liberals but more so than the conservatives, who are made up of the American Lutherans and the American Baptists. The fourth category is the fundamentalists—the Missouri Synod Lutherans and the Southern Baptists and the small sects who refuse to admit the possibility of doubt in their doctrinal affirmations. The Catholics, representing yet another group, are linked with the conservatives—that is to say, the American Lutheran group and the American Baptists, surely a position which may be somewhat disturbing to both sides of the comparison.

This typology of Glock and Stark, while it is not particularly original (the liberals and the moderates and the conservatives are generally to be found within the National Council of Churches, while the fundamentalists are outside of the NCC), is a useful one. However, it must be understood that, based on the Glock and Stark tables rather than on the two authors' interpretation of the tables, all that can be confidently said is that the liberals and the moderates find it easier to admit the possibility of doubt in the central doctrinal tenets of Christianity, and that there are more who definitely do not believe within these groups than within the more conservative or fundamentalist groups. (Twenty-one percent of the Congregationalists and 13

[6] Ibid., p. 120.

Table 3   Belief in God

"Which of the following statements comes closest to what you believe about God?"	Congregationalists	Methodists	Episcopalians	Disciples of Christ	Presbyterians	American Lutherans §	American Baptists	Missouri Lutherans	Southern Baptists	Sects ||	Total Protestants	Catholics
"I know God really exists and I have no doubts about it."	41%	60%	63%	76%	75%	73%	78%	81%	99%	96%	71%	81%
"While I have doubts, I do feel that I do believe in God."	34	22	19	20	16	19	18	17	1	2	17	13
"I find myself believing in God some of the time, but not at other times."	4	4	2	0	1	2	0	0	0	0	2	1

"I don't believe in a personal God, but I do believe in a higher power of some kind."	16	11	12	0	7	6	2	1	0	1	7	3
"I don't know whether there is a God and I don't believe there is any way to find out."	2	2	2	0	1	*	0	1	0	1	1	1
"I don't believe in God."	1	*	*	0	0	0	0	0	0	*	*	0
No answer	2	*	1	4	*	*	2	0	0	1	1	1
Per cent †	100	99	99	100	100	100	100	100	100	100	99	100
Number of respondents ‡	(151)	(415)	(416)	(50)	(495)	(208)	(141)	(116)	(79)	(255)	(2326)	(545)

* Less than ½ of 1 per cent.
† Some columns fail to sum to 100 per cent due to rounding error.
‡ The number of respondents shown for each denomination in this table is the same for all other tables in this chapter.
§ A combination of members of The Lutheran Church in America and the American Lutheran Church.
|| Included are: The Assemblies of God, The Church of God, The Church of the Nazarene, The Foursquare Gospel Church, and one independent Tabernacle.

Tables 3, 4, and 5 are from Charles Y. Glock and Rodney Stark, *Religion and Society in Tension*, © 1965 by Rand McNally & Company, Chicago, pp. 191, 192, 201, 116, 120. Reprinted by permission of Rand McNally College Publishing Company, Chicago.

Table 4 Belief in the Divinity of Jesus

"Which of the following statements comes closest to what you believe about Jesus?"	Congregationalists	Methodists	Episcopalians	Disciples of Christ	Presbyterians	American Lutherans	American Baptists	Missouri Lutherans	Southern Baptists	Sects	Total Protestants	Catholics
"Jesus is the Divine Son of God and I have no doubts about it."	40%	54%	59%	74%	72%	74%	76%	93%	99%	97%	69%	86%
"While I have some doubts, I feel basically that Jesus is Divine."	28	22	25	14	19	18	16	5	0	2	17	8
"I feel that Jesus was a great man and very holy, but I don't feel Him to be the Son of God any more than all of us are children of God."	19	14	8	6	5	5	4	0	0	*	7	3
"I think Jesus was only a man, although an extraordinary one."	9	6	5	2	2	3	2	1	1	*	4	1
"Frankly, I'm not entirely sure there was such a person as Jesus."	1	1	1	0	1	*	0	0	0	0	1	0
Other and no answer	3	3	2	4	1	0	2	1	0	1	2	2

* Less than ½ of 1 per cent.

Table 5 Additional Beliefs about Jesus

	Congregationalists	Methodists	Episcopalians	Disciples of Christ	Presbyterians	American Lutherans	American Baptists	Missouri Lutherans	Southern Baptists	Sects	Total Protestants	Catholics
"Jesus was born of a virgin." Percentage who said, "Completely true."	21	34	39	62	57	66	69	92	99	96	57	81
"Jesus walked on water." Percentage who said, "Completely true."	19	26	30	62	51	58	62	83	99	94	50	71
"Do you believe Jesus will actually return to the earth some day?" Percentage who answered:												
"Definitely."	13	21	24	36	43	54	57	75	94	89	44	47
"Probably."	8	12	13	10	11	12	11	8	4	2	10	10
"Possibly."	28	25	29	26	23	18	17	6	0	1	20	16
"Probably not."	23	22	17	12	12	6	6	4	1	2	13	11
"Definitely not."	25	17	11	6	8	7	5	1	1	3	10	12
No answer.	3	3	6	10	3	3	4	6	0	3	4	4

Tables 4 and 5 are from Glock and Stark, op. cit.

percent of the Methodists do not believe in life after death.) However, the dissenters are still a distinct minority; and whether they are any larger in number than they were one hundred or three hundred years ago will not be determined this side of paradise.

An Overview of the Denominational Society

Leaving behind for a moment statistical tables, we intend in this section to present a brief schematic overview of the complexities of the denominational society, an overview which, while based on reading of books and periodicals on American religion, must be conceded to be the highly personal perspective of the author. Such a personal overview is justified by the fact that flesh must be put on the statistical bones, and that in the present state of our knowledge of American religion the flesh is bound to be highly impressionistic, no matter what apparatus of scientific footnotes is produced to justify it.

The first assertion that can be made from American religion is that it is activist and not contemplative. From the Protestant sects eager to carve out a new world in New England to the Trappist monasteries advertising Monk's bread on radio and television, American religions, like everything else American, have been inclined more to be doers than thinkers. The Protestant ethic which Max Weber linked with the spirit of capitalism has survived in American society, though it is by no means limited to Protestants (some data suggest that the Jews are most achievement-oriented, Catholics the second most achievement-oriented, and Protestants the least "Protestant" of all). Churches, schools, hospitals, orphanages, colleges, even universities must be built; organizations must be founded; national offices opened; missionaries financed; welfare collections arranged; teen-age recreation programs begun, Sunday school or parochial school systems staffed; the laggards encouraged; the ignorant instructed; sinners admonished; and infidels converted. From the viewpoint of some of the more relaxed continental Christians, American religion is frantic to the point of madness. On the other hand, there is a contemplative strain in American religion; at one time, at least, half the members of the austere Trappist contemplative community were Americans. Going off in solitude to be alone with one's God is a folk image that is popular in American society and occasionally even honored, though it is generally understood that one comes back thereupon from the wilderness to throw oneself into even more activity. Reflection, meditation, contemplation are diligently praised from the American pulpits, though perhaps not quite so diligently practiced even by the occupants of the pulpits. It is not that we condemn the contemplative virtues; it is rather that we simply have not had time for them yet.

Second, American religion has been rather more pragmatic than theoretical. A new continent was to be tamed, a new nation to be built, and then a new world was to be won. In the midst of all the immense practical difficulties faced in the one hundred fifty years of expansion that has marked American history, there was little time for theorizing, and indeed the theoretician, like any other intellectual, was always held in grave suspicion by an important segment of American society. Even though the early colleges and universities were founded by religious denominations, their main purpose was generally very practical —to train ministers for the churches. Yet American religion has not been without its scholars and dreamers. Names like Channing, Emerson, and Bronson in the nineteenth century and a whole host of Protestant theologians in the twentieth century would indicate that the theoretical has not been completely ignored. The majority of divinity schools in the United States will compare with many in the world, and there is probably more theological activity in the United States than in any other country. Even the Roman Catholic Church, which because of its immigrant origins persisted in ignoring the theoretical longer than did some other denominations, is busy creating schools of theology in various parts of the country. The very size of American society, of course, makes it possible for an unbelievable diversity to exist within American religion, so that in this proposition, as in many of the others, we must speak paradoxically. There is much that is completely pragmatic in American religion, but also much that is extremely theoretical, and the theoretical element is, if anything, growing.

Third, most American religious groups have accepted the existing social order and served as integrators of American society; and yet at the same time one is forced to say that American religion has constantly been reformist and prophetic in its behavior, and it has been highly critical of both society and itself. The revival movement in the United States, dating back to the Great Awakening of the eighteenth century and extending all the way to Billy Graham, is but one tradition insisting on the constant renewal of the authenticity of faith. Similarly, American Protestantism was intimately connected with the abolition movement during the Civil War, with the progressive movement at the beginning of the present century and with the temperance movement which led to the passage of the Prohibition amendment. Most recently American foreign policy has been the target of criticism. Hardly anything has happened in the United States which some minister of religion has not risen to denounce. Those ministers and lay members marching for peace and black equality today should not think that they are the first religionists to become involved in politics, and should not further ignore the possibility that they could learn something from a study of the abolitionist movement. In general, however, American religion is basically conservative; and the overwhelming majority of Americans do not like to be disturbed by their religion more than they deem appropriate (though Americans have a highly elastic notion of what kind of disturbance in religion is appropriate).

Fourth, American religion from the beginning has been pluralistic, not monolithic. As we noted before, America was a denominational society before it became a nation. There never has been a formally established church, and there surely never will be. The establishment which exists is rather multi-denominational and a highly informal one. Perhaps no other single factor has been as important in shaping the denominational society and the whole history of American religion as the fact that there never has been one single official church. But this denominational pluralism has also had its impact within the denominational boundaries; for sheer size and geographic diversity, if nothing else, has produced different brands of, let us say, Methodism or Roman Catholicism in different parts of the country, and different strains and emphases within the denominational leadership and rank and file. If no one church is official, then no one school of thought can claim a monopoly on the orthodoxy within the various denominations. Despite all this pluralism, which at times may seem to the outsider to become dangerously close to religious chaos, particularly with its constant proliferation of new sects and new branches of denominations, there has also been a strong strain toward cooperation among American religious groups, and more recently, a quite powerful ecumenical movement. Theological dialogue between Protestants and Catholics has been quite recent, but cooperation in civic problems at the grass-roots level has existed for a long time. There is considerable conflict and competition among the American religious groups, but the conflict and competition is moderated, first of all, by the consciousness that certain rules must be kept lest the larger social structure be destroyed and, secondly, by the belief that at least some of the heretics and schismatics with which we are surrounded are also men of good will with whom we can cooperate. It does not seem too much to say that the social basis for ecumenism may well be stronger in American society than it is in many European countries where the heavy hand of history is more obvious than it is in the United States.

Fifth, there is a strong strain toward religious fundamentalism in American society and periodic demands that religion and its ministers return to the doctrinal and political foundations on which the society was built. But despite this fundamentalism, there is a considerable amount of flexibility and willingness to adjust; thus many of the denominations have been able to maintain their organizational membership intact, despite the changes in the social and economic composition of their population. Roman Catholicism has been especially able to do this as its immigrant population became thoroughly Americanized without having its loyalty to Catholicism impaired. Furthermore, despite this strain toward fundamentalism, the upper intellectual echelons of American religion are almost as open to the whims of fashion as the women's dress market.

Sixth, American religion has strongly insisted on the need for congregational independence and for democratic administration of church affairs, even though John England's attempt to democratize the Catholic diocese of Charleston in 1825 was not widely imitated (to put the matter mildly). A conviction of both leadership and rank and file in Roman Catholicism that the Church ought to be more democratic in American society has persisted and in the wake of the Vatican Council seems to be becoming operational. Further, while the varieties and forms of congregational independence vary greatly from denomination to denomination within Protestantism, the conviction that a maximum amount of participation of the laymen in decision making in the Church is an historic one in American religions. On the other hand, like most other American institutions, organized religion is powerfully inclined to the construction of bureaucracies. National offices and organizations proliferate at least as rapidly as do new sects and denominations, and the necessity to have conventions and magazines to facilitate and promote the work of national or regional organizations has been generally unchallenged. Even the so-called free churches, as Paul Harrison [7] has pointed out, have been forced to develop their own national bureaucracy, even though they will resolutely deny that it is a bureaucracy. While there is obvious humor in the statement that the National Council of Churches' building on Riverside Drive is the Protestant Vatican, there is more than some truth in the claim. Tension between the supposedly independent congregation and the higher levels of the organization of bureaucracy has been constant but does not seem to have seriously impaired either the existence of the local congregation or the continued expansion of the bureaucracy.

American religion, as befits its Protestant origins, is strongly individualistic. Man works out his salvation with his God. Roman Catholicism in the American climate has stressed its own individualistic

---

[7] Harrison, op. cit.

traditions. Nonetheless, American religion constantly produces new organizations and eagerly devotes itself to works of social betterment and charity. We Americans think of ourselves as individualists, but it would seem only as individualists who are almost pathologically eager to join groups. We may decry organizations, but we found them. We may extol the need for individualism, but we quickly seek out others with whom to work. We may insist that man must be responsible for himself, but we desperately seek someone whom we can help, whether he wants to be helped or not.

Seventh, folk religion—that is to say, the mixture of superstition and paganism with orthodoxy—has been rampant in American society, as we shall see in Chapter 7. Indeed, some forms of folk religion have even become institutionalized as small denominations. Americans may be a very skeptical people, but they are also a very gullible people, and the lust for the odd, the bizarre, the cultic, the mystical, and the supernatural does not seem to have been extinguished by the spread of science and education. Witchcraft, voodoo, black magic, and sorcery may not play prominent parts in American religion, but faith healing and miracle working are extremely important—to such an extent that they, too, have tended to become organized and institutionalized, much to the horror of the more liberal religionists who are aghast at plastic Jesuses on automobiles and towers of faith at Oral Roberts University. On the other hand, American religion has apparently succeeded in working out some sort of satisfactory coexistence with science (as we shall note in a later chapter), despite the claims made frequently on both sides that such a coexistence is impossible. Departments of chemistry, biology, physics exist in most of the church-related universities, and problems with evolution and Charles Darwin exist in only a small number of them at the present time. To some extent American believers have been able to avoid the conflict between science and religion by simply denying that it exists. Whether this is intellectually honest or not may be questioned, but the point remains that it has been successful; religion and science can go on their merry ways, not conflicting with each other very much, despite the arguments of some elite religionist and elite scientists that they should.

Finally, if it can be said that one of the basic themes of American society is that we are a people of plenty, it might also be said that American religion is a religion of plenty. Not only does the material abundance with which this country has been endowed shape the basic optimism and activism of American religion, it has also substantiated the conviction of American religionists that variety, diversity, plurality, paradox, and, if necessary, contradiction, are not particularly unhealthy. While we may very well (as will be suggested in a later chapter) be developing an overarching civic religion which subsumes the other religions, it is nonetheless a rather loose alliance of basic elements that make up this civic religion and within its framework (and it is a broad framework) almost anything can happen in American religion and probably already has, from monks in the desert praying by themselves to a cult of angelic beings arriving on flying saucers.

Summary

To summarize this chapter, while it is difficult because of lack of data from the past to say where on its pilgrimage American religion is, how it compares with its previous manifestations, and what the future manifestations will look like, it is still possible to say that at the present time it shows rather strong signs of vitality. More than two thirds of the American population are church members, more than one third of those members attend church services every week, the overwhelming majority accept the basic doctrinal tenets of Christianity, and education and upward mobility seem to strengthen religious activity rather than weaken it. American men, while less likely to be religious than American women, are still more religious than men in any other country in the Western world; and denominational differences, while basic and important, have not destroyed the overarching religious consensus which makes the denominational society possible. While the denominational society can be described as activist, pragmatic, conservative, sectarian, optimistic, superstitious, individualistic, and fundamentalist, it also displays strong strains of contemplation, theory, reform, cooperation, flexibility, social criticism, social consciousness, and theological innovation. From any viewpoint one would wish to take, there are many things wrong with religion in the denominational society, but it does not seem likely that the bookmakers of Las Vegas are going to give good odds on its going out of business.

Chapter 5

Religion as an Ethnic Phenomenon

American religion, as we have noted in the past two chapters, is both denominational and vigorous—both pluralistic in its behavior and pluraform in its shape. In the present chapter we intend to suggest that American religion is vigorous precisely because it is denominational—that it is able to be pluraform precisely because it is pluralistic. American religion, in short, is successful because American religious denominations are ethnic groups. The secret of the survival of the organized churches in the United States, we are contending, is their ability to play an ethnic, or at least quasi-ethnic role in American society.

By "ethnic" I mean a phenomenon by which the members of a religious denomination are able to obtain from their religion means of defining who they are and where they stand in a large and complex society. In some cases, this self-definition in social location may be the most important thing that religion does for a person. For other individuals, however, self-definition and social location are mixed with the belief system and ethical code according to which the person lives. The important question for the social scientist is not whether a religion stops being "authentically religious" when it becomes permeated by the ethnic phenomenon, but rather what the relationship is between religion as an ethnic phenomenon and religion as faith.

Within the Catholic Church a number of ethnic groups exist, usually built around a common language. Because they came with certain advantages, such as the English language, the Irish have been the dominant group in Church administration. During the nineteenth century, they were, however, challenged by German Catholics, whose period of influence was brought to a close by the First World War.

The Polish element, while numerically strong, has stayed much more to itself; and the Italians have much less loyalty to and involvement in Church affairs. To an outsider the Catholic Church may look monolithic, but a closer look reveals a diverse ethnicity under the Church's umbrella.

Ethnicity Defined

For Americans the ethnic group generally means the nationality or racial group. The Irish, the Jews, the Negroes, the Poles—these are thought to be the ethnics. In this frame of reference, it is trivial to say that American denominations are ethnic. Catholicism and Lutheranism are clearly divided into ethnic subdenominations—Irish Catholics, Polish Catholics, Italian Catholics, the German Lutherans, Scandinavian Lutherans—and Jews are simultaneously a religion in an ethnic group with, at least according to many of the more secular Jewish writers, the emphasis being on ethnicity rather than on religion. But we intend to say something much more than merely to assert that most Irishmen are Catholics. Rather, what we hope to do is answer the question of why most Irishmen remained Catholics when they came into Protestant American society, and why the American Irish are far more diligent in their church attendance and vigorous in their church affiliation than are their brothers and cousins who migrated to England.

We begin, therefore, by taking a more general definition of ethnic groups. In an extremely important essay on ethnic groups, Max Weber points out that "consciousness of kind" and a sense of a common origin may "become the bearer of communal social relationship." The American sociologist, E. K. Francis points out that ethnic groups in the Weberian sense have emerged in modern society precisely insofar as the old communal relationships of the peasant village have declined. Before migration to the industrial city, man thought of himself primarily as a member of the village community and not as belonging to some larger collectivity. But when he left behind the intimacy, the social support and control, it diffused particularistic [1] relationships of the village and substituted the more formalized, rationalized, and bu-

---

[1] By "particularistic," one means that what is important in judging a person is not some universal principle by which behavior is objectively measured but rather who the person happens to be. In the universalistic world, what you know is what counts; in the particularistic world, who you are is what counts. A role-opposite is simply someone who is one's partner in a pattern structured relationship.

reaucratized industrial metropolis. Man became an ethnic as part of his campaign to preserve some aspects of the peasant village in the metropolis; that is to say, to assure himself that there was available at least a certain number of role opposites with whom he shared a consciousness of kind—people whose origins were the same as his and who could therefore be expected, if not to give favored treatment, at least not to apply the rigid regulations of industrial bureaucracy with the same inflexibility as would someone with whom he had nothing in common. Nathan Glazer and others have pointed out that in the United States ethnic consciousness emerged among immigrants in many instances before it did among their families who stayed behind in the old country. Czechoslovakia was born in Pittsburgh, Pennsylvania, the Irish revolution was financed by Irish-American money, and the most important leader of the revolution was born in Brooklyn.

Will Herberg's description of the emergence of the ethnic groups in American society is by now classic:

> *In the Old World they had, let us remember, been men of their village or province, and known by that name; until well into the twentieth century most of them had no conception of national belonging, certainly no understanding of, or interest in, nationalism as an ideology. They were not Italians, but Apulians or Sicilians. They were not Poles, but Poznaniskers or Mazhevoers; not Germans, but Bavarians or Saxons or Prussians; not Greeks, but Thracians or men from Epirus. And the first societies they formed, as well as the first churches they tried to set up, were along such village and regional lines. But American life was too fluid to permit the indefinite perpetuation of these local identities. Men and women of many villages and regions were thrown together in the same "ghetto," and before long the new conditions of American life confronted the immigrant with a problem he had practically never had to face before, the problem of self-identification and self-location, the problem expressed in the question, "What am I?"*
>
> *This question is perhaps the most immediate that a man can ask himself in the course of his social life. Everyone finds himself in a social context which he shares with many others but, within this social context, how shall he locate himself? Unless he can so locate himself, he cannot tell himself, and others will not be able to know, who and what he is; he will remain "anonymous," a nobody—which is intolerable. To live, he must "belong"; to "belong," he must be able to locate himself in the larger social whole, to identify himself to himself and to others. There is*

nothing necessarily deliberate or conscious about all this. The process of self-location and identification is normally a "hidden" social process of which the individual is little aware; only at moments of disintegration and crisis does it emerge to the level of consciousness and require some measure of deliberate decision. Nor is actual social location ever one-dimensional; which aspect of a man's "belonging" becomes operative often depends on the concrete situation. So we can imagine a medieval villager, as long as he remained in his village, thinking of himself, and being thought of by others, in terms of his social caste—peasant, let us say. But once out of his village, the question, "What is he?", corresponding to the inner question, "What am I?", would very likely be answered in terms of his village, as indeed we can see from the structure of so many medieval names. This illustration suggests another significant fact. The way in which one identifies and locates oneself to oneself ("Who, what, am I?") is closely related to how one is identified and located in the larger community ("Who, what, is he?"). Normally they reflect, sustain, and illumine each other; it is only in abnormal situations that they diverge and conflict.

It was in such an abnormal situation of disintegration and crisis that the immigrant found himself as he attempted to rebuild his life in the New World. Who, what, was he? The question had rarely occurred to him in the "old home," but now it arose insistently before him and his children. Perhaps it seemed to him that there was no answer; but American reality not only raised the question, it also supplied the answer. "American experience taught these people to disregard the differences in dialect and custom among the various paesani. . . . Instead, immigrants found themselves drawn together by a larger affiliation the basis of which was the language that permitted them to communicate with each other. . . . So generally immigrant groups named themselves by their language rather than their place of origin": they became Poles and Russians and Slovaks and Greeks and Swedes and Hungarians, although very often the coverage of these names was not very clear in their own minds or in the minds of others. An emphasis on language gradually outlined the new character of the immigrant groups and answered the aching question of identity. Americans could understand such identification; indeed, they often referred to the immigrants as "foreign-language" groups. To Americans, and to immigrants who gave the matter any thought, language usually meant culture, and very soon nationality as well. The influence of intellectuals and busi-

*ness people, the former often nationalist ideologists and the lat-
ter eager to build up a cohesive group of "fellow countrymen"
as large as possible, encouraged the emergence of the new and
extended form of self-identification, but over and above everything else was the pressure of American reality. When finally
identification in terms of "national" group emerged and established itself, it seemed to the immigrants and their children as
though this kind of designation had been there from the very
beginning, almost a kind of biological label ("Why, of course, we
were Poles, or Italians, or Germans . . ."). But it had not been
that way; the new form of identification and self-identification
had been the product of* American *reality and* American *experience, and represented the first fruits of their Americanization.*

*This new form of self-identification and social location is what
we have come to know as the ethnic group. It soon became self-
evident to all Americans, and to almost all the immigrants and
their children, that the newcomers were falling into ethnic-na-
tional, or ethnic-cultural, groups within the larger American society. All immigrant life—and, therefore, in an important way,
all American life, since "the immigrants were* America"—*was
being rapidly reconstructed along the new lines. America became
the "land of immigrants," and over large parts of it, everyday
thinking and behavior followed "naturally" the patterns of ethnic
group relations. The ethnic group, because it was for so many
millions of Americans the primary context of identification and
social location, entered as a major factor into the economic, social, and political life of the total community, and into the most
intimate personal and social relations of the "ethnics" themselves.
Social-class structure, marriage selection, "availability" of political candidates, church and religious forms, all reflected the profound influence of the ethnic groups into which American reality
had organized the bewildered immigrants.*[2]

The essential point we wish to emphasize in the Herberg analysis
is that the emergence of the ethnic group was in response to the losses
man experienced in leaving behind *Gemeinschaft* society. The warm
and intimate supportive relationships of the village were not readily
given up and, as a whole, traditional sociological research for the last
three decades has established that informal, particularistic, diffuse relationships still play a major role in modern society. Production in an

industrial plant, marketing decisions, voting decisions, spread of information, the operation of the military establishment—all are strongly affected by friendship groups which, if they exist in the context of rationalizing, bureaucratized society, are not formed by it and often work against it.

The ethnic group is another manifestation, though on a somewhat larger scale, of man's attempt to sustain communal relationships in a contractual society. That such an attempt should focus on nationality groups in the United States is explicable in terms of the context in which the immigrant found himself and which Herberg described so acutely in the paragraphs we have quoted. It need not necessarily have been a nationality group. One can imagine in a different social context other bonds which would have provided the pool of preferred role opposites from which man could choose his friends, his spouse, his priest, his doctor, his lawyer and his contractor, his dentist, his undertaker, his real estate man, and his psychiatrist. We are using "ethnicity" in this volume to describe the tendency of urban man to create such pools of preferred role opposites when faced with the impersonality of the industrial metropolis. Ethnicity also can be used to describe nationality groups; it is appropriate because in the sense of having a common ancestor, it is the most appropriate and probably the first place where a man would look for a rationale for creating these preference pools. One might suspect that social class—that is to say, the consciousness of occupying a common position in the social structure, or, alternately, having a common set of enemies—would also be extremely useful in looking for a group of people to the members of which one could say, at least symbolically, "Your mother knew my mother."

Herberg argues quite vigorously that the transition in the United States is from a multiple melting pot of Protestant, Catholic, and Jew and uses' as his evidence the research of Ruby Jo Reeves Kennedy on marriages in New Haven, Connecticut, which shows an increase in interethnic marriages with little increase in religious intermarriages over a long period of time. Therefore, in his mind, Protestantism, Catholicism, and Judaism have become the three superethnic groups in American society. We would make two comments.

First of all, it is not clear that the old nationality groups have ceased being reservoirs of preferred role opposites. While American social scientists are reluctant to spend much time studying ethnic groups (and funding agencies equally reluctant to finance such studies), the information that is available would indicate that, at least in some large cities, nationality continues to be an extremely important factor of the social structure. (See especially Nathan Glazer and Daniel Patrick Moynihan, *Beyond the Melting Pot*.[3]) Furthermore, the yet unpublished work of Harold Abramson indicates that while intermarriage across nationality lines is increasing, there are certain definite patterns of such intermarriage with, for example, Irish Catholics far more likely to marry German Catholics than they would be to marry Polish or Italian Catholics. Thus the nationality group may still be an ethnic group (in our general sense of the word) in American society.

Secondly, we are going to suggest in this chapter, in an attempt to establish at least in some fashion in the remainder of the book, that the denominations in American society, even those which may not have any very clear nationality background, also play an ethnic role; it is their ability to provide a pool of preferred role opposites, and indeed, initiate interaction among members of the pool, that is the basic secret of the strength of organized religion in the United States. We are not necessarily intending to limit ourselves to saying that the ethnic effect is to be found merely in nationality groups and religious groups or in combinations of nationality and religious groups. Whether being an unaffiliated white Anglo-Saxon Protestant is to have an ethnic identity, or whether to be a Texan is to have an ethnic identity, whether to be a liberal intellectual is to have an ethnic identity, are questions which we consider much too complex to try to answer in the present volume. Neither does it seem feasible at present to attempt to untangle completely the complex nature of the relationships between nationality and religion. The early Irish immigrants were, one suspects, Catholics because they were Irish. The present American Irish may more likely be Irish because they are Catholic. It is altogether possible that, just as Lutherans, Methodists, and Baptists constitute quasi-ethnic denominations within Protestantism, so Irish Catholicism, German Catholicism, Polish Catholicism, and Italian Catholicism may also constitute "denominations" within Catholicism. But these questions are much too complex to be answered without far more data than are presently available to us. Our theorizing in this book is much more modest. We are arguing that denominational membership does make available to Americans a fellowship which is highly important in compensating for those intimate relationships of life which seem to have been lost when the peasant village was left behind. The religious denominations were available in American society to play this quasi-ethnic role, and therefore were eagerly seized upon.

[3] Nathan Glazer and Daniel Patrick Moynihan, *Beyond the Melting Pot*, 2nd ed. (Boston: The M.I.T. Press, 1971).

With some exaggeration we may say that instead of Americans belonging to churches because they believe in religion, there may be a strong tendency for them to believe in religion because they belong to churches.

The Ethnic Role of the Churches

It remains for us to delineate why the religious denominations were available to play this role. Once again we can turn to Herberg for a synopsis of an answer:

> *It must be remembered that in America the variety and multiplicity of churches did not, as in Europe, come with the breakdown of a single established national church; in America, taking the nation as a whole, the variety and multiplicity of churches was almost the original condition and coeval with the emergence of the new society. In America religious pluralism is thus not merely a historical and political fact; it is, in the mind of the American, the primordial condition of things, an essential aspect of the American Way of Life, and therefore in itself an aspect of religious belief. Americans, in other words, believe that the plurality of religious groups is a proper and legitimate condition. However much he may be attached to his own church, however dimly he may regard the beliefs and practices of other churches, the American tends to feel rather strongly that total religious uniformity, even with his own church benefiting thereby, would be something undesirable and wrong, indeed scarcely conceivable. Pluralism of religions and churches is something quite axiomatic to the American. This feeling, more than anything else, is the foundation of the American doctrine of the "separation of church and state," for it is the heart of this doctrine that the government may not do anything that implies the preeminence or superior legitimacy of one church over another.*
>
> *This means that outside the Old World distinction of church and sect America has given birth to a new type of religious structure—the denomination. The denomination as we know it is a stable, settled church, enjoying a legitimate and recognized place in a larger aggregate of churches, each recognizing the proper status of the others. The denomination is the "non-conformist sect" become central and normative. It differs from the church*

*in the European understanding of the term in that it would never
dream of claiming to be* the *national ecclesiastical institution; it
differs from the sect in that it is socially established, thoroughly
institutionalized, and nuclear to the society in which it is found.
The European dichotomy becomes meaningless, and instead we
have the nuclear denomination on the one side, and the periph-
eral sect on the way to becoming a denomination on the other.
So firmly entrenched is this denominational idea in the mind of
the American that even American Catholics have come to think
in such terms; theologically the Catholic Church of course continues to regard itself as the one true church, but in their actual
social attitudes American Catholics, hardly less than American
Protestants or Jews, tend to think of their church as a denomination existing side by side with other denominations in a pluralistic
harmony that is felt to be somehow of the texture of American
life.*[4]

Therefore, if the Irish Catholics immigrating to the United States
in the beginning of the nineteenth century chose to make Catholicism
an important part of their self definition and an important norm according to which one cleared one's pools of preferred role opposites,
it was because their Protestant predecessors had already done so. The
denominational nature of American society—that is to say, a society
composed of Congregationalists, Presbyterians, Unitarians, Methodists, Baptists, and so forth—can be traced back to the multidenomina-
tional origins of the colonies. Indeed, one could make a very strong
case that far from America's religious pluralism resulting from its
political pluralism, on the contrary, political pluralism became necessary because the nation even before it became a nation was already
religiously pluralistic. By pluralism I mean a situation in which society must balance not merely different social class groups but also different geographic, racial, religious and nationality groups. In its American form, political pluralism also involves many different levels of
governmental authority. Political power is not centralized exclusively
in a national government, but it also exists at the state, county, city,
and township levels. The first amendment to the constitution forbid-
ding the United States to establish an official religion was necessary
precisely because many of the states already had their own official
religion and the delegates to the Constitutional Convention came to
that meeting as representatives of denominational states. One must,
as a disciple of Max Weber, be careful not to go overboard. It would
be singularly ill advised to argue that religious pluralism caused politi-

---

[4] Herberg, op. cit., pp. 85–86.

cal pluralism, just as it would be ill advised to argue to the contrary. But it does seem safe to say that in the United States there has been, from the very beginning, a strong interaction process going on between political and religious pluralism and that the competition within the framework of cooperation which marks both our political and our religious society dates from the very origins of the thirteen colonies as denominational states.

In this view of things religion will come to play a quasi-ethnic role under two sets of circumstances: (1) a deprivation of intimate community as a result of the collapse of the *Gemeinschaft* village; and (2) the absence of an established church (official or unofficial), membership in which is almost coextensive with membership in society. Where these two conditions emerge, as in the United States, Canada, Switzerland, and Holland, religion will provide self-definition, social location, and a pool of preferred role opposites and will flourish in its organizational forms.

One point needs to be made about the social functions of religio-ethnic groups: they provide mobility pyramids that may turn into mobility traps. Because the ethnic subcommunity is, at least if it's big enough, a comprehensive substructure, it is possible for an upwardly mobile professional and businessman to build his career almost entirely within its confines. Not only a general practitioner, but even a surgeon, can have patients almost all of his own ethnic background; a Catholic academician can achieve a position within the system of Catholic colleges that he would not enjoy in the larger academic system; a political leader can gain far more power as the head of an ethnic faction within the party than he would if he tried to operate without such a power base; a contractor or an undertaker may do very well indeed servicing the needs of his ethnic colleagues, where he might be considerably less successful competing beyond the bounds of the ethnic group; even a racketeer, though he may be viewed with contempt by the larger society, may be respected for his success and affluence within his own substructure.

These mobility pyramids are, of course, very helpful for those who manage to achieve influence, affluence, and prestige that might well be less possible for them in the larger society. And such substructural mobility probably adds to the satisfaction and morale of the members of an ethnic community. On the other hand, there is the risk of a mobility trap. A promising academician who accepts his first major appointment at a Catholic college may move up very rapidly within the Catholic system but find the door closed to him for more meaningful mobility outside the system. Similarly, a doctor who has built his clientele within the ethnic community may feel that he has great prestige there, but when he goes to medical association meetings and finds himself outside the power elite of these associations, he may wonder if he might not have had even greater success beyond his own ethnic group.

A few individuals manage to avoid the ethnic trap, moving from positions within their own group to similar positions in the larger structure with increased influence and prestige. Thus, certain journalists whose careers originally were established within Catholic publishing journals have been able, because of their success on these journals, to switch over to important positions with secular newspapers and magazines. And the Kennedys, whose power roots lie in the ward politics of Boston, were able—with the aid of large sums of money and great personal dedication—to break out of the Irish Catholic political mold and make it in the big time. But the mobility pitfalls persist, and many ethnics eager for upward mobility are faced with Caesar's choice—whether to be first in the small pyramid or run the risk of being second (or lower) in Rome.

In fact, this thesis is a combination of Herberg with the Parsonian theoretical tradition. We are arguing that the major difference between American religion as we see it and American religion as it appears in Parson's otherwise brilliant essays is precisely that American religion functions as a quasi-ethnic group. Durkheim's religion provided integration and community, which held society together, Herberg's American religion provided a personal integration and a community (or at least a communal group—in Weber's sense, a group that facilitates community relationships).

In such a theory much of the busy social activity, the fellowship behavior, "religion in general," becomes intelligible. In a curious paradox, Americans may believe because they belong, but the fact that belief follows belonging to some extent weakens and limits the prophetic and challenging dimensions of belief. People do not change their religious beliefs, because to do so would deprive them of a tremendously important fellowship to which they belong; but since the fellowship is more important than the belief, it is possible to be part of the fellowship without necessarily penetrating or taking seriously all the dimensions of the belief. On the other hand, lest we fall victim to the same tendency which we criticized in O'Dea concerning the institutionalization of the church, we should note that the very fact that so many observers are prophesying about the non-prophetic nature of American religion is in itself quite interesting. The fact that American religion is organizationally strong precisely because of its belonging or fellowship dimension may very well make possible more prophecy (and certainly better paid prophets) than would be feasible if American organized religion was as weak as organized religion is in France and England. American religion truly has more than one "irony" in its fire.[5]

Catholic Ethnic Groups

Although American Catholicism is generally thought of as one denomination, there are some reasons for arguing that the various nationality groups were, at least to some extent, quasi-denominations within American Catholicism. On the national level the structure in the Catholic Church maintains some semblance of unity, but the large urban dioceses are often divided into ethnic enclaves, each of which has considerable power of its own in fact if not in canonical theory. They tend to be more suspicious of their Catholic counterparts than they are of Protestants. While some of these ethnic differences may be declining with the passage of time, they are still of major importance in cities like New York, Chicago, Boston, Philadelphia, Pittsburgh, Detroit, St. Louis, and Milwaukee where the majority of the American Catholic population is to be found.

The dominant Catholic ethnic group is, of course, the Irish who have had all the advantages vis-à-vis other Catholic nationality groups. The Irish came first; almost all of them were able to speak English; they were politically astute and organizationally skillful, particularly since the American political system was an Anglo-Saxon one (one which the Irish had necessarily exploited for centuries in order to survive); and they were also fiercely loyal religiously (again, due to the opposition of Mother England).

The Irish, therefore, have consistently controlled the American Catholic ecclesiastical structure. The first bishop, John Carroll, was a native American, since the Carroll family had been in the colonies many generations before the Revolution, but his background was Irish. For a brief period after his death the control of the Church slipped into the hands of refugees from the French Revolution and their English allies who strove to keep alive the Carroll tradition of the native American Catholic Church. The early archbishops of Baltimore—Maréchal, Whitfield, Eccleston, and Spaulding—were not Irish, but

[5] We hesitate to say that Americans are more religious than Englishmen and Frenchmen. We are not attempting to assert in any sense that there is more ultimate concern in the United States than there is in England and France or that qualitatively faith is better in the United States than it is in the two European countries. We are simply asserting that there is more organized religious activity in the United States and suggesting that the reason for it is a denominational society.

most of the other bishops were. Archbishop Kenrick of Baltimore was the first Irish-born prelate to hold that see (1851-1863). Every bishop of Baltimore, New York, and Boston since the time of Cardinal Gibbons (archbishop of Baltimore in the 1870's) has been of Irish origin. Of the more than a score of Americans who have become cardinals, all have been Irish save for three Germans (Mundelein and Meyer of Chicago, and Ritter of St. Louis) and one Pole (Krol of Philadelphia). While Polish and German Catholics have been heads of religious communities of their own nationality and also, occasionally, college presidents and bishops in some dioceses, the power structure of the American Catholic Church still continues to be largely Irish. Even in those dioceses where the Irish are not a majority of the Catholic population and where there may not even be an Irish bishop, the curial and administrative positions of the diocese still are staffed largely by Irish clergy. This cannot be written off merely as the result of political conniving, though surely there has been some of that; the Irish have flocked to the clergy and religious life, and they have proved themselves particularly able at organization and administration and at adjusting to the demands of American society.

Until recently the Irish have not been inclined to be particularly intellectual, but they have provided most of the leadership in the waves of self-criticism sweeping American Catholicism in the last decade and a half. Ecclesiastical administrators of Irish origin have generally tended to reflect the conservative elements in the Irish political and religious traditions, though Irish liberalism of a fierce and ornate variety has not been absent either in the hierarchy, or the clergy, or the laity. Among bishops, the names of England, Keane, Ireland, and Muldoon represent this tradition; labor priests such as the late Monsignor John Ryan and Monsignor George Higgins represent the clergy; and among the laity, the various Irish liberals who have sat in the United States Senate, even briefly in the White House, also reflect the more liberal elements in the Irish personality. Nevertheless, while there may be more liberalism in the Irish ethnic group than there is among some other groups, it still must be conceded that the Irish ecclesiastical mentality has frequently been narrow, digressive, puritanical and suspicious.

The German Catholic ethnic group was the first to resist Irish domination after the Irish waves swept over the French and English leadership of the native American Catholic Church. In fierce battles at the end of the nineteenth century, they managed to keep the Irish leadership at bay for the most part. The German tradition tends to be somewhat more intellectual, particularly because of its contact with the monasteries and theological faculties of Catholicism in Germany.

Table 6 Selected Attributes of Catholic Ethnic Groups in U.S.

	Irish	Germans	Italians	Poles	French
Have completed high school	77%	52%	51%	46%	42%
Hold prestige jobs	32	31	13	17	22
Earn over $14,000 a year	24	19	17	18	7
Belong to Democratic Party	70	65	67	77	70
Score high on general knowledge	18	9	7	3	5
Score high on open-mindedness	52	48	42	43	40
Consider themselves "very happy"	41	36	35	27	40
Score low on anomie	64	51	47	43	49
Score high on piety	32	31	13	30	22
Score high on religious extremism	19	20	24	34	28
Score high on racism	44	46	54	61	51
Score high on anti-Semitism	29	47	43	52	54
(Number of persons interviewed)	(328)	(361)	(370)	(184)	(177)

Tables 6 and 7 are from Andrew M. Greeley, *Why Can't They Be Like Us?* (New York: Institute of Human Relations Press, The American Jewish Committee, 1969), pp. 46, 48. Reprinted with permission.

A considerable amount of the theological and liturgical progressivism in American Catholicism has, in fact, come through these contacts, and particularly through the Benedictine Abbey of St. John's in Collegeville, Minnesota. Even though the late nineteenth-century German leaders who fought against the Irish "Americanists" were generally considered conservative, other Germans took very progressive positions on the social questions in the first part of the twentieth century and were active in the establishment of Catholic social services. Peter Dietz, one of the first of the labor priests, Frederick Kenkel, a layman, and the great Benedictine innovator, Virgil Michel, were all part of this German progressive element.

However, in many respects two world wars (particularly the first) spelled the end of the Germans as a distinct ethnic group in American society, because they definitively terminated the attempt to maintain a separate German-American culture with its own language, traditions, and institutions. In most dioceses there were only minor differences separating German Catholics and Irish Catholics, and most of the German national parishes are now inhabited largely by Polish or Negro groups. The German Catholics and Irish Catholics are quite content to live side by side in the same rectories and parishes and to form a common cause against more recent arrivals on the American shores.

The principal opponents to this German-Irish entente are the Poles, a group which will concede nothing to the Irish in the way of fierce loyalty to the Church, but which, unfortunately, had none of the advantages the Irish possessed. They came later to America, did not know the language, and lacked the Anglo-Saxon political skills of the Irish. They were able to maintain themselves as a distinct ethnic group and to found hospitals, orphanages, schools, cemeteries, and a vast array of religious and fraternal organizations. But beyond these boundaries they had very little power. The Irish-German leadership of the American Church was content to leave them alone, and the Poles remained a minority group which ultimately depended on the decisions of the Irish leadership.

Furthermore, many of the styles of religious behavior of the Polish clergy and laity were less at home in American society than were the styles of previous Catholic immigrant groups. Poles found themselves, then, twice unwelcome, both by the American society and by the controlling cliques within the Catholic Church. To complicate matters, the control of the Polish clergy over their people seems, to some observers at least, to be much less flexible than that of the earlier immigrant priests and thus to give rise to stronger friction between the clergy and laity than the other groups had to face. The Poles tend still to be found in large urban concentrations; they are moving from the working class to the lower middle class precisely at a time when the Irish and the Germans are moving from the lower middle class to the upper middle class, a phenomenon which merely aggravates the differences between the Poles and their predecessors. Many of these differences may ease with the passage of time, but both in terms of organization and religious style, Polish Catholics remain quite different from the earlier immigrant groups.

The fourth Catholic ethnic group, the Italians, are substantially different from the first three in that their religious style involves much less in the way of loyalty to the organizational church. While Italians would claim quite strongly that they are Catholics, their level of church attendance, their involvement in church organizations, and their financial support of the church, for reasons of the past history of their country, are substantially different from that of the Irish, the Germans, or the Poles. They do not, then, have the network of religious and fraternal institutions that the Germans had in the past and that the Poles have now. They are therefore more quickly assimilated into the American Catholic—that is to say—Irish Catholic structure. A number of Italian writers have recently noted (not altogether with pleasure) that third-generation Italians have a strong tendency to become very much like the Irish in their religious behavior. Affluence and success in American society demand that one be "religious" if one is to be a respectable member of the middle class. Since Italians are Catholic, and since the norms for respectable religiousness in American society come from the Irish, the Italians, as they move up the socioeconomic ladder tend to assimilate many Irish attitudes and to attend Catholic schools even to the college level. Even in the third generation, of course, their religious behavior is not as vigorously Catholic as are the other groups, but their assimilation of the Irish style involves much less difficulty because there is not a network of ethnic institutions impeding such assimilation. On the other hand, the absence of such a network has apparently contributed to a somewhat higher defection rate from the Church. Nevertheless, the overwhelming majority of Italian Americans still would define themselves as Catholic, and are likely to do so for the foreseeable future.

There are a number of other Catholic ethnic groups in the United States. The largest is probably the French Canadians concentrated in the New England area. In addition, there are Lithuanian, Bohemian, Croatian, and Slovenian Catholic groups, to say nothing of the very large if disorganized Spanish-speaking Catholic population. Furthermore, there are "Eastern Rite" Catholics among the Ukrainians, Armenians, Lebanese, and other immigrant groups who are loyal to Rome but have a liturgy and a tradition entirely their own. With the exception of the Spanish-speaking whose organizational commitment to religion is very weak, these smaller groups are in a position vis-à-vis the German-Irish elite similar to that occupied by the Poles. Needless to say, friction, tension, and occasional schisms are quite possible, but far more typical is a condition of suspicious but generally peaceful coexistence. The Irish-German leadership applies the minimum amount of control it deems necessary for organizational unity, and the leadership of the other groups demand that maximum amount of independence they feel imperative to maintain their own identity. The problem of course, is complicated by the fact that many of the second and third generations of the later immigrant groups are unhappy with the "old country" customs of ancestors and choose to become "American" Catholics, which is to say, to attend Irish-dominated churches. There is a possibility of a cultural revival in the next generation in which those "old world" customs will once more be valued; this possibility could create severe strains within American Catholicism. However, at the present time, it does not seem to be very likely.

As the accompanying tables show, Italian piety is lower than that of the other ethnic groups, and they are also more likely to defect from the Democratic party in later generations, perhaps as a revolt against the Irish domination of the Democratic party on the eastern seaboard.

Table 7   Selected Attributes of Catholic Ethnic Groups in U.S.—High-school
Graduates of Third or Later Generation Only

	Irish	Germans	Italians	Poles	French
Hold prestige jobs	31%	34%	12%	32%	21%
Work as professionals or managers	45	47	37	22	31
Earn over $14,000 a year	26	22	3	21	11
Belong to Democratic Party	67	61	51	62	76
Score high on general knowledge	26	17	20	11	9
Score high on open-mindedness	51	56	51	34	40
Consider themselves "very happy"	47	38	26	32	48
Score low on anomie	74	60	44	61	60
Score high on piety	32	32	10	20	39
Score high on religious extremism	14	15	20	31	26
Score high on racism	39	30	54	61	29
Score high on anti-Semitism	25	38	32	59	43
(Number of persons interviewed)	(131)	(102)	(29)	(24)	(31)

Greeley, *Why Can't They Be Like Us?*, op. cit.

Similarly, the Polish ethnic group is less likely to be socially mobile than the other groups and also more likely to score high on measure of ethnocentrism, quite possibly because they are now at the stage of their acculturation experience where large numbers of lower middle-class Poles are owning their own home for the first time, and thus feel themselves notably threatened by the in-migration of Negroes. This apparent racial prejudice of the Poles persists even among those with high-school education and among later generations, although it also seems to be a uniquely Middle Western phenomenon, perhaps because this is the area where there are the largest Polish ethnic concentrations. The Middle Western Irish, for some reason as yet unclear, seem to be much more devout in their religiousness than the East Coast Irish, and according to some observers (though the observation is not substantiated by our data), are also more inclined to be ecclesiastically and politically liberal. Finally, the research of the present writer and Peter H. Rossi [6] would seem to indicate that parochial school education has little impact on members of the Polish and Italian ethnic groups, while it has considerable impact on German and Irish Catholics. Furthermore, parental religiousness correlates with respondents'

[6] Andrew M. Greeley and Peter H. Rossi, *The Education of Catholic Americans* (Chicago: Aldine Publishing Company, 1965).

religiousness among the earlier immigrant groups much more strongly than it does among the later groups. These two phenomena have led Dr. Rossi to suggest that the Germans and Irish are more influenced by intergenerational values and Poles and Italians by intragenerational values. Thus, the Irish and Germans, at least in the present state of the acculturation process, will be influenced both by their parents and by their teachers in parochial schools, while Italians and Poles will be much more influenced by peer groups.

Summary

If one tries to define ethnicity, one finds a communal bond, which is an attempt to replace the *Gemeinschaft* relationships of the village or neighborhood left behind when an immigrant came to the industrial New World. Often language or nationality became the focal point for an ethnic group which in their country of origin would have centered around an area or village. In the United States the churches came to serve an ethnic role; they helped sort out "who one was" in a bewilderingly complex society. As a result the various denominations have been immeasurably strengthened, as they serve not only a religious need, but a social one as well. Sometimes the ethnic structures, which have been so useful to the newcomer as well as to the second and third generation, become traps out of which it is difficult for a talented person to escape. But overall, the ethnic bonds, often under the informal aegis of a church, have served a very useful function in helping newcomers to accommodate to a new and strange life.

American Catholicism, therefore, can hardly be thought of as a monolithic entity, and while it would perhaps be going too far to say that the nationality groups are denominations, it would be no exaggeration to say that they are quasi-denominations, and that as the young person is socialized within his religioethnic group, he thinks of himself not so much as a Catholic, but as a Polish Catholic, Irish Catholic, Italian Catholic, French Catholic, thus distinguishing himself not only from Protestants but also from Catholics of other ethnic backgrounds. There is probably a relationship between the length of time an immigrant group has been in the United States and its tendency to link religion and nationality as part of the process of self-definition and social location. Only further research will reveal exactly how religion and nationality blend with each other in the formation both of the personality system and of the social structure of the denominational society. But it would be a mistake on a priori grounds to exclude the nationality variable in any study of American religion. Just as no sensitive researcher would dream of lumping all American Protestants together (unless the sample was too small to split them into the various Protestant denominations), so no prudent researcher ought to lump all Catholics into one religious grouping. If the sample is large enough, the researcher should take into account the existence of the various nationality subcultures within the American Catholic Church.

Chapter 6
The Secularization Myth

It will seem to many readers that the situation described in the last chapter is a transient one. American religions may be vigorous because they are ethnic, but the immigration experience is receding into the past. Ethnicity is presumably declining in American society and, as the processes of secularization go on, both the ethnic function of religion and the importance of religion itself in the United States presumably will decline.

In two other and much briefer volumes, the author addresses himself to these questions and concludes that in this variegated and immense social structure in the United States ethnic or ethniclike groups show no signs of disappearing, and that by the year 2000 American religion is not likely to be substantially weaker than it is at the present time.[1] Nevertheless, it would be pertinent in the present volume to take a good hard look at the issue of secularization, particularly because a clarification of the issue will contribute substantially to our understanding of the present functioning of the denominational society.

That America is going through "secularization," or that it went through it long ago, is widely assumed by journalists, churchmen, intellectuals, and college students. "Secularity" means different things to different writers, and indeed it has so many possible meanings that it has become almost meaningless. But the essential notion that seems to underline much of the discussion of secularity—that is to say, that religion is becoming less important to Americans—is one that the sociologist finds himself forced to question, no matter how popular the notion might be in the fashion centers of contemporary American ideas or no matter how desirable the idea of secularity may appear to

[1] They are *Why Can't They Be Like Us?* op. cit., and *Religion in the Year 2000* (New York: Sheed & Ward, 1969).

the sociologist himself. In this chapter we will discuss some of the senses in which the word "secularization" is used, consider several of the theoretical positions taken by sociologists trying to understand the reality of secularization, and then will look at the empirical data that are available to us against which the secularization model might be tested. The conclusion that we will adhere to is quite similar to that of the sociologist, Seymour Martin Lipset, who suggests that there may very well be no conflict between religion and secularity, at least as the two are defined in American society, and that American religion not only can coexist happily with secularity, but has done so almost since its beginning. As a matter of fact, even more can be said: American religion (if one agrees with Lipset, and we do) embraced secularity to its bosom long ago without ever suspecting that the union might be illicit. From such a perspective it would appear that the current enthusiasm over secularism, far from being premature is, on the contrary, outdated.

Secularization Defined

There are a number of possible meanings that "secularization" seems to take in the current discussion.

First of all, to say that the modern world is secular may mean that science makes it impossible for modern man to believe. From the data presented in the last chapter it is apparent that—possible or not —men in great numbers do believe in religion. Science may make it difficult for some modern men to believe, particularly for those modern men who are most in contact with the intellectual currents of their time, but it does not seem that this problem of the intellectual and religion, which now is several hundred years old, has substantially affected the religious commitment of the masses, including even the college-educated masses. Further, we shall suggest later on that religion seems far from dead, even among the intellectual elites.

Second, secularism could also be interpreted as meaning that men are not motivated by religion in their daily lives. That this assertion is true, at least of many people much of the time, is hardly deniable. One suspects, however, that even during the great ages of faith there were many men who were not motivated by religion in their daily lives. Whether either the agnostic or the saint is less common today, sociology (and probably every other discipline) is unable to say.

Third, secularism can mean that fewer and fewer people are concerned with religion and that there is a tendency to drift from religious faith and commitment. If there is such a tendency, presumably it has been going on for a long time since the roots of religious unconcern—the scientific, technical, and industrial revolutions—have been with us for a long time. This proposition, while not clearly in error, is still very difficult to test because we have no substantial data about faith and commitment in any but the most recent past. However, the strength of religion and its pervasiveness in American society suggest that if there is a leakage away from religion, it is proceeding at a very slow rate indeed.

Fourth, it may be argued that religion and society are not in close contact and that there are vast areas of human behavior on which religion has no direct influence. This statement is certainly true, but again it is hardly new, and could have been said of most areas of human life for the last one hundred or one hundred and fifty years. As we shall see later on in this chapter, some sociologists, such as Talcott Parsons, contend that a better name for this dimension of secularization is "differentiation." According to that theory, in a more complex society religion's roles become more specific, and therefore its influence on society becomes more indirect but by no means vanishes or even is substantially weakened because it is indirect. The question here is extremely complicated and it is obscured even more by the lack of data. Religion and society were obviously in close contact in the Middle Ages, but whether this made for a more authentic religion or not in comparison with the present time is problematic. Religion influenced society more, but religion was also more of a prisoner of society and was faced with great difficulties in standing over against society and being critical of it. During that era it was hard for an individual to be integrated into the society and yet have the emotional and moral strength to be autonomous at the same time. It is certainly true that the relationships between religion and society have changed since the Middle Ages but, while it is true, it is also trivial unless one specifies in great detail the meaning of these changes. When one begins to do so, it is not immediately clear that this represents a net loss for religion. Further, since it is extremely difficult to define even today how one would measure the amount of influence that authentic religious faith has on behavior in man and his society, it is well-nigh impossible to make a comparison with the influence of authentic religion in the previous age.

Fifth, secularization can mean that religion is more and more relegated to the private sphere of man's activity and has no influence on the public's fear. One who holds this, of course, is faced with the problem of explaining the obvious impact of religion on, let us say, the civil rights movement or the war on poverty, but he must also wrestle with the Parsonian notion that by shaping man's values in the private sphere, religion exercises a powerful if indirect experience on the public sphere where its own ideals have already been to some considerable extent institutionalized and are taken for granted. The issue is a complex one but surely the complexity does not encourage the readiness with which the secularization hypothesis is embraced.

Sixth and finally, secularization can mean that nothing of the sacred or, not very much of it, is left in human life. Man has destroyed the gods, disposed of the myths, broken with the mythological and the metaphysical and embraced the rational, the scientific, and the technological in the marvelous new creation of the secular city. From what we've already said in this book, it should be evident that this sociologist is not altogether persuaded of the death of the sacred.

The sociologist tends to be skeptical of most of the theories of secularization that he reads even if he himself is thoroughly secularized. His statistics on religious activity and his knowledge of the importance that religion has always had in human society makes him wonder how secular modern man really is or is likely to become at least in the foreseeable future. Indeed, the sociologist asks himself who this modern man really is that writers like Harvey Cox, the Bishop of Woolich, and Thomas J. Altizer are so fond of describing—this man who rejects the mythical and the sacred and lives his whole life in the technical and the secular. He is not, as we shall show later on in this chapter, the typical college student or even the typical graduate student even in the best universities in the country. That there are some thoroughly unreligious and thoroughly secularized men in modern society, the sociologist is willing to concede. He is likely to be one himself and so are his professional colleagues. But such secularist agnostics seem to be few and far between in the general American population. When a religious magazine like the *Christian Century*, committed strongly as it is to the notion that the church is constantly in a crisis of secularization, nervously observes that a slight upswing in church attendance, as reported by the Gallup Poll, is not a sign that the crisis of religion is over, the sociologist is apt to be amused. From the perspective of his data, the crisis had never been terribly impressive in the first place.

That there are changing patterns in American religion does not seem to be in doubt. There apparently was an upswing in religious activity during and after the Second World War which persisted into the late 1950's. From then into the middle 1960's there was apparently a downswing in religious activity, which may have come to an end at the time of the present writing. But these swings, as we shall see later in the chapter, are not particularly new in American society, and do not seem to affect more than a relatively small minority of the population. Data reported on later in this chapter were collected in 1952 and 1965, representing presumably the high point of the postwar religious revival and something close to the low point of the post-1960 "crisis of secularization." Changes in belief and practice in this period were minor.

But even if changes are to be recorded across time in American religious attitude and behavior, we must be careful not to view these changes as necessarily indicating a long-run trend. The Gallup Poll's report on Sunday church attendance has indicated that in the past decade the high percentage was in 1955 (49 percent of the American population attended church weekly, a somewhat higher attendance record than was recorded in Table 1) and the low percentage in 1966 with 44 percent attending every week, a figure which had begun to creep up in 1967 and turn down again in 1969. On the other hand, comparisons to be made later in this chapter between 1952 and 1965 indicate an increase in those thirteen years of eight percentage points for Catholic weekly church attendance and five percentage points for Protestants with a decline of eight percentage points for Jews. It is a mistake to make too much of either set of figures. Even granting that the annual fluctuation is caused by something more than sampling variation, the newspaper headlines and the anxious editorials in the denominational journals about either the religious revival or the religious decline are premature in the extreme. For reasons we do not fully understand, there are cyclical patterns in religious behavior with upswings and downswings following each other at intervals of perhaps from five to ten years. It may be correct to say that traditional religion is in serious trouble in the middle 1960's but it was in serious trouble in the middle 1860's and in the middle 1760's when, according to one observer, there were more than 30,000 atheists in the city of Paris alone.

The end of organized religion or its transformation into some new form of religion has been cheerfully predicted by both the friends and the foes of religion for at least three centuries and yet religion has managed to survive. Whether the current set of predictions represents anything new under the sun remains to be seen. They might, but this sociologist will be forgiven for expressing doubt until he sees more convincing evidence.

Theories of Secularization

Even though more popular theologians such as Harvey Cox and Daniel Callahan are constantly referring to the findings of sociologists, they ignore systematically the most important theoretical contribution by a sociologist to the question of secularization, the work of Professor Talcott Parsons. In a long essay in a volume honoring the work of the sociologist, Pitirim Sorokin, Parsons takes sharp issue with Sorokin's view of the deterioration of the influence of religion and by implication many of the popular theories of secularization.[2] Parsons' basic critique of Sorokin is the latter's "assumption that religiousness *ipso facto* implies other-worldliness, supplemented only by spontaneous altruism." Parsons, writing from a strongly Protestant perspective, contends on the contrary that a predominantly inner-worldly orientation, such as is found in medieval Christianity, but most evidently in "ascetic Protestantism," can just as validly be described as religiousness. Furthermore, Parsons, in the theoretical viewpoint in his own theory of action, argues:

> *Like all other aspects in the course of social, cultural, and personality development, it (religion) undergoes a process of differentiation in a double sense. The first of these concerns differentiation within religious systems themselves; the second, the differentiation of the religious element from the nonreligious elements in the more general system of action. In the latter context the general developmental trend may be said to be from fusions of religious and nonreligious components in the same action structures, to increasingly clear differentiation between multiple spheres of action.*[3]

Parsons then traces the history of Christianity from St. Paul through to the modern world showing how this twin process of differentiation went on. This basic argument is that as society became more complex and diversified and as religion itself also became more complex and diversified, the religious component both of society and of the individual personality became more and more differentiated from the rest of society so that, for example:

> *Luther broke through—to make the individual a religiously autonomous entity, responsible for his own religious concerns, not only in the sense of accepting the ministrations and disciplines*

[2] Parsons, "Christianity and Modern Industrial Society," op. cit., p. 276.
[3] Ibid., p. 37.

of the church but also through making his own fundamental religious commitments.[4]

In Parsons' view, this change, far from making religion or faith less important, made it more important because now it became a matter for conscious choice. As we have noted before, Parsons feels that while many of the institutions of modern society are not at all directly under the influence of Christianity and may not even explicitly acknowledge the ethical values of Christianity, nonetheless, these institutions have, by the very fact that they have evolved in the process of differentiation from the society where the Christian ethic (at least in this Protestant manifestation) was strong, assumed into their structure many Christian ethical values. He further argues that in the process of differentiation religion is directly exercising only its essential function of providing a value system with regard to ultimate questions and to one's basic moral postures that have a powerful indirect influence on society because it becomes a major component in the individual's action system.

As we noted in Chapter 2, Thomas Luckmann is less convinced of the indirect impact of Christianity on many of the secular institutions. He contends that these systems have allowed their own rationale and their own value systems, which are functional to their specific purposes and have nothing to do with Christianity or with organized religion, to prevail. The reality may be somewhere in between. Modern large corporations in the United States, for example, may engage in all sorts of socially enlightened behavior both within themselves and in relation to the larger society—behavior that can only be remotely justified in terms of the profit motivation, which is presumably the basic principle of the productive economy. This socially enlightened behavior may be rationalized for boards of directors and stockholders in terms of its long-range benefit to the total corporation. It may be further argued that the survival of the corporation has now become more important than maximizing profits, and that socially enlightened behavior is functional for its survival. If the disciples of Parsons still ask why a corporation must be socially enlightened to survive, it could be answered that such activities as donations to higher education are merely means of assuring a steady supply of skilled personnel for the corporation. Surely there is an element of truth in such a claim, yet most corporation grants to higher education do not automatically guarantee employees for the specific corporation. And many of the social activities of the corporations seem to be dedicated more to enhancing its image than to producing

[4] *Ibid.*, p. 50.

immediate results. If it is necessary for the corporation to have an image of being socially conscious or charitable, then it seems safe to say that in some fashion social consciousness and charity have been institutionalized in the value system of both the larger society and of the nonreligious organizations which is precisely Professor Parsons' point. Modern man, working in a large corporate structure that is infused somewhat by Christian ideas, with himself directed somewhat by the Christian ethic, may be behaving religiously a good deal of the time, though the fact that he is influenced by religion may not be immediately clear to him because the influence is both indirect and implicit.[5]

That Christian motivation affects the essential decision making of the large corporate bodies may be more difficult to prove. Men will act ethically in their decision making when they can, and when they cannot, will be content with ethical rationalizations for what they are doing. But even if they need ethical rationalizations, it suggests that religion has yet to be banished completely from the marketplace, the government office, or the university campus.

So Parsons may have the better of it in a discussion with Luckmann, at least to the extent that modern man's behavior in the large corporate bodies is probably motivated by a mixture of religious values and values that are strictly functional for the purposes of the organization. This mixture may not on balance represent anything that is less religious than the behavior of human beings in organizations of the past. The medieval barons were presumably Christians and devout members of their church, but their behavior both as feudal lords and as military commanders was strongly motivated, one suspects, by a combination of Christian values and the functional requisites of economic or military survival with a good deal of rationalization going on to justify it. In this perspective the mistake of those who are so eager to see secularization of values is to assume that at some not necessarily specific time in the past religion was less differentiated from the rest of society and man's action system was somehow less a mixture of religious and self-serving values. They assume further that the fact of differentiation and specification somehow makes religious motivation less possible when in fact it might be assumed with equal plausibility that differentiation merely makes hypocrisy more difficult.

[5] We are using the word "Christian" in the present context because it is Christianity with which Professor Parsons is concerned in his essay. One could just as easily speak of Judaism, perhaps more so, because of the very strong social consciousness of the Jewish religion and particularly in its American manifestation.

In the words of Parsons' student, Bellah:

Private voluntary religious association in the West achieved full legitimation for the first time in the modern situations. . . . The tendency in more recent periods has been to continue the basic pattern but with a much more open and flexible pattern of membership. . . . The assumption in most of the major Protestant denominations is that a church member can be considered responsible for himself. This trend seems likely to continue with an increasingly fluid type of organization in which many special purpose subgroups form and disband.[6]

But Bellah does not see these trends as representing either indifference or secularization but rather the acceptance of the notion that the individual must work out his own ultimate solutions and the most the church can do is provide a favorable environment for doing so without providing a prefabricated set of answers.

Parsons concludes his long essay on Christianity and modern industrial society with some astute comments on the tension that must exist between at least the Christian religion and any society in which it is institutionalized.

It seems probable that a certain basic tension in relation to the "things of this world" is inherent in Christianity generally. Hence any relative success in the institutionalization of Christian values cannot be taken as final, but rather as a point of departure for new religious stock-taking. But in addition to this broad internal consideration, the confrontation on such a new basis with the non-Christian world presents a new and special situation. We are deeply committed to our own great traditions. These have tended to emphasize the exclusive possession of the truth. Yet we have also institutionalized the values of tolerance and equality of rights for all. How can we define a meaningful orientation in such a world when, in addition, the more familiar and conventional problems of suffering and evil are, if not more prevalent than ever before, at least as brought to the attention through mass communications, inescapable as facts of our world?

It is the inherent tensions and dynamism of Christianity and the unprecedented character of the situation we face which, to my mind, account for the intensive researching and questioning, and indeed much of the spiritual negativism of our time. The explanation in terms of an alleged moral collapse would be far too simple, even if there were more truth in it than the evidence

---

[6] Bellah, op. cit., p. 372.

*seems to indicate. For this would imply that we did not need new
conceptions of meaning, all we would need would be to live up
more fully to the standards familiar to us all. In no period of
major ferment in cultural history has such a solution been adequate.*[7]

Both Parsons and Bellah operate on a very high level of abstraction
dealing with value systems and action orientations. They concede the
obvious fact that there is much less direct contact between the religious institution and the economic, social, governmental, and educational institutions in modern society than there was in the past. But
they explain this as a differentiation and reject the notion of a religious
or moral decline. If secularization means differentiation, then Parsons
and Bellah would be happy to concede that modern society is in the
process of continuing secularization. But if secularization means that
organized religion, indeed Christianity, is no longer socially important
because it no longer shapes either the world views and the action
systems of individuals or the behavior of social institutions, then both
on theoretical and empirical grounds Parsons and Bellah would deny
that the theory of secularization is a valid one. Minimally, it must be
conceded first that the word "secularization" is used with inexcusable
looseness in contemporary discussion. If it is to serve any purpose
at all in such discussion, its precise meaning ought to be much more
clearly specified by those who rely upon it as a category. One may
choose not to accept the theoretical framework of Parsons and Bellah
but neither can one afford to reject it or ignore it in attempting to
specify precisely what one means about secularization. Secondly, it
ought to be hoped that journalists, theologians, and ecclesiastical
viewers-with-alarm would be more careful in claiming the universal
assent of sociologists to the notion that the influence of religion is
diminishing rapidly in contemporary society. Parsons and Bellah, the
two most distinguished American sociologists to devote themselves
directly to the question on the theoretical level, strongly disagree. As
we shall see later, Seymour Martin Lipset, who approaches the issue
on the more empirical level, can hardly be said to be in agreement
with naive notions of secularity either.

A Look at the Data

We now turn from the rarefied atmosphere of general theory at which
Parsons and Bellah operate to the much more grubby world of survey

[7] Parsons, "Christianity and Modern Industrial Society," op. cit., pp. 69–70.

researchers collecting empirical data. As we have noted frequently in the course of this volume, we have practically no information on religious behavior in past centuries or even in the early part of this century, but we do, fortunately, have information on religious behavior in the 1950's; and there exists at least one time series study in which questions asked a national population sample in 1952 were repeated in 1965. Thirteen years is not a long period of time and yet, given the immense publicity to secularization trends and the death of God, one would have expected notable changes in religious attitudes and behavior in the course of a decade and a half. To report, as we are going to in this section, that there is almost no confirmation for such an expectation is not to reject, on empirical grounds at least, the possibility of a long-range decline in the importance of religion. But one is forced to assert that if there is such a long-range decline, it is of so slow a nature in American society at the present time that it does not substantially affect our religious attitudes across a period of thirteen years.

Table 8 shows the basic continuity among gentiles in the thirteen-year period in belief in God, in Christ, in the Trinity, in prayer, in

Table 8   Continuities in Religious Beliefs and Behavior

Religious Beliefs and Behavior	1965			Change from 1952		
	Protestant	Catholic	Jewish	Protestant	Catholic	Jewish
Continuities:						
Believing in God	99%	100%	77%	0%	0%	−21%
Believing Christ is God	73	88	—	−1	−1	—
Believing in Trinity	96	86	—	−2	−1	—
Believing in prayer	94	99	70	0	0	−19
Praying three times a day or more	23	25	5	+2	−3	− 4
Believing in life after death	78	83	17	−2	−2	−18
Believing in heaven	71	80	6	−4	−3	−15
Active church member	75	80	62	0	+3	+12

From *Religion in the Year 2000* by Andrew M. Greeley, © Sheed and Ward Inc., 1969.

life after death and heaven. Martin Marty, in commenting with some surprise on this continuity, said that one would have expected in the period of theological and organizational ferment in the churches that the last thirteen years have been, there would have been considerably more changes.

On the other hand, the differences in Jewish attitudes and behavior in the thirteen years are striking. Belief in God is down twenty-one percentage points; in prayer, nineteen percentage points; in life after death, eighteen percentage points; and in heaven fifteen percentage points; while, at the same time, active church membership among American Jews has gone up some twelve percentage points.

Table 9 indicates that there have been some changes in doctrinal attitudes and religious practice among gentiles that are something more than trivial. Even though church attendance is up, belief that religion is important in one's own life is down. Catholics are somewhat less likely to believe that the Bible is inspired than Protestants, but both Catholics and Protestants are somewhat more likely to report that they read the Bible once a week. Finally, American Jews are seventeen percentage points less likely to believe that religion is important in their life and the same number of points more likely to attend church at least once a year.

The picture in Tables 8 and 9 is a mixed and puzzling one, and the considerable analysis that is reported elsewhere does not particularly solve any of the puzzles. Why people can go to church more and simultaneously say that religion is less important may seem almost incomprehensible unless one is inclined to believe that religion in American society provides belonging as well as meaning and that the belonging function underpins and supports the meaning function, which of course is precisely the thesis of the present volume.

But the empirical data at least lend relatively little support to the notion that there have been major changes in religious belief in the last thirteen years and indicate that there has been, if anything, an increase in religious practice for gentiles. The Jewish problem is more complex and we shall return to it in greater detail in the chapter in which we treat American Jews. Suffice it to say at the present time that doctrinal orthodoxy may be less important to one's self-definition as a Jew than it is to Catholics or Protestants. If it were possible in the past to accept the Jewish doctrine without conscious or formalized choice of church membership (a Jew was a Jew in any case), it may also be equally possible in the present to maintain a formal choice of congregational membership without explicit acceptance of their teachings. If such an interpretation be accurate, then one could say that the Americanization impact on the Jews has produced two quite di-

Table 9   Changes in Religious Beliefs and Behavior

Religious Beliefs and Behavior	1965			Change from 1952		
	Protestant	Catholic	Jewish	Protestant	Catholic	Jewish
Changes:						
Believing religion important in own life	74	76	30	−2	− 7	−17
Attending church weekly	33	67	4	+5	+ 8	− 8
Attending church at all	67	87	61	—	—	+17
Believing Bible inspired	85	82	17	0	− 6	−28
Reading Bible at least once weekly	47	37	31	+7	+15	+17
N	(3,088)	(1,162)	(128)			

Tables 9, 10, 11, 12, and 21 are from *What Do We Believe?* by Martin E. Marty, Stuart E. Rosenberg, Andrew M. Greeley. Copyright © 1968 by Meredith Corporation. Reprinted by permission of Hawthorn Books, Inc., 70 Fifth Avenue, New York 10011.

verse tendencies. Since religion is much less important to being a Jew than it is to Protestants or Catholics, there were no organizational barriers to protect the interpretive scheme from the powerful onslaught of scientific secularism in American society, particularly on the Jews who would be deeply involved in precisely those scientific areas where secular agnosticism would be most powerful. On the other hand, since being a Jew is still important and since being anything religious requires congregational affiliation, it is also possible in American society for Jews to become much more conscious and formalized in their religious adherence than they were in the past, despite the simultaneous decline in propositional orthodoxy. We are thus suggesting that Judaism, faced with the acculturating and assimilating influences in American society, made possible a situation where conscious and formal affiliation would increase while adherence to the interpretive scheme would decrease. Such a paradox is not possible in the Protestant or Catholic groups, or at least at the present time is much less possible, because of the much more intimate connection between the interpretive scheme and affiliation in these groups.

In the third table of this chapter (Table 10), we note that there have been considerable changes also among American Catholics, but

Table 10 Changing Attitudes Among Catholics

Attitudes	1952	1965
A. *Sex mores:*		
Percent disapproving divorce	51%	36%
Percent disapproving mechanical means of birth control	51	37
B. *Attitudes toward clergy:*		
Percent describing clergy as "very understanding"	72	62
Percent saying sermons are "excellent"	43	30
Percent thinking clergy too concerned about money	11	19

Table 11 Trends in Attitudinal Change Among Catholics by Age and Education

Trends in Attitudinal Change	Age			Education		
	18–34	*35–55*	*Over 55*	*Grammar School*	*High School*	*College*
Disapproving divorce	31%	41%	33%	41%	32%	41%
Disapproving birth control	33	41	35	38	33	43
Clergy not "very understanding"	53	44	32	30	50	28
	(40)*	(38)	(30)	(30)	(35)	(45)
Sermons not "excellent"	85	67	68	60	73	74
Too "concerned about money"	26	14	5	10	18	20
N	(329)	(530)	(253)	(203)	(703)	(246)

* Percentages in brackets indicate comparable Protestant responses.
Tables 10 and 11 are from Marty, Rosenberg, Greeley, op. cit.

not so much in their doctrinal orthodoxy or their organizational affiliation as in their attitudes toward the sexual morality of the church and toward their clergy. A very notable decline in American Catholics' willingness to accept the traditional teaching of their Church on birth control has in great part resulted from the ferment of the Second Vatican Council and the very strong possibility that there will be a substantial modification in the Church's teaching on birth control. Similarly, the restructuring of the relationship between clergy and laity in the Church resulted from both the Americanization of the Catholic population and the dramatic changes of the Second Vatican Council. However, thus far in the history of Catholicism in the United States, the changing attitudes toward the clergy and changing sexual morality have not affected either the basic doctrinal loyalty of Catholics or their organizational involvement. (One can presume that, certain Catholic leaders to the contrary notwithstanding, birth control and divorce are not at the center of the Catholic doctrinal system.)

The data reported in previous paragraphs are admittedly thin. They do not prove that the secularization hypothesis is wrong but they certainly call it into considerable question. The issue remains, however, as to how there can be so much evidence in the press, both secular and religious, that religion is going through a crisis and how much agitation in the theological faculties about the meaning of the crisis, when national sample data find little, if any, indication that there is a crisis. Sociologists would reply that, with some exceptions (and the behavior of American Jews seems to be one of those exceptions), massive social changes take a long time. While allegations of dramatic change make extremely good journalistic copy and may impart a sense of crisis and guilt to theologians (many of whom would be at a loss as to what to do if they were not caught in a mixture of crisis), they do not seem to be actually taking place. At least the observer who has been trained in the social sciences will maintain a professional skepticism about accounts of massive social change which are not backed up by strong empirical data. He will also remember, particularly if he is considering the subject of religion, that the demise or decline of organized religion has been announced many times before the 1960's and does not seem to have occurred. A crisis, of course, there is; doubt and confusion over religion there is; but it tends to be limited to a very small group of the population—those who are particularly concerned about religion—that is to say, divinity school faculty and students, editors of religious journals, and organizational bureaucrats within the denominations. The average member of a denomination who learned his religious commitment from his earliest years, perhaps went through some sort of crisis in his adolescence, but presently finds his religious posture too important a part of his life to put it aside because the theologian announces that God is dead. It is important, not because he thinks of it all the time, or because it pervades everything he does, but because rather it provides him with both a reassuring answer to ultimate questions and a fellowship which enables him to find himself over against others in his society. Dedicated religionists may argue that this is not much of a religion; that it shows no prophetic intensity or concern, and those who are going through the agonies of the "crisis of faith" and the "secularization of religion" are much more authentically committed to the principles of true religion. They may very well be, but those who have shown authentic religious commitment in the sense that elite groups within Christianity would define authentic commitment, have been few and far between in the history of human religions. And religion can be important in a man's life, extremely important, without necessarily being authentic as religious elites would define authenticity.

Religion and Youth

Those who herald both the rise and decline of religion are particularly concerned with young people, partly because America is a society that worships its youth (while at the same time imposing severe ordeals upon them); and since youth represents the adult population of the future, the attitudes and behavior of youth are taken to be a prediction of the future. Such an assumption, of course, is a weak one. Rebellious youth have historically shown strong predisposition to settle down to conservative middle age. The religious behavior of young people is not at all necessarily a predictor of the religious behavior of the same people when they reach forty. Identities and ideologies are indeed being shaped in the late teens, but the social forces directing these shapes toward an adult life style that is not terribly dissimilar from one's parents are strong indeed. If apathy, doubt, and indifference mark the religious posture of the young person, it by no means follows necessarily that when he has settled down to the business of developing his career and raising his family, he will not adopt the same middle-class religious posture of his parents. To say that young people are experiencing grave doubts about the religions they have from their parents is not necessarily to affirm a social change. Given the fact that late adolescence is a time when there is at least an opportunity to evolve one's own value system and some independence from that of one's family, religious problems would seem to be inevitable. It may well be that these problems can be discussed more openly today than in the past, though even then the young person who feels that his generation is the first one to explicitly call into question his family's religious commitment demonstrates some lack of historical sense. The so-called religious crisis on campus is not a new phenomenon and one can find literature of the 1920's and the 1930's agonizing over the same problems.

Nonetheless, data on the religious attitude and behavior of young people may be relevant to our discussion of the secularization question, for if we cannot find even among young people any evidence of a decline of religious faith, the secularization hypothesis, at least in its more popular forms, is going to be in very serious trouble. In Table 12 of the present chapter, we compare the respondents in the 1965

Table 12   Religious Attitudes of Young People

	Catholic		Protestant	
	18–25	*Over 25*	*18–25*	*Over 25*
There is a God	100	99	100	97
Bible is inspired	76	83	74	86
Pray	99	99	90	94
Life after death	85	81	72	77
Heaven	84	79	68	70
Hell	76	70	57	54
Against mixed marriage	62	62	65	74
Against birth control	21	38	17	18
Divorce wrong	37	36	12	10
Church member	87	90	62	76
Clergy not very understanding	59	43	58	50
Sermons not "excellent"	93	70	76	68
Church too concerned about money	23	16	12	15
N	(135)	(1,027)	(259)	(2,829)

From Marty, Rosenberg, Greeley, op. cit.

survey who are under twenty-five with respondents from 1952. (Jews are not considered in this table because the very small sample of Jews makes it impossible to find enough under twenty-five for serious analysis.) Catholic young people are less orthodox than their predecessors in the matter of the inspiration of the Bible, but they are as likely to believe in God and more likely to believe in life after death and heaven and hell. They are as opposed to mixed marriage and divorce as members of the older generation, but only one fifth accept the official teaching on birth control. Furthermore, they are more likely to be critical of the Church's quest for money, of the sermons, and of the understanding and the sympathy of the clergy. They are also slightly less likely to consider themselves church members, though this may simply be due to the fact that young people have not settled down into a parish in which they can consider themselves formally involved.

Catholic young people, therefore, demonstrate quite a bit of consistency with the general Catholic population as it was described earlier in this chapter. Their religious faith and their religious practice suggest that their relatively high level of devotion and of doctrinal orthodoxy currently existing in the American Catholic church will continue into the future. Furthermore, their attitudes toward the clergy and birth control seem to suggest that opposition to the status of the clergy and the Church's sexual morality will increase in American Catholicism. Young Catholics, like their parents, therefore, are both doctrinally stable and ethically and organizationally restless. Their restlessness represents a continuation and an expansion of a problem that has notably increased in American Catholicism in the last two decades. If one wishes to project into the future the development of American Catholicism based on the responses of its young people to the questionnaires in the 1965 survey, one can say that church attendance, church affiliation, and doctrinal orthodoxy will continue to be high among American Catholics for the remainder of the century, but the willingness to accept the Church's sexual teachings and to respect the privileged status of the clergy will continue to decrease between now and the year 2000. If young Catholics represent the most revolutionary elements of the Church, it must be admitted that the revolution is a highly selective one.

The picture among Protestant young people is somewhat more ambiguous. In previous sections of this chapter, we noted the differences between Protestants in 1952 and 1965 were generally slight. While younger Protestants are more likely to believe in God, they are somewhat less likely to pray, and to believe in life after death, and to accept the existence of heaven, though, curiously enough, they are more willing than their elders to subscribe to the possibility of a hell. They are less opposed to mixed marriage than their predecessors but still a trifle more unsympathetic to mixed marriage than younger Catholics. They are also less impressed with sympathy for the sermons of their clergy than the previous generations of Protestants, though their criticisms do not represent such dramatic shift of attitudes as is apparently going on in the Catholic population. Therefore, insofar as the very sketchy indicators in the table are an adequate measure of reality, the future of American Protestantism, if the youth continue into the future with their present attitudes, is one of relative stability with some doctrinal erosion. Therefore the data generally tend to support our contention that there is no revolutionary religious change to be observed among American gentiles, despite the overwhelming publicity to the contrary. Whatever their crisis of faith might have been, young American Protestants and Catholics are, if anything, more likely to believe that God is not dead than their parents.

A research done at the National Opinion Research Center on the behavior of 1961 college graduates confirms the findings reported in the previous paragraph. It was assumed that the group most likely to be affected by a secularization trend would be those who were in the Ph.D. programs in the top twelve graduate schools [8] in the country, for in these graduate schools the strongest conflict between religion and academic secularism presumably would be encountered. The accompanying Table 13 shows, first of all, that there is some erosion of

Table 13   Religious Affiliation of Arts and Sciences Graduate Students in Top Twelve Universities

Religious Affiliation	Original Religion	Current Religion
Protestant	54%	38%
Catholic	17	16
Jewish	19	15
Other	5	6
None	5	25
Total	100	100
N	908	

Tables 13–17, reproduced in this section, are reprinted from "The Religious Behavior of Graduate Students," by Andrew M. Greeley, *Journal for the Scientific Study of Religion,* 5, No. 1 (1965). Reprinted by permission of the author and the Society for the Scientific Study of Religion.

church affiliation among the arts and science graduate students in these top twelve universities but that the erosion is something less than a massive apostasy. Ninety-five percent of the students were raised in affiliation with organized religion while only 75 percent still maintained a religious affiliation. This, of course, is a considerable loss for the organized church but it must be remembered that this loss occurs among those young people where presumably the loss will be most massive and that, even here, the loss still constitutes only one-fifth of

[8] The top schools were Harvard, Chicago, Columbia, California (Berkeley), Yale, Princeton, Cornell, Michigan, Illinois, Wisconsin, California Institute of Technology, and MIT.

the population. The most notable losses are among American Protestants who suffer a decline of sixteen percentage points between the original religion and the current religion of the graduate students. The Catholic loss is only one percentage point and the Jewish loss, at least as far as religious affiliation goes, is four percentage points.

Table 14 accompanying this section turns to the question of church attendance of the graduate students. Quite astonishingly, the Catholic graduate student at the top twelve universities is considerably

Table 14   Church Attendance of Graduate Students by Religion (Original Religion)

Church Attendance	Protestant	Catholic	Jewish
Weekly	21%	78%	1%
2 to 3 times a month	14	4	3
Monthly	12	5	7
2 or 3 times a year	26	9	38
Yearly	12	0	14
Never	15	4	38
Total	100	100	101
N	(510)	(158)	(180)

From Greeley, "The Religious Behavior of Graduate Students," op. cit.

more likely to go to Mass every week than would be the typical Catholic in the general population. Protestant church attendance is substantially under the general population of Protestants though one-fifth of the Protestant students attend church every week in the top twelve graduate schools and almost half attend at least once a month. Interestingly enough, the percentage of Jews attending church at least once a year is only one percentage point different in the graduate school population (62 percent) than it is in the general Jewish population as previously reported. Thus one can say in summary that while there is some erosion in weekly church attendance among Protestants studying for Ph.D.'s at the top twelve graduate schools, there is no evidence of a notable secularization of either the Catholic or Jewish respondents and that the general picture of church attendance and affiliation among the graduate students is one that indicates astonishingly high religious behavior.

One might suspect that the graduate students in the hard sciences would be the most likely to have problems between their religion and their science. Table 15 indicates that no such close relationship exists across the three major religious groups. The Catholics in the hard

Table 15   Church Attendance by Religion by Field

Church Attendance	Protestant		Catholic		Jewish	
	Sciences	*Arts and Letters*	*Sciences*	*Arts and Letters*	*Sciences*	*Arts and Letters*
Weekly	16%	24%	89%	68%	1%	1%
2 or 3 times a month	17	13	—	7	4	3
Monthly	14	11	2	7	7	8
2 or 3 times a year	26	25	5	13	30	41
Yearly	16	10	—	—	12	17
Never	11	17	5	4	45	31
Total	100	100	101	99	99	101
N	(198)	(310)	(64)	(94)	(73)	(107)

From Greeley, "The Religious Behavior of Graduate Students," op. cit.

sciences (physical sciences and biological science) are more likely to be weekly churchgoers than Catholics in the arts and letters, while the reverse is true for Protestants. The Jews in the hard sciences are also the most likely to be among those who never attended church services. The reasons for the differences among Catholics may simply be sampling variation or may have to do with the fact that Catholicism has made its peace with Galileo and Darwin but not yet with Kant, Freud, and Comte.

The picture that emerges, therefore, from the first three tables is that of a graduate student population of which one fourth belongs to no denomination and one fourth goes to church every week. If there is conflict in the minds of these young people between their scholarship and religion, it would be presumed that those who are religious would be the most likely to have problems with the academic environment in which they are studying and that, therefore, they would score lower on academic values, lower on plans for academic careers, lower on self-rating as intellectuals, and higher on dissatisfaction with the schools they attend which, by hypothesis, should stand for values that cannot be reconciled with religious faith.

Table 16 shows that while there is some slight support for such expectations, the religious students (Catholics who go to church every week, Protestants who go two or three times a month, and Jews who go once a month) are less likely to have an academic career (73 percent versus 79 percent), and less likely to choose "working in the world of ideas" as a career value (78 to 89 percent). However, there is no difference in the choice of "opportunity to be original and creative" and in self-definition as intellectual nor is there any difference in their evaluation of the schools they have attended. Furthermore, the religious students show no particular signs of emotional strain in their position. They are more likely to describe themselves as happy and have less worries than their nonreligious counterparts. There was only a slight difference in the proportion reporting an "A" average.

On two of the items, therefore, there is a negative correlation between religion and academia. But the strength of the correlation is

Table 16   Religion and Attitudes Toward Academia

Attitudes toward Academia	Religious * (320)	Non-Religious (564)
Occupational values:		
Original and creative	85%	86%
World of ideas	78	89
College or university as career employer	73	79
Rating school as "excellent" in:		
Research facilities	72	63
Curriculum	43	43
Students	38	38
Faculty	77	78
Self-description:		
"Intellectual"	45	47
"Happy"	24	17
"Liberal"	32	37
Average number of worries	3.0	3.5
Percent with grade average of "A"	10	8

* Catholics going to church weekly, Protestants two or three times a month, Jews once a month. (Those whose original religion was "other" are excluded.) From Greeley, "The Religious Behavior of Graduate Students," op. cit.

rather weak and does not establish any major conflict apparently for the vast majority of religious students.

While NORC's promises to the schools that participated in the study make it impossible for us to review data for individual institutions, we can say that the patterns reported in these paragraphs persist through all of the twelve graduate schools and that no particular school seems to be more irreligious than any of the others.

To some extent, the rather striking religiousness exhibited by these graduate students in the early 1960's may be related to the appearance on the campus of large numbers of Catholic graduate students, apparently for the first time in the history of American higher education. This is not to argue that Catholics have increased the level of church attendance among other students. It is quite possible, however, that the religious participation levels for Jews and gentiles are about what they always were but that the inclusion of many Catholics has substantially affected the proportion of the future academicians who are also religious. It just may well represent a beginning of a major change in the composition of American academia if churchgoing Catholics in the future hold as many major university appointments as Jews.

Table 17 indicates that the churchgoing Catholics are not very different from other graduate students in their values and career plans. They are more likely to consider themselves intellectuals than the

Table 17   Religious Catholics and Attitudes Toward Academia

Attitudes toward Academia	Percent
Values:	
Original and creative	86
World of ideas	68
College or university career	79
Self-description:	
"Intellectual"	54
"Happy"	24
"Liberal"	47
Percent with grade average of "A"	8
N	(121)

From Greeley, "The Religious Behavior of Graduate Students," op. cit.

nonreligious of all faiths, more likely to describe themselves as politically liberal, just as likely to plan academic careers, just as likely to value originality and creativity, and less likely to value working in the world of ideas. The last fact is the only evidence that there is any conflict between the ideals of secular academia and fervent Roman Catholicism and it is slender evidence to substantiate the secularization theory.

How can one reconcile the apparent diversity between the statistical data reported in this section and popular impressions? These impressions are summed up by the editorial writer of the *Christian Century* who remarked, "One need only to talk to young people for five minutes to know that something important was going on."

First of all, it might be remarked that the five minute conversation was not exactly a sustained interview. Be that as it may, it might be that the measures available in the surveys we relied upon do not tap the dimensions of religious restlessness and revolution that actually exist. Secondly, it could well be that the revolutionary elites are so small that they do not turn up in a national sample. Those who have been seriously influenced by atheistic or secular theology may be too small a proportion of the national population of young people to affect any change on average figures of religious attitude and behavior. Thirdly, it may be that our impressions are based on the "dog bites man" approach to reality. That most young people differ very little in their religious attitudes from their parents is not news and doesn't attract much attention. But that some think very differently from their parents is news and we do notice it, even though the group that represents disagreement and change may be a very minute part of the total population. It is also possible, of course, that there may be dramatic changes between 1964 and 1965 when the data in this section were collected and 1970–1971 when this volume is being written. But as we have noted before, the sociologist is always skeptical of dramatic changes because the general behavior of large populations tends to be relatively stable. When someone says to a sociologist that things have changed since the data were collected he is forced to reply that they may have but that there was no indication in his data that such a change was impending. He will be skeptical of it until he sees data as strong as his indicating that a change has occurred. It is also possible that considerable numbers of young people go through agonies over their religious faith but somehow or other they manage to survive the agony without changing very much their basic orientation concerning religious doctrine and practice. Our data may indicate that, while the crises of faith are more serious and more frequent than they were in the past, they are not yet necessarily the beginning of a loss of faith or departure from organized religion. Nevertheless, we are forced to assert on the basis of our data that while the problem of growing up religiously may be more acute in contemporary American society, or it may be simply more explicit, its ultimate resolution seems not to differ very much from that arrived at by the generations over twenty-five.

The secularization hypothesis, therefore, is simply not substantiated by any of the empirical data available to us; neither is the hypothesis of grave crisis. It ought to be remembered by those scholars and journalists who go about the country speaking of crises, and then find a number of crisis-ridden young people talking to them after their lectures, that those who discuss a lecture after it is over are far from typical and that those who are bothered by doubts are the ones most likely to bring these doubts to the attention of the speaker who has discussed precisely that subject. Of such thin data are crises frequently made.

Secularity and Religiousness

Thus far in this chapter, we have assumed an opposition between religiousness and secularity because this opposition is the way the issue has been discussed by popular writers in the field and also by sociologists such as Glock and Stark, and also, to some extent at least, by Parsons and his students.

Seymour Martin Lipset in a lengthy essay on "Religion and American Values" suggests rather the opposite—that the American value system has always been a mixture of the secular and the sacred and so indeed has American religion. "American religion, like all other institutions, has made major adjustments in response to changes in the size and the scope of the nation, but as the institution most intimately linked with values, it has shown the tenacity exhibited by the value system itself." [9]

Lipset, first of all, establishes that the prominent European visitors who wrote on American life, such as Martineau, Trollope, de Tocqueville, Brice, and even Max Weber, all remarked on the intense religious interests of Americans. Lipset quotes Robert Baird, an American Presbyterian minister who spent eight years in Europe in the middle of the nineteenth century, as saying:

In no other part of the world, perhaps, do the inhabitants attend church in larger proportions than in the United States; certainly no part of the Continent of Europe can compare with them in that respect. The contrast between the two must strike anyone who, after traveling much in the one, comes to see any of the cities of the other.[10]

Lipset then goes on to try to master the intricate problems of the statistics of church membership. In attempting as he is to establish the continuity of religious behavior of the past, Lipset suggests that from the end of the eighteenth to the middle of the twentieth century, approximately three fifths of the American people have been affiliated with churches at least in the sense that the word "affiliation" has come to mean today. He also points out that the ratio of clergymen to general population has fluctuated from 1900 to 1960 between 1.1 and 1.2 without much in the way of notable change. Lipset, of course, was interested in proving that the religious revival of the post-World War II era was really not a revival but merely a continuity.

---

[9] From *The First New Nation* by Seymour Martin Lipset, Basic Books, Inc., Publishers, New York.

[10] Ibid., p. 1421.

But, if the continuity evidence can be used to refute a revival, it can equally effectively be used to refute the thesis of a decline.

Lipset next turns to the question of the secular nature of American religion and quotes many of the nineteenth-century observers on the practical and ethical, rather than the dogmatic and theoretical nature of American religion. In de Tocqueville's words, "Go into the churches (I mean the Protestant ones). You will hear morality preached, of dogma not a word; nothing which can at all shock the neighbor, nothing which can arouse the idea of dissent." And Harriet Martineau noted:

> *One circumstance struck me throughout the country. Almost as often as the conversation between myself and any other person on religious subjects became intimate and earnest, I was met by the supposition that I was a convert. It was the same in other instances. Whenever there was a strong interest in the Christian religion, conversion to a particular profession, it was confidentially supposed. This fact speaks volumes.*[11]

Lipset suggests that the secularity may result from the separation of church and state in American society.

> *The separation of the church and state has increasingly given religion per se a specific rather than a diffuse role in American society. The minister, the priest and the rabbi, all deal in generalizations that extend beyond the confines of the church itself; but the members of the congregation do not necessarily carry these with them to their other activities, because they judge the religious leader in his specific role. Democracy's giving religion a specific role in American society—as Sunday Religion—may have, oddly enough, contributed to its all-pervasive and secular qualities. The only mention of religion on "weekdays" must be in terms of generally agreed upon morality which cannot be identified with the teachings of any given denomination. In so far as the secular and all-pervasive characteristics of American religion are a result of this emphasis on role specificity in American society, they have become accentuated with urbanization and industrialization. However the consistency over time of foreign observers' remarks to the effect that American religion is unique in these characteristics shows that neither of them has grown simply as a result of these modern trends.*
>
> *Thus the consistency with which both secularization and widespread adherence have distinguished American religion through-*

out its history is a result of the fact that democratic values have continued to influence the growth of religious institutions as the society has changed. In this respect, the persistent traits in American religion resemble the constant traits in American character. They have continued to distinguish America from other countries precisely because they have stemmed from the basic American values that have remained stable as the economy, population, and society of the country have changed.[12]

Lipset's theory is a remarkable one and, to the present writer's mind, a persuasive one. American religion has persevered through two centuries precisely because it has been flexible enough to adjust to the changes in American society and stable enough to maintain a constant relationship with the stable traits of the American value system. It has always been widespread and popular and it always has been able to cope with the secularization trends (or, in Parsons' words, the trends in differentiation) by incorporating the values of secularity into its own system and by providing a value system broad enough to be useful and untroubling in secular corporate institutions. In other words, religion as an interpretive scheme has survived precisely because religion as a social organization has been plastic enough to provide fellowship and belonging for Americans. In Lipset's scheme of things, it is easy enough to say that from its beginning the American republic has been simultaneously sacred and secular and American religion has survived and flourished because it, too, is able to be simultaneously sacred and secular. Harvey Cox's [13] secular city was founded by Thomas Jefferson, and it has been sacred and secular through its history.

Perhaps therefore the crisis of secularization is merely the conscious realization on the part of some Americans that there may be a conflict between the secular and the sacred in their religion. Surely much of the criticism directed by people like Herberg, Marty, and A. Roy Eckhardt (see Bibliography for specific titles) on American religion (which we shall discuss in a later chapter) is based on the fact that it is too secular, too much oriented toward fellowship and belonging, and not enough toward meaning and prophecy. On the other hand, writers like Harvey Cox and Daniel Callahan [14] were inclined to lament the fact that religion is not secular enough and that secularity somehow or other exists apart from the outmoded sacral

[12] Ibid., pp. 168–169.
[13] Harvey Cox, *The Secular City* (New York: The Macmillan Company, 1966).
[14] Daniel Callahan, *The Secular City Debate* (New York: The Macmillan Company, 1966).

religions. One could put together from writers such as Lipset and
Parsons the following response to these observers: not by prophecy
alone does man live, and the very fact that American religion has been
flexible enough to incorporate the secular within itself and to reinforce
the broad value system of American society has enabled the prophetic
elements within it to stay alive and to find a large audience to which
to preach. Only when the meaning components of religion are taken
at least with some seriousness by major elements of the population
is prophecy likely to get a hearing. In those societies in the Western
world where religion has not been secular enough and has not been
able to provide the fellowship and the belonging and the social integration that American religion does, the meaning component of religion
has vanished completely and prophetic words fall on empty ears.
Those who say that religion is irrelevant in American society because
American society is secular are quite wrong. So was Harvey Cox
when he said that American religion must become secular if it is to
survive. American society has always been secular and American
religion has been able to keep up with the rest of society precisely because it has been able to incorporate the sacred and the secular in a
synthesis which is providing both belonging and meaning for most
Americans.

Summary

In this chapter we have strongly suggested that the "pop" sociological model which suggests that society is evolving from the sacred
to the secular ought to be carefully reexamined. There are powerful
forces in society today which take men's minds off religion and the
sacred but also unquestionably there have always been such powerful
forces. For some people today religion is of little importance but there
is no reason to think that any time in the past religion was important
for everyone. Some people today need religion only occasionally in
their lives but there is no reason to think that those who are occasionally religious were any less frequent in the past than in the present.
Finally, today there are some men and women for whom religion is
very important for any number of reasons. There is no evidence that
they are any less numerous today than they were in the past. There
is, of course, tension between religion and secular life. It is hard to
be deeply involved in the world and still keep one's mind on things
which are not, at least in the immediate sense, part of this world. It

may also be true that there are great cycles of religious devotion, with one period in time being more religious than the other. It is well worth remembering, however, that the conflict between religion and science has gone on now for perhaps three hundred years. Neither side seems to have definitely eliminated the other and, with the resurgence of all kinds of weird forms of religions on the college campuses, one can even be more confident than one was five years ago when one says that religion is likely to be around in the foreseeable future.

Chapter 7

The Civil Religion

Robert Merton,[1] in his now famous essay on functional theories of religion, posed the extraordinarily pertinent question of how religion can be said to integrate a society when that society has many religions. Since that essay a number of writers have suggested that religion exists in the United States on two levels: the level of the individual denominations and then the level of some super religion in which all denominations participate in some fashion. This super religion or, as Will Herberg has aptly called it, "the religion of Americanism" provides the context of social unity in which the diversity of the denominational society can occur. In this chapter we will reappraise this civil religion of Americanism, particularly with the help of the insights of Robert Bellah, and conclude that it may not be nearly as worthless a phenomenon as some writers have thought. Instead of being a "watering down" of denominational religion, it might also be considered as a distillation of what is best in the denominations.

The Religion of Americanism

Even though the Constitution of the United States prohibits the establishment of an official religion in the United States, and even though the Supreme Court has interpreted very broadly the meaning of the "wall of separation" between church and state, a cursory investigation of American society establishes that there is an official religion if not an official church in the American republic. This reli-

---

[1] R. K. Merton, *Social Theory and Social Structure* (New York: The Macmillan Company, 1949).

gion has its solemn ceremonials, such as the inauguration, its feast days, such as Thanksgiving, Memorial Day, the Fourth of July, and Christmas.[2] The armed forces have chaplains as do both houses of Congress. The national motto sometimes is *E Pluribus Unum* but on our coins it is "In God We Trust." The national anthem is the *Star Spangled Banner,* which is not without religious allusions, but *God Bless America* is much easier to sing. An allegiance is pledged to the flag with the annotation that those so pledging are doing so "under God." Oaths of office, loyalty oaths, and the other pledges by which Americans pronounce their loyalty to the government and its Constitution generally call for God's help in living up to that which is pledged. Religious functionaries usually representing all three of the major faiths are proudly exhibited at major and even not so major public and private functions. Churches, church property, and church schools are generally tax exempt. Clergymen need not serve in the armed forces. Professed atheists or agnostics are at a distinct disadvantage in seeking public office, and "crusades" are waged with a frequency and enthusiasm which one suspects would have dismayed the twelfth century.

The sociologist, accustomed as he is from reading Durkheim and Weber to expect religion in the society, is not terribly surprised by these sacral underpinnings of the American consensus. He is surprised that others are surprised, however, and is rather dubious about the likelihood of success of those professional secularists who dedicate themselves to eliminating "myths" from the public life of the republic, especially since, at least on occasion, secularists seem to have their own myths.

2 Perhaps Christmas should more appropriately be called the "holidays" since insofar as it is part of America's civic religion, Christmas has long since lost its Christian meaning and has become a week-long celebration of family unity, friendship links, and hope in the future. It might be wise to make the separation total and change the name of the feast from Christmas to "the holidays," or "midwinter festival," or "winter solstice." It might also be historically and culturally accurate to call it by its former name, the "saturnalia." The Christians could then celebrate the coming of Christ quietly at some other time of the year and the major functions of the midwinter festival, that is to say, the reaffirmation of intimate ties, the reinforcement of the economy, and the providing of employment for college students home for "the holidays" could be maintained without affronting the more secular elements in American society who resent the vague Christian aura which still surrounds Christmas. Only a few things need be lost if such a campaign to "take Christ out of Christmas" were to be successful. Christmas crèches would disappear, sentimental readings of the nativity story would never be heard on radio and television, and some Christmas carols might be dropped. It might also be necessary to rewrite the words of *Adestes Fidelis,* although the song is usually sung with such gusto that the words really aren't all that important.

For those readers lacking a sense of the ironic, be it herein established before crank letters are written to the author that the previous paragraph is ironic.

The civil religion was not discovered by the critics of the religious revival of the 1950's. Alexis de Tocqueville said that the American religion "powerfully contributes to the maintenance of a democratic republic among the Americans."

One would suspect then that if St. Paul should have visited the shores of this republic any time during its history, he would have been forced to repeat his words to the Athenians, probably with the same irony with which he uttered them on the Acropolis, "Sirs, I perceive that you are very religious people."

But if, as has been observed for a long time, there is a sort of civil religion in the United States which transcends the denominations but in which all participate, it was only in the 1950's when a number of important spokesmen for organized religion began to express doubts as to whether the unofficial alliance between the denominations and the civic religion was a good thing. Will Herberg was the first one to raise these questions and no one has described them as astutely. For Herberg, the American Way of Life is in fact the religion of the land:

> *It seems to me that a realistic appraisal of the values, ideas, and behavior of the American people leads to the conclusion that Americans, by and large, do have their "common religion" and that that "religion" is the system familiarly known as the American Way of Life. It is the American Way of Life that supplies American society with an "overarching sense of unity" amid conflict. It is the American Way of Life about which Americans are admittedly and unashamedly "intolerant." It is the American Way of Life that provides the framework in terms of which the crucial values of American existence are couched. By every realistic criterion the American Way of Life is the operative faith of the American people.*[3]

Nor is this American Way of Life religion merely a common denominator which takes the least objectionable parts from all the denominations and combines them. Rather, it is a religion in itself:

> *It should be clear that what is being designated under the American Way of Life is not the so-called "common denominator" religion; it is not a synthetic system composed of beliefs to be found in all or in a group of religions. It is an organic structure of ideas, values, and beliefs that constitutes a faith common to Americans and genuinely operative in their lives, a faith that markedly influences, and is influenced by, the "official" religions*

[3] Herberg, op. cit., p. 88.

of American society. Sociologically, anthropologically, if one pleases, it is the characteristic American religion, undergirding American life and overreaching American society despite all indubitable differences of region, section, culture and class.[4]

This American Way of Life religion pulled together in one set of beliefs those qualities which Americans would claim are basic to the political and social greatness of their republic:

If the American Way of Life had to be defined in one word, "democracy" would undoubtedly be the word, but democracy in a peculiarly American sense. On its political side it means the Constitution; on its economic side, "free enterprise"; on its social side, an equalitarianism which is not only compatible with but indeed actually implies vigorous economic competition and high mobility. Spiritually, the American Way of Life is best expressed in a certain kind of "idealism" which has come to be recognized as characteristically American. It is faith that has its symbols and its rituals, its holidays and its liturgy, its saints and its sancta; and it is a faith that every American, to the degree that he is an American, knows and understands.

The American Way of Life is individualistic, dynamic, pragmatic. It affirms the supreme value and dignity of the individual; it stresses incessant activity on his part, for he is never to rest but is always to be striving to "get ahead"; it defines an ethic of self-reliance, merit, and character, and judges by achievement; "deeds, not creeds" are what count. The American Way of Life is humanitarian, "forward looking," optimistic. Americans are easily the most generous and philanthropic people in the world, in terms of their ready and unstinting response to suffering anywhere on the globe. The American believes in progress, in self-improvement, and quite fanatically in education. But above all, the American is idealistic. Americans cannot go on making money or achieving worldly success simply on its own merits; such "materialistic" things must, in the American mind, be justified in "higher" terms, in terms of "service" or "stewardship" or "general welfare." Because Americans are so idealistic, they tend to confuse espousing an ideal with fulfilling it and are always tempted to regard themselves as good as the ideals they entertain: hence the amazingly high valuation most Americans quite sincerely place on their own virtue. And because they are so idealistic, Americans tend to be moralistic: they are inclined to

[4] Ibid., p. 77.

see all issues as plain and simple, black and white, issues of morality. Every struggle in which they are seriously engaged becomes a "crusade." To Mr. Eisenhower, who in many ways exemplifies American religion in a particularly representative way, the second world war was a "crusade" (as was the first to Woodrow Wilson); so was his campaign for the presidency ("I am engaged in a crusade . . . to substitute a good government for what we most earnestly believe has been bad government"); and so is his administration—a "battle for the republic" against "godless Communism" abroad and against "corruption and materialism" at home. It was Woodrow Wilson who once said, "Sometimes people call me an idealist. Well, that is the way I know I'm an American: America is the most idealistic nation in the world"; Eisenhower was but saying the same thing when he solemnly affirmed: "The things that make us proud to be Americans are of the soul and of the spirit."

The American Way of Life is, of course, anchored in the American's vision of America. The Puritan's dream of a new "Israel" and a new "Promised Land" in the New World, the "novus ordo seclorom" on the Great Seal of the United States reflect the perennial American conviction that in the New World a new beginning has been made, a new order of things established, vastly different from and superior to the decadent institutions of the Old World. This conviction, emerging out of the earliest reality of American history, was continuously nourished through the many decades of immigration into the present century by the residual hopes and expectations of the immigrants, for whom the New World had to be really something new if it was to be anything at all. And this conviction still remains pervasive in American life, hardly shaken by the new shape of the world and the challenge of the "new orders" of the twentieth century, Nazism and Communism. It is the secret of what outsiders must take to be the incredible self-righteousness of the American people, who tend to see the world divided into an innocent, virtuous America confronted with a corrupt, devious, and guileful Europe and Asia. The self-righteousness, however, if self-righteousness it be, is by no means simple, if only because virtually all Americans are themselves derived from the foreign parts they so distrust. In any case, this feeling about America as really and truly the "new order" of things at last established is the heart of the outlook defined by the American Way of Life.

In her Vermont Tradition, *Dorothy Canfield Fisher lists as that tradition's principal ingredients: individual freedom, personal*

*independence, human dignity, community responsibility, social
and political democracy, sincerity, restraint in outward conduct,
and thrift. With some amplification—particularly emphasis on
the uniqueness of the American "order" and the great importance
assigned to religion—this may be taken as a pretty fair summary
of some of the "values" embodied in the American Way of Life.
It will not escape the reader that this account is essentially an
idealized description of the middle-class ethos. And, indeed, that
is just what it is. The American Way of Life is a middle-class
way, just as the American people in their entire outlook and feeling are a middle-class people. But the American Way of Life as
it has come down to us is not merely middle-class; it is em-
phatically inner-directed. Indeed, it is probably one of the best
expressions of inner-direction in history. As such, it now seems
to be undergoing some degree of modification—perhaps at certain points disintegration—under the impact of the spread of
other-direction in our society. For the foreseeable future, however, we may with some confidence expect the continuance in
strength of the American Way of Life as both the traditional and
the "common faith" of the American people.*[5]

It is hard to quarrel with Herberg's astute observations. Like all
official religions in Herberg's view, the American Way of Life religion
is designed to provide faith in the society in which the believer is a
part and also to strengthen the society in confrontation with his enemies:

*In a more directly political sense, this religiosity very easily
comes to serve as a spiritual reinforcement of national self-
righteousness and a spiritual authentication of national self-will.
Americans possess a passionate awareness of their power and of
the justice of the cause in which it is employed. The temptation
is therefore particularly strong to identify the American cause
with the cause of God, and to convert our immense and undeni-
able moral superiority over Communist tyranny into pretensions
to unqualified wisdom and virtue. In these circumstances, it
would seem to be the office of prophetic religion to raise a word
of warning against inordinate national pride and self-righteousness as bound to lead to moral confusion, political irresponsibil-
ity, and the darkening of counsel. But the contemporary religious
mood is very far indeed from such prophetic transcendence.
Aside from occasional pronouncements by a few theologians or*

---

[5] Ibid., pp. 78–81.

theologically-minded clergymen, religion in America seems to possess little capacity for rising above the relativities and am-biguities of the national consciousness and bringing to bear the judgment of God upon the nation and its ways. The identification of religion with the national purpose is almost inevitable in a situation in which religion is so frequently felt to be a way of American "belonging." In its crudest form, this identification of religion with national purpose generates a kind of national messianism which sees it as the vocation of America to bring the American Way of Life, compounded almost equally of democ-racy and free enterprise, to every corner of the globe; in more mitigated versions, it sees God as the champion of America, en-dorsing American purposes, and sustaining American might. "The God of judgment has died."

Insensibly, this fusion of religion with national purpose passes over into the direct exploitation of religion for economic and political ends. A good deal of the official piety in Washington, it is charged, is of this kind, and much of the new religiousness of businessmen and business interests throughout the country. Certainly, when we find great corporations such as U. S. Steel distributing Norman Vincent Peale's Guideposts *in huge quan-tities to their employees, when we find increasing numbers of industrial concerns placing "plant chaplains" on their staffs, we are not altogether unjustified in suspecting that considerations of personnel policy have somehow entered into these good works of religion. On another level, there seems to be a concerted ef-fort to turn President Eisenhower's deep and sincere religious feeling into a political asset. How otherwise are we to interpret the paragraph in the resolution officially adopted by the Republi-can National Committee on February 17, 1955, in which it is de-clared: "He (President Eisenhower), in every sense of the word, is not only the political leader, but the spiritual leader of our times"? The fusion of political and spiritual leadership in the person of one national leader is in accord with neither the Amer-ican democratic idea nor the tradition of Jewish-Christian faith; yet the statement of the Republican National Committee, making explicit the political exploitation of the "President's religion," seems to have aroused no comment in American religious circles. If indeed religion is the "spiritual" side of being an American, why should not the President of the United States be hailed as the "spiritual leader of our times"? [6]*

[6] Ibid., pp. 263–265.

It is very difficult to quarrel with Herberg's description of the civic religion or with his assertion that the doctrines and attitudes of the civic religion permeate the three major faiths and the several religious denominations which made up America's denominational society. Not since Emile Durkheim has anyone so astutely described the social-integration dimension in a religion.

Nor would one be in much of a position to disagree that such a religion, which is really nothing more than "faith in faith" and which provides Americans with results, peace of mind, happiness and success, lacks the prophetic dimension of historical Christianity and Judaism. The civic religion and the three major faiths insofar as they are affected by the civic religion do not sit in judgment on the society as a whole nor on the cherished commitments and self-righteousness of the society. In addition, in turning God into a sort of senior partner in American terms, the civic religion eliminates the ambiguous, the transcendental, and the self-critical elements of religion. It is a faith in faith without content, without substance, without judgment, and without anxiety. However, Herberg may be too quick in saying that his civic religion has nothing to do with traditional Christianity. In many respects both in content and style, the religion of the American Way of Life is little more than a doctrinal development of Max Weber's Protestant ethic.

Even more severe in their criticism of the civic religion than Herberg are Martin Marty and A. Roy Eckardt. Marty speaks of America's "religion in general," that is to say, a religion without content other than faith in faith. According to Marty the God of religion-in-general is cut in the American cloth:

> *First, He is understandable and manageable. When men are bewildered in foxholes they want a cozy relationship with a comfortable God. Earthly knowledge has become too high for us; we cannot attain it. It has become too complex for us; we must contain its source. . . . Second, religion-in-general's understandable God is comforting . . . if God must calm the terrors of men, He must also be on hand to sanction their assurances. . . . A third mark of the God of religion-in-general is that He is one of us, an American jolly good fellow. Popular songs . . . reveal this. In this connection, Bible-believing Miss Jane Russell's reference to God as a "livin' Doll" has been most frequently quoted.*[7]

---

[7] Martin E. Marty, *The New Shape of American Religion* (New York: Harper & Row, Inc., Publishers, 1959), pp. 37, 39. Reprinted by permission of Harper & Row, Inc., Publishers.

Eckardt, in his attempt to analyze the so-called religious revival of the fifties, advances the following hypothesis:

We suggest, in sum, the following hypothesis as a possible orientation to the question of the roots of the surge of American piety: If the religion of the fathers, either as it was or, more probably, as it is imagined to have been, helps to provide essential social fulfillment along with psychological aid and comfort, and if, accordingly, it has become rather un-American to be unreligious, then piety can and will break out just about anywhere —from the best-seller lists in the local bookstore to the prayer group in the nation's Capitol, and from the recently established department of religion in a thoroughly secular university to the juke box in the corner saloon. It follows that the important issues before us go beyond such a question of personal opinion as, "What do you think of Billy Graham?" The real issues involve the peculiar and ongoing socio-psychological processes of American life.[8]

Eckardt sees the civic religion as being essentially a "domestication of faith, a creation of a folk religion which underpins the institutional arrangement of American society."

For the American citizen, the Protestant, Catholic, and Jewish faiths tend to furnish a psychosocial resting place. This is in contrast to the sort of faith which allegedly enshrines the final truth of God, a being to whom men ought to commit themselves quite independently of specific "good" consequences that may follow. The background for the American brand of folk religion —let us say its necessary, although not sufficient, condition—is our general religio-political arrangement, which provides religion with freedom and importance but always within the restrictions noted above. When the trinitarian character of American institutional religion is associated with this religio-political arrangement, the over-all picture is one of faith under arrest and piety under restraint. Protestantism, Catholicism, and Judaism combine with less institutional aspects of American folk piety to form a body of religion distinguished and limited by elements of utilitarianism, this-worldly activism, and moral concern, surrounded by an atmosphere of religious pluralism, tolerance, and optimism. The Protestant teaching that salvation is a free gift of divine grace quite apart from all human effort, the Catholic in-

[8] A. Roy Eckardt, *The Surge of Piety in America* (New York: Association Press, 1958), pp. 38–39.

*sistence that the Church of Rome is the one true church, and
the Jewish persuasion that the Jews are the peculiarly chosen
people of the Lord have alike either been soft-pedaled or essentially reformulated to accord with the responsibilities of the faithful as citizens of this democracy.*[9]

The high priests of the folk religion, according to Eckardt, are
Billy Graham, with his focus on simple solutions to complex social
problems, and Norman Vincent Peale, the high priest of the cult of reassurance, which guarantees to Americans that religion will provide
them with self-centeredness and success. The folk religion is a mutual
admiration society which supports piety, free enterprise, the American
tradition, and the American Way of Life, and underwrites upper middle-class suburban life styles and conformity as the measures of salvation.

While Herberg's analysis is astute, the reader in the 1970's may
be inclined to find both Marty and Eckardt to be irritable and irritat-
ing. It must be remembered, however, that they were faced with the
so-called religious revival of the 1950's and as good professorial
Protestants were properly horrified by the vulgar and tasteless (to
their minds) manifestations of popular folk religion of which Messrs.
Peale and Graham were the best and not the worst. It must have
seemed to Marty and Eckardt that the plastic Jesus on the automobile
dashboard was rapidly becoming *the* central symbol of the American
Way of Life. Furthermore, the so-called religious revival seemed to be
identified with the political turn to the right represented by the Eisenhower administration and the moralizing and pietism which they
thought they saw in both the president and his secretary of state. It
was a religious revival which from their point of view was worse than
a religious decline because it was the simplicisms and the vulgarities
of folk piety that were being revived. It seemed to endorse the war on
Communism, the tastelessness of the new suburbs, right-wing politics,
middle-class sexual values, togetherness, conformity, and all those
other evils which academicians felt bound to condemn in the 1950's.
As good university professors, both Eckardt and Marty were properly
humiliated to see organized religion, and particularly organized Protestantism, identified with such horrors.

Of course, now that we are supposedly in a time of religious
decline, Professor Marty is busy emphasizing the crisis that Christianity faces in its confrontation with secular society and Professor Eckhardt emphasizes the Christian obligation to support the state of Israel
in its struggle against Arabs. Middle-class folk religion and the Amer-

[9] Ibid., pp. 57–58.

ican Way of Life still receive periodic drubbings from these authors and others writing from the same perspective, but since the Graham-Peale religious revival is supposedly a thing of the past, it need no longer be subject to so much concern.

The perspective taken in this volume, based to some extent on the data provided by Lipset and referred to in a previous chapter, is that the so-called religious revivals and religious declines are merely cyclic changes in fashion which affect a relatively small proportion of the population, though perhaps a relatively somewhat larger proportion of space in the mass media. The iceberg changes its shape periodically but the unseen part of it is still there. Folk religion, popular religion, the religion of the American Way of Life, the cult of reassurance, the faith of upper middle-class suburban conformity, have been part of American religion since its beginning, as have indeed been the tendency of popular religion resolutely and devoutly to support American foreign policy. Further, the only connection between America's civic religion and a comforting, reassuring, conforming, success-generating faith in the American Way of Life has also been intimate from the very beginning. The need to excoriate or to defend or to ignore this civic religion both in its elite and folk manifestations is, one suspects, more relevant to the sociology of knowledge than to the sociology of religion, or at least to the sociological study of changing intellectual fashions. It ought not to be particularly surprising that religious denominations, accepting as they do in American society the obligation to provide the function of belonging (*Gemeinschaft,* "fellowship") for Americans, can very easily settle down to play a role similar to that which magic plays for Malinowski's Trobriand Islanders, that is, to assure that no harm will come when one ventures out on the high seas.

But it ought to be possible to draw a distinction between the folk elements in American religion, even in America's civic religion, and other elements which run contrary to the cult of reassurance, conformity, and self-fulfillment. Thus, Herberg, Eckardt, Marty and a large number of writers, ministers, and church leaders who feel as they do, are themselves the product of American religion, and the books and journals they write in are eagerly snapped up by large numbers of other people who are also the products of American religion and of the American way of life. One suspects further that both these critical writers and their readers do watch presidential inaugurations on television with at least some sense that the ceremony transcends ordinary, everyday experience and that they also participated in the great televised trilogy of mourning at the death of John Kennedy, perhaps the most mammoth collective representation in all human history and surely one of the greatest symbolic events in the development of the American civic religion (into whose pantheon, by the way, the first Catholic president was admitted without any religious test).

All of this is merely to argue that, given the absence of an established church or a national racial consciousness around which historic myths could assemble, it was practically inevitable that a society like the United States would evolve its own civic religion and that that religion by its very definition would tend to reinforce the values on which the republic was supposedly founded. These values can easily be simplified, distorted, abused, and corrupted, as can any set of religious values. The republican religion which de Tocqueville identified in the United States can be noble or vulgar, and probably will at most times manifest itself in both fashions. However, it also includes within its creed at least one stubborn dogma which decades of pressure have not struck down—the right to dissent, to criticize, and to protest. Even though the American civic religion can readily be corrupted, and even though its influence on the denominations can lead them toward corrupting the prophetic, toward disturbing and challenging elements in their own tradition, the right, and indeed the obligation, to dissent and criticize has produced countervailing forces which have refused to permit the aberrations of folk religion or of official piety to go unchallenged. Dissent further refuses to permit the denominations becoming so committed to the American Way of Life that no one will criticize them for their superpatriotism. One is tempted to go so far as to say that never before have there been so many members of the American denominations who have subscribed so vigorously to the dogma of criticism, dissent, and protest as there are at the present time. Clergymen who protest war and racial injustice do it in the name of their own religious traditions as well as in the name of that dogma of the civic religion. Nor are they the first to do so, as a brief perusal of the history of both abolition and prohibition would establish.

Civil Religion Evaluated

It would therefore seem appropriate to take a somewhat more lenient view of America's civic religion. Granted that one was necessarily inevitable, we could have done a lot worse.

Such a more restrained view is taken in the recent article by Robert Bellah. Bellah contends that:

> . . . *not only that there is such a thing [as civil religion] but also that this religion—or perhaps better, this religious dimension—*

has its own seriousness and integrity and requires the same care and understanding that any other religion does. . . . the Durkheimian notion that every group has a religious dimension, which would be seen as obvious in southern or eastern Asia, is foreign to us. This obscures the recognition of such dimensions in our society.[10]

Bellah is also quite impatient with those who write off national ceremonials, such as the inauguration of the president, as being "only a ritual." "What people say on solemn occasions need not be taken at face value, but is often indicative of deep-seated values and commitments that are not made explicit in the course of everyday life." [11]

Bellah was particularly intrigued by the references to God in inauguration addresses, since only one inauguration address in the history of the republic has omitted reference to the Deity, and that was George Washington's second inauguration which was only two paragraphs long.[12]

In his examination of John Kennedy's inaugural address, Bellah notes that the references to God are at both the beginning and the end, providing as it were a framework for the rest of the address. Bellah suggests that this framework provides the rationale for both democratic government and the political processes.

The will of the people is not itself a criterion of right and wrong. There is a higher criterion in terms of which this will can be judged; it is possible that people may be wrong. The president's obligation extends to the higher criterion.

When Kennedy says that the "rights of man come not from the generosity of the state but from the hand of God," he is stressing this point again. It does not matter whether the state is the expression of the world of autocratic monarch or of the

---

[10] Reprinted by permission of *Daedalus,* Journal of the American Academy of Arts and Sciences, Boston, Mass., Winter 1967, *Religion in America.*

[11] Ibid., p. 2.

[12] Bellah notes the curious fact that the Deity was mentioned by the proper name only in Monroe's second inaugural in 1821. He was described in previous addresses as "the Almighty Being who rules the universe," "the great author of every public and private good," "an invisible hand," and "the benign parent of the human race" by George Washington. John Adams called Him "Providence," "the Being who is supreme over all," "the patron of order," "the fountain of justice," and "protector in all ages of the world of virtuous liberty." Thomas Jefferson spoke of "the infinite power which rules the destiny of the universe," and "that Being in whose hands we are." Madison thought of God as "that Almighty Being whose power regulates the destiny of nations," and "Heaven." Monroe stuck to "Providence" and "the Almighty" in his first address, but, finally, in the second one got around to calling God by His right name, that is to say, "God."

"people"; the rights of man are more basic than any political structure and provide a point of revolutionary leverage from which any state structure may be radically altered. That is the basis for his reassertion of the revolutionary significance of America.

But the religious dimension in political life as recognized by Kennedy not only provides a grounding for the rights of man which makes any form of political absolutism illegitimate, it also provides a transcendent goal for the political process. This is implied in his final words that "here on earth God's work must truly be our own." What he means here is, I think, more clearly spelled out in the previous paragraph, the wording of which, incidentally, has a distinctly Biblical ring:

Now the trumpet summons us again—not as a call to bear arms, though arms we need—not as a call to battle, though embattled we are—but a call to bear the burden of a long twilight struggle, year in and year out, "rejoicing in hope, patient in tribulation,"—a struggle against the common enemies of man, tyranny, poverty, disease, and war itself.[13]

One can, of course, be cynical about both the American civil rights and the political experiment which it gratifies and justifies; yet, it must be admitted that the twin concepts of the inalienable rights of man, which no power can take from him, and the obligation to struggle against tyranny, poverty, disease, and war are noble political ideals. A political process which is dedicated to these ideals as well as to the civil religion which underwrites them can be criticized indeed for failing to live up to them but hardly for the ideals themselves. Americans can become very pious and self-righteous about being a chosen people; they can forget that "chosen people" seen in the Judeo-Christian tradition does not mean that the people cannot err, but rather they are people with a mission. If the mission of the United States is indeed to eliminate tyranny, poverty, disease, and war, the people have no grounds for self-justification or self-righteousness. A people which feels itself sent on such a mission may quite properly be condemned for not honoring their vocation or for twisting and distorting it beyond recognition, but they surely cannot be criticized for having taken on themselves an easy, insignificant task. In Bellah's words:

The whole address can be understood as only the most recent statement of a theme that lies very deep in the American tradition, namely the obligation, both collective and individual, to carry out

[13] Bellah, "Civil Religion in America," op. cit., pp. 4–5.

God's will on earth. This was the motivating spirit of those who founded America, and it has been present in every generation since. Just below the surface throughout Kennedy's inaugural address, it becomes explicit in the closing statement that God's work must be our own. That this very activist and non-contemplative conception of the fundamental religious obligation, which has been historically associated with the Protestant position, should be enunciated so clearly in the first major statement of the first Catholic president seems to underline how deeply established it is in the American outlook.[14]

"The Times of Trial"

Bellah speaks of two "times of trial" which are essential to the mythology of civil religion. The first time of trial was the Revolutionary era and shows how the leaders of this time—Washington, Hamilton, and Jefferson (especially, in the Declaration of Independence)— stressed the same two themes which John Kennedy stressed in his first inaugural. Religion, the guaranty of democratic rights ("the inalienable rights by which men are endowed by their Creator"), and the providential mission of the United States. Washington, in his first inaugural address, this first saint of the civil religion, said:

No people can be bound to acknowledge and adore the Invisible Hand which conducts the affairs of man more than those of the United States. Every step by which we have advanced in the character of an independent nation seems to have been distinguished by some token of providential agency.[15]

Thomas Jefferson, in his second inaugural, observed:

I shall need, too, the favor of that Being in whose hands we are, who led our fathers, as Israel of old, from their native land and planted them in a country flowing with all the necessities and comforts of life.[16]

Bellah points out that this theme of America as Israel is a frequent one.

---

14 Ibid., p. 5.
15 Quoted in ibid., p. 7.
16 Quoted in ibid., pp. 7–8.

As recently as President Johnson's inaugural address, the same theme could be seen:

They came here—the exile and the stranger, brave but frightened —to find a place where a man could be his own man. They made a covenant with this land. Conceived in justice, written in liberty, bound in union, it was meant one day to inspire the hopes of all mankind; and it binds us still. If we keep its terms we shall flourish.[17]

Bellah says that this religion is both Biblical and American. The "Biblical archetypes"—Exodus, Chosen People, Promised Land, New Jerusalem, Sacrificial, Death and Rebirth—are clearly Biblical themes.

But it is also genuinely American and genuinely new. It has its own prophets and its own martyrs, its own sacred events and sacred places, its own solemn rituals and symbols. It is considered that America be a society as perfectly in accord with the will of God as man can make it, and a light to all nations.[18]

Bellah explicitly rejects the notion that this is merely "religion in general." It has highly specific content, and indeed—contrary to Herberg, Eckhardt, and Marty—extremely challenging dogma. It is not Christianity, though it shares much with Christianity, but neither was it thought to be by its founders as a substitute for Christianity:

There was an implicit but quite clear division on function between the civil religion and Christianity. Under the doctrine of religious liberty, an exceptionally wide sphere of personal piety and voluntary social action was left to the churches. But the churches were neither to control the state or be controlled by it. The national magistrate, whatever his private religious views, operates under the rubrics of the civil religion as long as he is in an official capacity. . . . This accommodation was undoubtedly the product of a particular historical moment and of a cultural background dominated by Protestantism of several varieties and by the Enlightenment, but it has survived despite subsequent changes in the cultural and religious climate.[19]

It is not difficult, of course, to fit this observation into the theme of the present volume. The civil religion emerged precisely because the denominational society needed some basic underpinning which

[17] Quoted in ibid., p. 19.
[18] Ibid., p. 18.
[19] Ibid., pp. 8–9.

committed it to the goals that all denominations shared and, in support of which, the members of the denominations had established the new republic.

The second great trial, according to Bellah, was the Civil War, which tested the commitment of American society to its own goals and extracted from the society a price: tragedy and suffering which at least in the myth was essential for its survival. The Civil War, of course, also produced the great saint of the pantheon of the civil religion— Abraham Lincoln:

> *With the Civil War a new theme of death, sacrifice, and rebirth enter the civil religion. It is symbolized in the life and death of Lincoln. Nowhere is it stated more vividly than in the Gettsyburg Address, itself a part of the Lincolnian "New Testament" among the civil scriptures. Robert Lowell has recently pointed out the "insistent use of birth images" in this speech explicitly devoted to "these honored dead": "brought forth," "conceived," "created," "a new birth of freedom."* [20]

From the Civil War, in addition to a saint and a myth of suffering and rebirth has also come sacred places and sacred days.

> *. . . the Gettysburg National Cemetery, which Lincoln's famous address served to dedicate, has been overshadowed only by the Arlington National Cemetery. Begun somewhat vindictively on the Lee estate across the river from Washington, partly with the end that the Lee family could never reclaim it, it has subsequently become the most hallowed monument of the civil religion. Not only was a section set aside for the Confederate dead, but it has received the dead of each succeeding American war. It is the site of the one important new symbol to come out of World War I, the Tomb of the Unknown Soldier; more recently it has become the site of the tomb of another martyred president and its symbolic eternal flame.* [21]

Similarly, the feast day which commemorates the Civil War, Memorial Day, has become:

> *. . . a major event for the whole community involving a rededication to the martyred dead, to the spirit of the sacrifice, and to the American vision. Just as Thanksgiving Day, which incidentally was only securely institutionalized as an annual national holiday under the presidency of Lincoln, serves to integrate the family*

---

[20] Ibid., p. 10.
[21] Ibid., p. 11.

*into the civil religion, so Memorial Day has acted to integrate the
local community into the national cult. Together with the less
overtly religious Fourth of July and the more minor celebrations
of Veterans Day and the birthdays of Washington and Lincoln,
these two holidays provide an annual ritual calendar for the civil
religion. The public school system serves as a particularly important context for the cultic celebration of the civic rituals.*[22]

Even at the present time, Bellah notes, such themes as the New
Frontier and the Great Society are clearly historical continuations of
the civil religion. When a crucial issue faces the republic, such as the
civil rights controversy, the leadership of American society falls back
on the dogmas of the civil religion, as President Johnson did in his
March 15, 1965, speech on the voting rights bill:

> *Above the pyramid on the great seal of the United States it says
> in Latin, "God has favored our undertaking."*
> *God will not favor everything we do. It is rather our duty to
> divine his will. I cannot help but believe that He truly under-
> stands and that He really favors the undertaking that we begin
> here tonight.*[23]

Summary

It is easy to be cynical about America's civil religion, as we have
noted before, but then it is easy to be cynical about the principles of
any religion because the most noble of religious ideals are anything
but universally honored in practice, no matter what the religion be or
what the society in which the religion operates. Folk religion, the religion of comfort and reassurance, the religion of self-righteousness,
are not new in the world. Neither is turning religion into a justification
for pursuing the selfish goals of the community, but the difference between the theory and the practice should not cause the observer to lose
his respect for the theory and for its power to be a norm against which
the failures of the practice can be evaluated. In Bellah's words:

> *It has often been used and is being used today as a cloak for
> petty interests and hungry passions. It is in need—as is any living
> faith—of continual reformation, of being measured by universal
> standards. But it is not evident that it is incapable of growth and
> new insight.*

[22] Ibid., p. 11.
[23] Quoted in ibid., p. 14.

It does not make any decision for us. It does not remove us from moral ambiguity, from being, in Lincoln's fine phrase, "an almost chosen people." But it is a heritage of moral and religious experience from which we still have much to learn as we formulate the decisions that lie ahead.[24]

There is a curious irony in a comparison of Bellah with Marty, Eckardt, and Herberg. In the 1950's, during a time of so-called religious revival, the professional religionists denounced America's civic religion, while in the 1960's, a time of supposed religious decline, the professional sociologist defends what he calls the civil religion. There is validity in both viewpoints but, as in so many other dimensions of American religion, one can keep one's perspective only if one balances the paradox which is involved in affirming that both the best and the worst in the American religious tradition can be found in the nation's civil religion.

[24] Ibid., pp. 18–19.

Chapter 8

Diversity Within Unity

In the overview of American religions presented in Chapter 4 we provided some basic statistical information about the principal American denominations. Then we described the quasi-ethnic role they play in American society, noting that even the Roman Catholic Church contains separate and distinct ethnic groups. We learned in Chapter 7 that American denominations operated within a context of social unity made possible by common acceptance of the civil religion, which is not surprising given the fact that the civil religion and its practices are distilled from the Judeo-Christian tradition itself. But while there is a common heritage that holds the denominational society together, history and social class in their institutional formats are different in the different denominational traditions. In this chapter, we will summarize the diversity to be found within the unity of the denominational society.

Protestants

Protestantism has had the longest and most eventful history of any of the major religious groups in the United States. In the colonies Protestant denominations were established churches—Congregationalists in New England, Anglicans in the southern States. Even though this special privilege never existed on a national level and was eventually phased out on the state level, Protestantism was still the religion of the overwhelming majority of Americans until well after the Revolutionary War. In his book, *Commentaries on the Constitution*, Mr. Justice Story argued that the United States was a Protestant nation and that Christianity was part of its common law.

However, even before the beginning of the nineteenth century, established Protestantism was in trouble. Franklin Littell describes the colonial situation:

> *In sum, we have a colonial record in New England with an oppressive establishment of mixed Congregational and Presbyterian order, with an internal inconsistency carrying the seeds of its own destruction. In the southern colonies, Anglicanism enjoyed up to the time of the Revolution a position of privilege which—when it collapsed—left whole sections of the population unchurched. In New York State the picture was more ambiguous, although both Friends and Presbyterians were compelled to fight for their rights under the Anglican establishment. Only in Pennsylvania, and the colonies which for some time shared its history (the Jerseys and Delaware), was the shift to religious liberty and voluntary support accomplished without severe readjustment. Pennsylvania, indeed, despised by New Englanders and southerners alike as a "swamp of sectarianism," foreshadowed in its religious life the variety and lay activism which were later to become characteristic of the whole American religious scene.[1]*

However, this order was in deep trouble; even though the Congregational establishment in New England had begun as a sect, it had become a church and by the middle of the eighteenth century suffered from many of the weaknesses of the established church. For all its stranglehold on life in New England, most of the citizens of the areas were not particularly religious. Similarly in the South, the Anglican establishment had only a very superficial hold on society. Zealous ministers realized how much work there was to be done, and in 1740 there began what was perhaps the most decisive event in the history of American Protestantism: the Great Awakening. With Theodore Freylinghausen working among the Dutch Reformed, William Tennent and his son, Gilbert, among the Presbyterians, and Jonathan Edwards attempting to recapture religious fervor in New England, the way was prepared for the arrival in Philadelphia of George Whitefield who, along with John Wesley, can be described as the co-founder of Methodism. Although it was only the first of many religious revivals, the Great Awakening was the most important because it inserted into the bloodstream of American Protestantism a mixture of enthusiasm, fundamentalism, and pietism which is still very much a part of the

---

[1] From *From State Church to Pluralism* by Franklin Hamlin Littell. Copyright © 1962 by Franklin Hamlin Littell. Reprinted by permission of Doubleday & Company, Inc.

Protestant tradition. The distance from George Whitefield to Billy Graham is not, after all, such a great one. In Littell's words:

Although revivalism began in New Jersey under the preaching of the Dutch Pietist, Domine Freylinghausen, its consequences can be divined most readily by considering the career of Jonathan Edwards and the effect of the Wesleyan revivals in the southern colonies. . . .

The Great Awakening must be conceived as the first major manifestation of a motif which, more than any other, has shaped modern American church life: mass evangelism. Even though the camp meeting had not yet appeared, and other carefully planned techniques of the later evangelism had not become routine, the Great Awakening was a forecast of things to come. The New England establishment resisted the Great Awakening fairly successfully, sacrificing even Jonathan Edwards to the commitments of culture-religion. Even late in the nineteenth century there were still discriminatory clauses in New England state constitutions. In the South, however, the Awakening carried right up to the Revolutionary War. By the time the new states were writing their constitutions and proclaiming religious liberty, the revival emphasis was already fairly advanced in Methodist, Baptist, and "New Side" Presbyterian circles. The work which had begun in an effort to enliven a stagnant Christendom was now carried forward as an offensive to reclaim the people for the church on a voluntary basis. This is the primary distinction between the Great Awakening and later revivals, between the Second Great Awakening in Connecticut and the contemporary impulse in the Cane Ridge Revival in Kentucky; in one case the revivals were functioning within the setting of a reluctant and even resistant "Christendom," in the other, evangelism had blended with that characteristically American institution, "Home Missions," of which the European establishments have no counterpart to this day.[2]

From the Great Awakening there emerged what Littell calls "the Revival churches"—the Disciples of Christ, the Methodists, and the Baptists. The Methodists, even though they were founded in England as part of the Anglican church, and only reluctantly separated from that body, developed into a great success as a distinct denomination in the United States as the result of the Great Awakening. And the Baptists were a relatively small New England sect founded by Roger Williams until the Great Awakening gave them a powerful impetus, particularly in the South. The Disciples of Christ, however, were thor-

[2] Ibid., pp. 18, 19–20.

oughly American, combining initially Baptists, Methodists, and Presbyterians under the leadership of a dissident Presbyterian minister named Thomas Campbell. Initially, the Disciples were intended to be an ecumenical body, promoting Christian reunion by reducing theological and institutional liturgical discipline to a minimum. Unfortunately, like many other such attempts along these lines, the Disciples became not a comprehensive church but rather a new denomination.

These three revival churches introduced another element into the American Protestant tradition which has had far-reaching political effects and, indeed, made possible the evolution of the denominational society, for they replaced ecclesiastical establishment with voluntaryism. In Littell's words:

> *It was mass evangelism and the style of church life that it produced that made voluntaryism a permanent part of religion in America. The common interpretation is that voluntary support dates from the separation of church and state at the beginning of the Republic. In fact, however, the church accustomed themselves but slowly and reluctantly to the prospect of voluntary support of religious education and church life. Again and again, confronted by special problems or opportunities, they reverted to the old custom of using government or tax monies to support church work. It was the revivals, however, that made voluntaryism a possibility. They brought the laity alive and produced a sympathetic co-operation of clergy and laity such as the best of the establishment rarely saw.*
>
> *In the East and even across the Alleghenies the churches used tax monies for schools, colleges, care of Indians and freedmen, chaplaincies in public institutions, etc. In the valleys of the Ohio and Mississippi, where voluntary support came into its own, it was the central place held by camp meetings and revivalistic techniques that made voluntary giving and support a practical possibility. The very founding of churches, once the old centers of transplanted European Christendom were left behind, depended upon the winning of members afresh through home missions and the organizing of support and discipline on a strictly voluntary basis. Unfortunately, the anxiety of the American churches— deriving chiefly from "the Left Wing of the Reformation"—has led them to stress their tie to the sixteenth century Reformers and depreciate the unique aspects of the American setting. More than that, there has been insufficient appreciation of the fact that for half of American history establishments of the European type dominated the scene and that religious voluntaryism and plural-*

ism is a comparatively new thing even in America. The romantic myth about separation of church and state and the "Founding Fathers" has served simply to confuse thinking about the issue.[3]

The final eighteenth-century development was the collapse of the Congregational establishment in New England and the emergence of Unitarianism. The vigor of the Massachusetts orthodoxy gradually weakened through the seventeenth century and the now successful and affluent citizens of that state had grown weary of Puritan discipline.

The standing order in Massachusetts began the eighteenth century with loosened discipline. During the time when the awakenings revitalized the churches of the Connecticut Valley and reached far into former Anglican territory in the South, many parishes in Massachusetts resisted "enthusiasm" bitterly. And it was finally the incoherence between congregation and parish which destroyed the theocracy. Without a strong association between covenanting congregations, the churches were compelled to lean upon the legislature for coherence; and property control and final decision rested with the parishes, not the covenanted congregations within them. By the end of the eighteenth century the parishes in and around Boston were thoroughly liberalized, with the exception of Old South. When Jedidiah Morse was called to the church in Charlestown, Massachusetts, in 1789 it was already too late to save the cause of orthodoxy in that area.[4]

It was but a step, then, to the emergence of Unitarianism, a form of Protestantism so liberal that its links with the Puritan past were slender indeed. Given the power of the local congregations in the Congregational church, it was not all that difficult for many of the parishes to move from Trinitarian Congregationalism to Unitarian Congregationalism, so that in the towns of New England, the "First" Congregational Church will have (Unitarian) after it, and the "Second" will be the Trinitarian Congregationists. Weakened on the left by Unitarianism and on the right by the enthusiasts of the two Great Awakenings, the New England establishment was finished. To quote Willard L. Sperry:

Unitarianism will be grossly misunderstood, however, if it is judged solely, or even primarily, in the terms of its anti-Trinitarianism. It was a revolt against the whole grim doctrine of human nature and the mechanical means for man's salvation which had become the convention in American Calvinism by the

[3] Ibid., pp. 47–48.
[4] Ibid., p. 39.

middle of the eighteenth century. Unitarianism, with its more cheerful view of human nature, and its confidence in man's power to help himself spiritually and morally, was the theological parallel to the political perfectionism presupposed by the American Republic. The parsons who preached revolution from 1750 to 1775 were the theological liberals of New England, pre-Unitarians.

According to Congregational polity the majority of the members of a given church, or its "society," are the owners of the property. When the schism between the Trinitarians and the Unitarians became imminent in Massachusetts, the Unitarians often outnumbered and thus eventually outvoted their orthodox brethren. With the resultant right to determine the faith and practice of a single church, as well as to hold the church building, they virtually forced the orthodox minority out. The seceders from a "First" church usually organized a "Second" church. Thus it is that, in many a New England city and village today, the old colonial meeting house is that of "The First Congregational Church (Unitarian)," while the more recent and usually less graceful church across the way is "The Second Congregational Church (Trinitarian)." Of the 300 Unitarian Churches in America to-day nearly half are in Massachusetts alone.[5]

And in Littell's words:

New England Unitarianism, originally a movement to defend simple New Testament religion against hard Calvinist scholasticism, became thereby a type of Bostonian culture-religion, and lost the restitutionist zeal which bid fair to sweep the Continent.[6]

But it would be a mistake to assume that New England lost its influence on the shaping of the American Protestant tradition to the twin assault of revivalism and Unitarianism. It persisted particularly in the Middle West for decades to come. In Littell's words:

On the one hand, the Unitarian movement represented an effort to maintain the goals of Christianity, of a continuum of Christ and culture. This tradition the Unitarians still carry on, although more recently a considerable section has identified itself almost completely with the spirit of the times (humanism and secularism). . . .

Long after the Puritan oligarchy had lost out in the East, it

---

[5] Willard L. Sperry, *Religion in America* (Boston: Beacon Press, 1963), p. 88. Reprinted by permission of Cambridge University Press.
[6] Littell, op. cit., p. 35.

was possible—right up to the time extreme mobility and the high pace of industrialism changed the whole style of American civilization—to find towns and rural areas in Ohio, Indiana, Illinois, Iowa, the Dakotas, Nebraska, Kansas, etc., where New England culture-religion survived intact. In these Puritan communities the Protestant clergy still played a strong and sometimes controlling role in politics; the churches dominated the cultural, moral, and educational life of the villages or townships. The New England standing order did not break up suddenly: it has survived in scattered areas right into the twentieth century. Much of the anti-Catholicism, anti-Semitism, anti-refugee sentiment, racialism, and nativism which mark the Protestant underworld today derives its support from islands of defensive culture-religion which resent being passed by in the flow of national history. In a degenerate and negative way they live with eyes cast backward, as unworthy of the fathers who once stormed a continent as they are of the present hour.[7]

Therefore, for the century and a half after the beginning of the republic, there were two main and opposing thrusts in American Protestantism on the one hand toward the missionary evangelical field, based on voluntarism and internal discipline and, on the other hand, a strong strain toward involvement in political life and the use of government and law to enforce church judgments and positions. Abolitionism in the nineteenth century, prohibitionism in the early twentieth century, and even the present deep involvement of Protestant churches in the peace and racial issues can be traced to the New England tradition. On the other hand, the revivalist movement guaranteed periodic resurgences of enthusiasm as devout and dedicated men and women strove to rekindle religious fervor among the unchurched or the apathetic. Enthusiasm seems to be particularly effective among the lower classes for whom the established church or, in later years, middle-class churches have little or no appeal. The real heirs to the enthusiasts of the late eighteenth century are not the churches which they founded, but the fundamentalist and Pentecostal sects which today are so popular among the lower strata of society. Wesley himself saw the problem. If his Methodists were the sober and respectable persons that he persuaded them to be, then they would become successful. But as they became successful, they would lose interest in the vigor and enthusiasm of Methodism. But neither Wesley nor any of his followers were able to solve the problem, so that the revivalist impulse has produced new denominations and new subdivisions within

[7] Ibid., pp. 58 and 59.

denominations in almost every attempt that is made to revivify established denominations.

At the end of the Revolutionary War, therefore, Baptists, Methodists, and Disciples were making great progress, particularly on the frontier. Congregationalism was disestablished and in disarray in New England, though at least its ecclesiastical form and its concern about governmental policies would continue to have a strong influence on American Protestantism. The Unitarians would produce a brilliant intellectual movement in New England, particularly in their transcendentalist offshoot, but would have no influences on the masses of Americans. Episcopalians, now firmly disestablished in the Middle Atlantic states, would remain a relatively small denomination but an influential one because of many well-to-do members. As the years went on, the Anglo-Catholic revival had a strong influence on this denomination, and its High Church branch would be increasingly dominant over the Low Church branch. Scotch-Irish Presbyterians retained some of their strength in the Middle Atlantic states, particularly in Pennsylvania, but neither their institutional form nor their strict Calvinism were particularly suited to holding large numbers of their members, and severe losses to the Methodists, Baptists, and Disciples were experienced. Lutherans and Dutch Reform denominations would grow—the former more rapidly than the latter—through immigration and spread to the Middle West; and the Quakers would remain a small but influential denomination. Thus, the basic shape of American Protestantism was formed; and the framework that was developed was relatively stable, though there would be constant instability within it as dissensions and revivals spawned new denominations and new divisions within old denominations, and uniquely American phenomena such as Mormonism and Christian Science emerged.

The Civil War was a severe blow to Protestantism because many of its denominations split into northern and southern branches, divisions which at least in some still persist, and in others were healed only with great difficulty. However, division, combination, and then more division were by now part and parcel of the life of American Protestantism; middle-class Protestant churches found themselves constantly threatened by liberal temptation on the left and the fundamentalist revivalism on the right. Some of the denominations—Congregationalists, Methodists, and Presbyterians—have moved substantially to the left of their earlier doctrinal position, while the Lutherans and the Baptists have generally resisted such movement, largely because of the very strong conservative elements within their denominations, the Missouri Synod Lutherans, for example. The Episcopal church has been able to be flexible enough to combine within its membership the most advanced liberals with the most enthusiastic of rosary-saying Anglo-Catholics. The evangelical and fundamentalist groups on the right successfully resist the temptation to liberalism, but at a price of cutting themselves off from the Protestant establishment, particularly as it is represented by the National Council of Churches. From the Middle Western Unitarian on the far left to the hard-shell fundamentalist on the far right, American Protestantism covers a vast variety of beliefs and practices, not excluding those of its members who would be perfectly content in a united church to accept the Pope as the head of that church.

Divided, then, by origin, social class, geography, race, and nationality background, united at least in part and at least for a time by resistance to Rome and by its confidence that it was, after all, the American religion, Protestantism approaches the end of the twentieth century with a host of new problems, most of which are also old problems.

First of all, it must wrestle with the principle of congregational independence versus the need for denominational organization. If schools are to be supported, ministers trained, effective national bureaucracies established, then there has to be some central governing body within the denomination—a central governing body staffed by men who tend to be cosmopolitan in their outlook and somewhat intellectual in their training. Hence, it is not infrequent that they stand in opposition on many important issues to what members of the local congregation feel are their own vital interests. Catholicism is able to cope with this difficulty by vesting its hierarchy with sacred powers. But Protestantism does not have this theological option available, and as modern society grows more complex and requires an even more sophisticated denominational bureaucracy, tension between congregation and bureaucracy can grow more acute.

Secondly, Protestantism is faced with ambivalence toward scholarly activity. Even though it maintains first-rate seminaries and divinity school faculties and is far superior to Catholicism or Judaism in its theologizing, it has not yet solved, and probably cannot solve the kind of tension which appeared at the end of the eighteenth century between Unitarianism and revivalism. Not only is Protestantism a collection of denominations, but many of the individual denominations are caught between the poles of revivalistic fundamentalism (or at least insistence on biblical traditions) and advanced liberal theologizing. Catholicism has solved this problem, at least until recently, by making clear the subjection of theologians to ecclesiastical authority. But this option is not available to Protestants.

A third perennial problem for Protestantism is the conflict between political involvement on the one hand and skepticism about
human effort on the other. The tradition of free church dissent, trans-
ferred from England to the United States, produced a commitment to
political activity which, while never quite as strong as Oliver Crom-
well's Commonwealth, nonetheless has played a major role in the development of American life, particularly through the abolitionist and
prohibitionist movements. Then, a somewhat different strain of the
Protestant tradition is extremely skeptical about the ability to find
easy answers, or, indeed, any answers at all that can be called Christian, to political and social problems. It is Lutheran in its origin, neoorthodox in its current orientation, and shaped and directed most recently by Reinhold Niebuhr.

Finally, Protestantism continues to wrestle with the problem of
unity and diversity. While the ecumenical mergers currently taking
place are probably more realistic and will endure longer than other
mergers made in the past, it still must be acknowledged that the cen-
trifugal and centripetal forces in American Protestantism have generally cancelled each other out, and that the current enthusiasm for
ecumenism leaves large sections of Protestantism, particularly of the
fundamentalist or conservative variety relatively untouched. Protestant
principles of individual choice and the voluntarism dating in the
United States from the Great Awakening is a strong and inevitable
counterforce working against ecumenical tendencies. This is not to
say that Protestant ecumenism is impossible, but it does face considerable difficulties.

Protestants will argue, of course, and quite correctly in their
frame of reference, that these dilemmas are part of the human religious condition, at least as that condition has manifested itself in the
Protestant churches; whatever tensions they introduce are merely part
of the price one has to pay for the openness and freedom that the
Protestant principle makes possible. While one can hardly quarrel with
such an argument, nonetheless it must be affirmed that under such
circumstances American Protestantism will always be in a state of
flux, crisis, and instability, to which the Protestant will quite properly
reply that this is more or less the way he wants it.

These tensions complicate for Protestants the basic issue with
which this book is concerned—the relationship between the meaning
and the belonging functions of religion. The emphasis which a given
individual or congregation or denomination may choose to take on the
various continua described in the previous paragraphs will shape
the relationship between the meaning and belonging functions. Thus,
for example, a fundamentalist sectarian, congregationally oriented

Protestant will find himself necessarily committed to many specific doctrinal positions and devotional practices in order that religion may provide him with a sense of self-definition and self-location. However, as compensation for the commitments he must make, self-definition is much clearer and more precise. On the other hand, a liberal ecumenic and denominationally oriented Protestant will not be required to accept in any great detail a Protestant interpretive scheme, but neither will his religion provide him with anything like the clear sense of identity that other Protestants may experience. To put the matter somewhat differently, there is a wide variety of possible relationships between the meaning and belonging function in Protestantism, ranging from some that are even more rigidly specified than for Roman Catholics to some that are even less clearly specified than they are for Jews. The issues are more complex in the Protestant denominations because Protestantism is, in the most general sense of the word, the principal American church. As the majority religion comes closest to being "established," it is easier for Protestantism than it is for the other two major religious groups to become a cultural religion. Thus, about 10 percent of the American population will describe itself simply as Protestant, without giving any other denominational affiliation.

In other words, it is possible for the majority religion to become a residual category and include within its bonds a fair number of people whose ties with the Protestant religious tradition are, at best, tenuous, and whose Protestantism is, in fact, merely a sign that they are Americans who do not happen to be Jewish or Roman Catholic. Thus, for many Protestants formal religion provides little in the way of either meaning or belonging and is almost indistinguishable from the American civil religion previously described. On the other hand, however, it also must be emphasized that there are some Protestant groupings, particularly of the fundamentalist variety, whose interpretive schemes and sense of community are much more powerful than one could find among all but a handful of Roman Catholics.

Of the two principal functions of religion—meaning and belonging—with which this volume is concerned, it must always be asked which meaning, and what kind of belonging, and for whom, when one is speaking of American Protestants. The answers to these questions will be very complicated indeed. Nonetheless, it was the various Protestant denominations, shaped up as they were by the Great Awakening and the Unitarian schism, that formed the denominational society in the years preceding and immediately after the Revolutionary War. A sharp sense of self-definition and self-location that their denominations provided for the Protestants of that era made religious pluralism essential and contributed greatly to making political pluralism possible. Despite the intensity of the self-criticism in which Protestants engage (and recently they are imitated by Roman Catholics), they may still look with some pride to the denominational society they have created. It may be filled with tensions and contradictions, but it works, politically and religiously.

Catholics

An adequate understanding of the present condition of the Roman Catholic Church in the United States requires comprehension of two essential points: (1) Roman Catholicism came to the United States as a religion of immigrants; (2) the immigrant era is over and its aftereffects are rapidly vanishing.

Even though the history of the Catholic Church in the United States is the history of an immigrant church adjusting to a new society, it is worthwhile noting that at least in its origins it was "made in America." John Carroll, the first bishop of Baltimore, was a fifth-generation American. He served with Benjamin Franklin on a mission to Quebec during the Revolutionary War; his cousin, Charles Carroll of Carrollton was a signer of the Declaration of Independence, a close friend and business associate of George Washington, and almost the second president of the United States. His brother, Daniel Carroll, was one of the signers of the Constitution. Even though his flock numbered only about 1 percent of the total population and suffered under a fair number of legal and social restrictions, its loyalty to the new republic and its principles was never questioned. The Carroll clan was part of the colonial establishment and as such their religion was considered the religion of native Americans. When John Carroll presumed to address congratulations to the new president of the United States, Washington did not dismiss him as the head of some tiny immigrant sect but graciously responded to the congratulations of a man whom he knew well, whose cousin had been a close supporter in the days of Valley Forge, and who himself had served the patriot cause on a mission to Canada. Carroll's immediate successors in the archdiocese of Baltimore were also part of the native American aristocracy or French refugees closely allied with it. American Protestants had no love for the Church of Rome, but they did not view the Carrolls or their successors in Baltimore as a threat of a foreign invasion.

But the day of the American Church and the goodwill that it established were to be overpowered by 1820, when the immigrant waves swept up on the American shore. Catholicism was no problem when it was only 1 percent of the population, but hordes of Irish and later German immigrants pouring into the seaports on the east coast were another matter. By 1830 nativist bigotry had hit its stride and would continue to be a major factor in American society until well into the twentieth century. The Carrolls were forgotten, and Catholicism had become a religion of unwanted immigrants.

There were two basic styles available to the leadership of the immigrant church: one was to view the United States as a Protestant nation hostile to the faith of the immigrants. Under such circumstances, the only possible posture was to stop at nothing in the fight to defend immigrants and their faith from the encroachments of a hostile Protestant society. The other approach was to argue that American freedom and democracy offered a climate in which Catholicism could flourish, and it was therefore necessary for the Catholic Church to become as American as it possibly could without sacrificing any of its basic doctrines. John Carroll freely chose the latter style, as did the brilliantly liberal genius, John England, the first bishop of Charleston. As early as 1825 England had entrusted the financial governance of his diocese to an elected board of five priests and ten lay people and governed the diocese under a "constitution," his name for the group which met frequently in the course of his twenty-year administration of Charleston.

But while John England represented a happy combination of Irish liberalism with American democracy, most of his fellow bishops were not willing to take the risks involved. John Hughes, truculent archbishop of New York, summarized his approach to the new society in the following words:

Now my lot was cast in the great metropolis of the whole country. My people were composed of representatives from almost all nations. They came under episcopal government in a new country, and in circumstances such as they had not been accustomed to in their own. It was necessary that they should be brought to coalesce as one Catholic flock. They were surrounded by many inducements to diverge from the unity of the Church, both in profession and in practice. Many snares were laid for them; and, under these circumstances, I found it expedient to adopt a mode of government resulting almost by necessity from the peculiarity of my position. I had to stand up among them as their bishop and chief; to warn them against the dangers that surrounded them; to contend for their rights as a religious community; to repel the spirit of faction among them; to convince their judgment by frequent explanations in regard to public and mixed questions; to encourage the timid, and sometimes to restrain the impetuous; in short, to knead them up into one dough, to be leavened by the spirit of Catholic faith and of Catholic union.

*   *   *

Convents have been burned down, and no compensation offered to their scattered inmates; Catholic churches have been burned down, while whole neighborhoods have been, under the eye of public officers, reduced to ashes. People have been burned to death in their own dwellings; or if they attempted to escape have been shot down by the deadly messenger of the unerring rifle. Crosses have been pulled down from the summit of God's sanctuary. Priests have been tarred and feathered. Ladies have been insulted for no crime except that of having devoted themselves to the service of their divine Master in a religious state, in the hope of conferring aid or consolation on their fellow-beings. . . . These things were the work of what is called mobs; but we confess our disappointment at not having witnessed a prompt and healthy, true American sentiment in the heart of the community at large in rebuke of such proceedings, and so far as reparation was possible, in making it to the injured parties whom they had failed to protect.[8]

The Hughes style, rarely stated so bluntly, however, became a typical approach of Roman Catholicism in American society. The nineteenth and the early part of the twentieth centuries can be viewed as a struggle between the Americanizers and the anti-Americanizers within Catholicism. While those who favored as rapid Americanization as possible generally had the best of the theoretical discussions, in practice fears for the faith of the immigrant combined with the defensive attitude which characterized nineteenth-century Catholicism and in most parts of the world produced a practical policy that was designed to protect the Catholic immigrants from losing their faith in a largely Protestant society.

The compromise which was evolved would permit Catholic church leaders to be fervent supporters of American political democracy and American foreign policy while at the same time remaining paternalistic autocrats within the Church defending their people from Protestantization. In the two decades at the end of the century a new

[8] John Rose Greene Hassard, *The Life of the Most Reverend John Hughes, D.D., First Archbishop of New York* (New York: D. Appleton and Co., 1866).

generation of leaders emerged, principally James Gibbons, the cardinal archbishop of Baltimore; John Ireland, the archbishop of St. Paul; John Keane, the first rector of the Catholic University of America; and Lancaster Spaulding, bishop of Peoria. They argued that American religious freedom and American religious virtues should provide a model which the rest of the Catholic world could profitably imitate. The Americanists, as these reformers were called, were open-minded, liberal, progressive men, but they encountered bitter opposition from their fellow bishops, hostility from nativists (who destroyed John Ireland's attempt to arrange a modus vivendi between the Catholic and public schools), and suspicion in Rome. The Americanists themselves were never formally condemned, though Rome did issue a warning against the so-called heresy of Americanism, which the Americanists denied ever existed in this country. The sending of an apostolic delegate to supervise the Church in the United States effectively terminated the Americanists' enthusiasms by the first decade of the twentieth century.

While the Americanists' attempt to create a modus vivendi between the Catholic Church and other American religions was unsuccessful, it is worth noting that many of their ideas became official practice of the Church at the Second Vatican Council. However, the return to a conservative and defensive posture after the Americanist interlude so obscured the work of Ireland, Spaulding, and Keane that few Americans realized how many of the Vatican reforms had been anticipated in the United States in the late nineteenth century.

Although men like Carroll, England, and the Americanists are the heroes of American Catholic history, it must be confessed that the internal organization and structure of American Catholicism from 1820 until the present has not been liberal, but has rather been based on the premise that the Catholic Church in the United States must defend itself in a hostile society which would if it could destroy the faith of its people. Separate school systems, separate charitable organizations, strong social controls, anti-intellectualism, fear of close contact with Protestants, belligerent defense of one's own rights, suspicion of attempts at intercreedal activity, strong loyalty to Rome, vigorous emphasis on sexual morality, and close alliance with international Catholicism—these were the characteristics of immigrant Catholicism. The Church was a garrison at war, and there was precious little room for individual freedom, much less dissent within the garrison, or communication with the enemy on the other side of the garrison walls. The parish Church and its vast array of social and religious activities became the bulwark of Catholicism in the United States. Its pastor was the unquestioned lord spiritual of the neighborhood and, together with the precinct captain, also the lord temporal. While the Church perhaps never had quite the power over its membership that many outsiders supposed, and while there was plenty of bitterness, criticism, and politicking within it, the necessity of presenting a united front to the nativist world outside was questioned by very few Catholics. Indeed, the issue of individual versus communal religious expression could never have occurred in the immigrant Church.

It is essential to note that the immigrants themselves, far from questioning the Church's demand for fierce loyalty, cheerfully accepted it. Religion and ethnicity, or rather more precisely, religioethnicity, had become crucial for their own personal identity. To be a loyal and devout Catholic had become a means of self-definition and self-location which few of the immigrants were willing to give up, no matter how great the pressure. It can be understood why the church leaders were afraid that the immigrant would lose his faith, and why well into the twentieth century the claim would be made that not many millions had, indeed, left the Church. But in retrospect it can be seen that their fears were unjustified. The nativist opposition which the immigrants encountered, far from weakening their faith, rather reinforced it. The nativists resented and condemned the immigrants because they were Irish Catholics, Italian Catholics, Polish Catholics, or German Catholics, but in the act of so doing they also defined the immigrants as Catholics in such a way that religious loyalty became an important part of the immigrants' self-concept. There were enough immigrants, and they were well enough organized that when the larger society made fun of them for being, let us say, Irish Catholic, they would respond, not by trying to cease being Irish or Catholic, but rather by proclaiming pride in their religious and ethnic origins, and their intention to prove that they could be as good Americans as anyone else, indeed if need be, better. The Catholic superpatriotism of the years immediately after the Second World War can be seen as a legacy of this reaction to nativist prejudice.

The immigrants saw that other Americans living as they did in a religiously pluralistic society defined themselves by their religion, and since the immigrants aspired to be good Americans, they behaved in exactly the same way and defined themselves by their own religion. The adoption by the immigrants of religious denominationalism as a means of self-definition explains perhaps more adequately than any other single factor why the working class did not leave the Catholic Church in the United States as it did in most European countries. It is worth noting, for example, that very few of the Irish immigrants in the United States stopped being Catholic, that, indeed, in many respects they became even more militantly Catholic than did their cousins who remained in the Emerald Isle. On the other hand, Catholics who migrated to England have left the Church in fairly large numbers precisely because religion in England is not nearly so important as a means of self-definition.

We can see, therefore, that for a century and a quarter (1820 to 1945) the shape of American Catholicism has emerged from an interaction between a clergy fearful for the faith of its people and a people proudly loyal to a Church which, even though it made them unwelcome, at least gave them something to cling to during the years of acculturation into American society.

Even when the immigrant era was over, loyalty to Catholicism in the face of the continuing hostility of American Protestants (as manifested, for example, by the defeat of Al Smith and by the near defeat of John Kennedy) was unquestioned by the children and the grandchildren of the immigrants. The inauguration of Kennedy, coinciding as it did with the dramatic change brought about by Pope John and the Vatican Council, marked the end of the immigrant era, the end of wide-scale nativism, and the beginning of the end of ecclesiastical organization built on the two rocks of fear of Protestantism and immigrant loyalty.

But a social organizational style appropriate for an immigrant era would have become obsolete for American Catholicism even if there had not been a John Kennedy or a John xxiii. By 1960, the occupational, educational, and financial achievements of Catholics under forty were no different from those of white American Protestants living in the same areas of the country in which Catholics lived. Catholicism had become a middle-class church, as it were, and was well on its way to becoming an upper middle-class church. The immigrant ghettos in the inner city had been left behind, and the Catholic population was every bit as likely to graduate from college and continue on to graduate school as it was to make a pilgrimage to the professional suburb. Catholic intellectualism, which had been in a sorry state as recently as 1950, was undergoing a dramatic change as Catholic graduates now were just as likely to go to the top quality arts and sciences graduate schools, to finish their doctorates at these schools, to plan academic careers, and to turn in superior academic performances as were Protestants. Under such circumstances a new breed of younger clergy and laity, for whom the struggles of the immigrant were not even a dim memory, was bound to emerge. The crisis which the Roman Catholic Church in this country presently faces would have occurred in any event, but the dramatic events of the Vatican Council accelerated the pace of change and created a dynamic and fluid situation almost overnight.

It is perfectly clear to anyone who reads the Catholic press that many things which were in the past discussed only in whispers have now become front page news. Priests leave the Church to get married, not in secret, but with half-page ads in the *New York Times*. Clergy and laity openly criticize bishops and at times even defy them. Ecclesiastical teaching on divorce and birth control is questioned by the majority of the Catholic population. Substantial elements of both the clergy and the laity think that celibacy ought to be optional for the clergy. Newly educated laity demand the right to participate in ecclesiastical decision making and financing. Unofficial organizations of both priests and lay people emerge to engage in collective bargaining with their church leaders. Protestants have ceased to be heretics and have become separated brothers. Indeed, Protestant church leaders are treated with far more respect and courtesy in many Catholic journals than are bishops. Control of Catholic colleges is turned over to boards of trustees, the majority of whose members are lay people. A nun who is president of a Catholic college leaves her religious order and continues as president of the college. A religious underground emerges and engages in drastic experimentation with the ceremonies of the Mass in defiance, at times public, of canon law. And the Canon Law Association of America, once the bastion of conservatives and traditionalists, takes the lead in demanding the abolition of the present church legislation. In the space of a very few years Roman Catholicism in the United States has passed from a situation where the individual would not dream even of thinking of his personal religious activity being at variance with the prescribed activity of the official Church to a situation where a substantial number of Roman Catholics seem to be taking religious matters into their own hands, sometimes without the leadership of their bishops and clergy, and sometimes in direct opposition to this leadership. While one might have expected on a priori grounds that the social and economic changes within the Catholic population would have brought about such phenomena, the suddenness with which they have appeared is somewhat surprising.

It is difficult to be certain how widespread the restlessness and ferment is within Roman Catholicism in the United States. Many church leaders are firmly persuaded that the unrest, the agitation, is limited to a small minority. But several recent surveys would indicate that on matters related to sexual morality and to ecclesiastical leadership, the dissatisfaction has extended to a large minority of the Catholic population. The question arises as to how drastic an impact this will have on the Roman Catholic Church. Some liberal Catholic critics insist, with little effort to conceal their joy at the prospect, that the institutional Church as it has been known until now is destined for sure destruction. Yet, younger Catholics are apparently just as devout and just as doctrinally orthodox as their parents, but they are more critical of the clergy and more skeptical of the Church's teachings on birth control than the previous generation. The revolt of the individual against the institution within Roman Catholicism in the United States, thus far at least, is limited to highly specific and generally very personal issues. The basic loyalty to the Church of the grandchildren of immigrants does not yet seem to have been affected; and, indeed, many of the most severe critics writing in the Catholic and secular press still make their criticism in the context of their strong commitment to the Catholic ideal.

Even though many in leadership positions are worried that the pace of change is too fast for the faithful (in line with the traditional concern about defending the faith of the "simple people"), survey material suggests that the opposite is the case. The English liturgy, ecumenism, change in styles of authority, even the possibility of a married clergy, and certainly change in birth control, far from upsetting most American Catholics, seem to be warmly welcomed. The demythologization of authority—papal, episcopal, and clerical—has now become a fact of life in American Catholicism, and the attempt of some American Catholic leaders to prevent this from happening is rather like the farmer padlocking the door of his barn long after it has been emptied.

As the bonds of loyalty to their Church grow more selective, and American Catholics can engage in individual religious activity quite independently of the Church without experiencing any guilt feelings, it does follow that the organizational structure of the Church is substantially weakened, but it is not necessary to assume that Catholicism in the United States is faced with imminent collapse. What is far more likely is that the Roman Catholic Church in this country will be "Protestantized," or perhaps more aptly, "Americanized." This is not to say that Catholics will become Protestant in their doctrinal beliefs or will abandon their union with the Roman pontiffs, but the organizational style and posture of American Catholicism will become more and more like that of the Protestant churches. Popular participation in decision making and selection of leaders, more independence for the clergy, the committee approach to church governance, the emergence of a scholarly clerical elite, the evolution of a social service concept of the ministry, a good deal more room for personal decision making, both in the clergy and the laity, a much more relaxed attitude toward authority, the collapse of the caste barriers between clergy and laity (and the possible appearance of a married clergy), much greater freedom for discussion and criticism, and more openness toward non-Catholic religions—all these seem to be an inevitable part of the future of the Roman Catholic Church in this country as it realizes that such styles of ecclesiastical organization are inevitable when one is dealing with a thoroughly Americanized population. But such changes in styles do not mean the collapse of religious organization. There has been precious little erosion of Protestant doctrine or practice under such organizational styles. Popular publicity to the contrary, God does not seem to be dead for American Protestants, and He is not likely to die for American Catholics either, at least in the foreseeable future.

Two points must be noted about this "Protestantization" or "Americanization" of the Roman Catholic Church in the United States. First of all, most of the changes we are projecting would be considered highly desirable from the point of view of the church reform undertaken at the Vatican Council. Secondly, almost all of them have been advocated in the past by the folk heroes of the American Catholic Church—Carroll, England, Spaulding, and Ireland. Those advocating drastic change in the Catholic Church in the United States can find excellent theoretical justification for their demands to adjust to the change in the status of the Catholic population.

It seems likely, therefore, that the present frictions and uncertainties will eventually abate, particularly when a younger generation comes to leadership in the Catholic Church; a new balance between individual and community will be established in which there will be a great deal more room than there is at present for personal religious choice and decision. The important question for the Catholic Church at the present time is not whether such changes will come but, rather, how soon they will come, and how much of the old organizational structure will have to be destroyed before a new balance is struck. A cautious estimate at the present time would be that the failure of most elements of ecclesiastical leadership to recognize the implications of the present situation will delay the appearance of a new balance and will lead to a substantial organizational loss (a notable reduction of Catholic schools, for example) but little loss in membership.

Jews

By almost any standards one cares to use, American Jews have been the most successful of all the immigrant groups who have come to American society. The majority of them were relative late-comers, arriving at the end of the nineteenth and beginning of the twentieth century. They were numerically small, linguistically disadvantaged, and religiously unpopular. They came, for the most part, as refugees from areas where they had been persecuted for centuries; yet within less than a half century, they have emerged as well-to-do, educated, politically and socially powerful, and culturally sophisticated. Despite the residue of anti-Semitism, which survives in American society in the twentieth century, Jews have been far and away the most skillful practitioners of the American way of life. The rapidity of their acculturation and economic success surely must be viewed as one of the most astonishing social phenomena in the whole history of the republic.

Both Jews and gentiles, one suspects, are ambivalent about this success. The Jews can point to it with pride, of course, as a measure of their dramatic accomplishments in American society; and yet they are also a bit nervous about the wealth and power they have acquired because of the very legitimate fear that gentile animosity toward such success might lead to an increase in anti-Semitism. Gentiles, on the other hand, are frequently torn between pride that American society was open enough to permit a group against which there was and still is considerable prejudice to be so successful and outright envy, if not to say suspicion, of Jewish success. Social scientists may be a little bit skeptical about both reactions. Jews have been successful in American society not because of any innate superiority in Jewishness or because of any particular dishonesty in business practices. The explanation for their success is to be found in social and cultural variables. Jewish commitment to learning, particularly the practical learning, and the study of their own religious books predispose them to make the most of the education that was available to American society. The intellectual and emotional quickness which had been necessary for their survival as a permanently persecuted minority in Europe equipped them to face the American economy with the same prospect of success that the Irish faced in American urban polity. While the Jews came to the United States as poor and frequently uneducated, they did not come as peasants but rather as an alert and intelligent people whose survival in the past had frequently depended on diligence, wit, and the ability to take risks. Even though the American society was not eager to welcome them and still discriminates against them on the level of social interaction and occasionally of occupational employment, it was open enough to provide Jews with an opportunity to exercise the skills which they had acquired through the centuries. The result of this combination of social openness and social skills produced a success which, while impressive, was nonetheless predictable; and attempts to explain it in the terms of anti-Semitism or even anti-anti-Semitism are ludicrous.

When one starts to discuss American Judaism as a religion one has to be wary of using the same categories that one uses in speaking of gentile groups. While Judaism is a religion, it has not been, at least for several thousand years, either a church or a denomination, even though we may refer to it as a denomination in developing a theory of a denominational society. We must realize that it is not a denomination like other denominations or a church like other churches; one either uses the categories which apply to other religious groups analogously when speaking of Jews or one finds an entirely different set of categories.

The first American Jews were of Spanish, Portuguese, and Dutch origins. They came to the United States in the late part of the seventeenth century. These Sephardim were joined shortly thereafter by Ashkenazim, the German Jews and their descendants. But in the middle of the nineteenth century, the American Jewish population was minute, with only fifteen thousand Jews living in this country in 1840. Twenty years later the Jewish population had increased tenfold, and by 1880, there were a quarter of a million Jews in the United States. Almost all of them were of German origin. Many of these German Jews had been profoundly influenced by the emancipation which had occurred in Europe at the end of the eighteenth and the beginning of the nineteenth century; the Jews were now freed both from the rigorous laws of their own religion and also the discriminatory laws imposed upon them by gentiles. Under such circumstances many German rabbis had begun to experiment with a form of Judaism which would be more acceptable to those Jews who had chosen a path of substantial acculturation into German or French society.

Reformed Judaism, which in belief, practice, and ritual looked rather like German Protestantism, was in many ways much more successful in America than in Germany. Under the leadership of Isaac Mayer Wise it rapidly became the dominant force in nineteenth-century American Judaism. While there were various degrees of Reform Judaism, it was nonetheless estimated that in 1880 only twelve congregations were strictly Orthodox.

By the end of the nineteenth century, however, something of a reaction set in with the emergence of Conservative Judaism among the immigrant Jewish group. This movement included those who did not want to return to the strict Orthodoxy of the past yet were dubious about the great similarity between Reform rabbis and Unitarian, Congregational ministers. Sabatamo Rais, its founder, was concerned with maintaining a much more authentically Jewish religious tradition, complete with the study of the rabbinical literature, a love of the Hebrew language, and the fidelity to the Jewish law.

But between 1880 and 1900, the Jewish population grew from one quarter of a million to three quarters of a million. Another million and a quarter Jews arrived on the American continent by the time of the First World War. Both Reformed Judaism and Conservative Judaism were then quite literally inundated by waves of Orthodox Jews from Poland and Russia fleeing pogroms and persecutions unleashed in these countries at the end of the nineteenth century.

Most of these Jews were religiously Orthodox; many others were socialists, anarchists, Zionists, or devotees of other radical secular movements. To the Orthodox immigrant Jews, the Reform Jews were scarcely better than gentiles, and to the radical and Zionist Jews, the Reform congregations were merely bourgeois hypocrites and exploiters. The established German Jews were not terribly happy about their Eastern European confreres either.

> *To the established, middle-class, Americanized German Jews of the 1880's, the East European immigrants were a frightening apparition. Their poverty was more desperate than German Jewish poverty, their piety more intense than German Jewish piety, their irreligion more violent than German Jewish irreligion, their radicalism more extreme than German Jewish radicalism. It is not surprising that the American Jews viewed this immigration, initially, with mixed feelings, and some even suggested the possibility of deflecting or preventing it. In 1884, according to Irving Aaron Mandel's study of the Jewish press in this period, "the State of New York had passed restrictive immigration laws, and The American Israelite (edited by Isaac Mayer Wise) suggested the use of these laws by the immigration authorities to return some 200 indigent Russian refugees who were about to arrive on the steamer 'California' "!* [9]

To a very considerable extent, the Yiddish-speaking Eastern European immigrants have given shape to contemporary American Judaism both in its more orthodox religious variety and also in its secular and radical manifestations. The main religious beneficiary of the immigration has been the middle-of-the-road approach to the Jewish religion, particularly the Conservatives who stand in the middle

---

[9] Nathan Glazer, *American Judaism* (Chicago: University of Chicago Press, 1957), p. 66. Copyright © by The University of Chicago. Published 1957. Third Impression 1960. Composed and printed by The University of Chicago Press, Chicago, Ill., U.S.A.

of the middle-of-the-road; for American Jews, at least at the present time, require that their religion be both modern enough so as not to impede their acculturation into American society and yet traditional enough to guarantee their distinctiveness as Jews.

However, from the point of view of the wider norms of traditional Judaism the immigration experience was a tremendous blow, for only a relatively small minority of American Jews can be considered observant in the traditional sense of the word. To quote Nathan Glazer:

> *The Jewish migration out of the areas of second settlement was a migration of just those elements in the past most immune to Jewish religion, the second and third generation of the East European group. The areas of second settlement, we have seen, were the strongholds of Jewish irreligion and of Jewishness. It was in these almost totally Jewish areas, paradoxically, that Jews could live lives almost completely unaffected by Jewish religion and that the proportion of synagogue members was always lowest. It was in these areas, too, that any special movement in Jewish life, one, let us say, combining attachment to Yiddish, rejection of Zionism, socialism, and insistence on the need for territorial concentration in some area not Palestine, could be reasonably sure of finding a few adherents; for Jews were so numerous that some of any outlook could be found. And it was in these areas, too, that one could live a completely Jewish life from a sociological point of view and yet have no connection with any Jewish institution, religious or non-religious. It was here, in other words, that one could have only Jewish friends, eat Jewish foods, follow Jewish mores and culture patterns, and yet have little consciousness of being a Jew. But, as these neighborhoods have broken up under the impact of prosperity and new settlements of much lower density have been created on the outskirts of the metropolitan centers, a number of social influences have begun to be felt which have simultaneously strengthened Judaism and weakened Jewishness.*[10]

There was, therefore, a considerable apostasy among the second-generation Jews, at least from the Jewish religion, and perhaps some attempted apostasy from any association with the Jewish tradition. However, a number of factors impeded this development. First of all, it was not so easy to stop being a Jew, for even if you ceased to think of yourself as Jewish, the larger society was still prepared to define you as a Jew unless you became formally a member of a gentile de-

[10] Ibid., pp. 116–117.

nomination, something which few Jews were willing to do. Secondly, the disaster of the Second World War to European Judaism produced a reaction in most American Jews that precluded any denial of their Jewishness. Even though most of the traditional dietary customs had long since fallen into disuse and the frequent synagogue attender was relatively rare, being Jewish remained essential for most American Jews. While some secularist Jews insisted that Judaism was an ethnic group or people and not a religion, the point was difficult to make in the face of the religiousness of one kind or another of many of their Jewish counterparts, with the result that large numbers of relatively secularized Jews still maintain affiliation with the synagogue and attend services occasionally, even though they have no religious beliefs and practice none of the traditional Jewish customs. Such affiliation with a synagogue or congregation is viewed as a means of maintaining Jewishness and of passing it on to one's children.

In addition to varying degrees of religiousness as a means of maintaining continuity with the Jewish past, the various networks of Jewish paternal and charitable organizations provide an alternative and overlapping mode of Jewish behavior. Some Jews will be active primarily in purely religious organizations and others primarily in charitable or welfare organizations, and a very considerable number are active in both, with the exact blend of Jewishness varying from person to person. A certain number of Jews have chosen to keep alive the traditions of radical political involvement, be it Zionism or socialism or militant unionism. However, these modes do not seem to be increasing in popularity, and it is safe to say that the major portion of the Jewish population can be found somewhere along a continuum with the rigidly Orthodox Hasidim at one end and the thoroughly secularized middle-class Jew who is heavily involved in Jewish welfare activity at the other, with the middle majority of Jews involved moderately both in religious and nonreligious activity.

In Chapter 6 we presented a table showing that in a twelve-year period there had been a rapid decline in assent to certain religious propositions among American Jews but an increase in the percentage of those who went to religious services at least occasionally and of those who were affiliated with a religious congregation. It may be that propositional assent has never played the important part in the Jewish religious tradition that it has in the Christian; since it is quite possible in American society to be a Jew without assenting to any religious propositions, the meaning function and belonging function of religion are considerably more distinct for Jews than they are for gentiles. Thus the ethnic group function of religion can be fulfilled for Jews by their religion without requiring nearly as much overt religious behavior as would be required of gentiles. In this supposition, precisely because of the differences in their historical traditions, Jews could be much more flexible in the belonging and meaning functions of religions in American society than could gentiles. As Jewishness became more important for them in the third and fourth generation, they could even increase their level of affiliation while at the same time reject those elements of the Jewish tradition which did not seem particularly suitable for a modern secularist scientific society.

In a study of a well-to-do Jewish suburb of Chicago, Marshall Sklare discovered a considerable decline in the observance of traditional Jewish practices, with the respondents reporting a mean level of 2.8 practices as opposed to 5.2 by the parents.[11] Similarly, synagogue attendance had declined from 5 times a year in the parental generation to 3.7 times a year. On the other hand, Sklare observed an increase in both home observance and synagogue attendance among later generations of Jews when the level of parental observance was held constant. Thus the third-generation Jews of eastern European descent were more likely to practice some home observance and to go to synagogue five times a year or more than were second-generation respondents when the level of their parental observance was held constant. Similarly, fourth-generation German Jews were also more likely to go to synagogues and to practice home observance than were third-generation German Jews.

While Sklare's data are limited to one suburb and based on a small number of cases with a fairly low cutting point for religious observance, the trend is still suggestive and indeed remarkable. It is confirmed by the data reported in the previous chapter about the increase in congregational affiliation and attendance of religious services for the total population of American Jews in the last twelve years. Hence it might be said that for American Jews secularization has hit rock bottom, and institutional affiliation is now increasing as well as the performance of ritualistic practices in the home. The reason is not

[11] The practices which Sklare discusses were:
1. Bacon or ham never served.
2. Kosher meat bought regularly.
3. Special dinner on Friday night.
4. Lighting of candles on Friday night.
5. *Kiddush* on Friday night.
6. No smoking allowed in house on Sabbath.
7. Seder on Passover.
8. Bread not eaten in home on Passover.
9. Either or both parents fast on Yom Kippur.
10. Candles lit on Hanukkah.

From *Jewish Identity on the Suburban Frontier* by Marshall Sklare and Joseph Greenblum, Basic Books, Inc., Publishers, New York.

Table 18 Level of Religious Observance by Generation, Descent, and Parents' Level of Home Observance

| | Generation of | | | |
| | German Descent | | East European Descent | |
Among those reared by highly observ-ant parents (9–11), percent with	*Third*	*Fourth Plus*	*Second*	*Third*
3+ home observance	*	*	67	85
5+ synagogue attendance	*	*	45	50
N	(*)	(*)	(76)	(20)
Among those reared by moderately observant parents (5–8), percent with				
3+ home observance	*	*	42	60
5+ synagogue attendance	*	*	23	28
N	(*)	(*)	(34)	(25)
Among those reared by low or nonob-servant parents (0–4), percent with				
3+ home observance	4	10	30	47
1+ home observance	33	61	73	90
3+ synagogue attendance	46	59	46	63
1+ synagogue attendance	63	85	83	93
N	(24)	(39)	(30)	(40)

* Too few cases.

The thing to be observed in Table 18 is that among those of eastern European descent, the third generation is more likely than the second to report both home observance and synagogue attendance. This is true regardless of whether they came from highly observant or moderately observant or low observant back-grounds. Similarly, among those of German descent, there are in each case higher scores of observance in the fourth generation than in the third.

From Sklare and Greenblum, *op. cit.,* p. 84.

that there is any close relationship of such activities to religious doc-trine but that they are seen as being important for maintaining Jewish-ness in the midst of American life. Jews may have reached a com-promise through which they have rejected much of the beliefs and practices of the past and yet maintained a continuity with their reli-gious condition by a minimum level of observance and affiliation, a level which, if anything, is tending to move slightly upward. Their adjustment in the denominational society was different from the gen-tile adjustment; but functionally, it was the same. The moderate in-crease among fourth-generation German Jews reported by Sklare could be considered the functional equivalent of the relatively stable doc-trinal orthodoxy of Catholics and Protestants.

However, this apparently successful Jewish compromise must face two critical questions: First of all, to what extent is it strong enough to be able to resist that dread enemy of Jewishness—assimilation? Jewish leaders, both secular and religious, are generally strongly opposed to intermarriage, arguing that an increase in it would threaten the existence of the Jewish tradition. Although there is no convincing evidence that the rates of Jewish intermarriage have gone up very much, at least in the centers where the Jewish population is concentrated, the specter of it still threatens the leadership of the Jewish community. And the threat is more real for Judaism than it is for gentiles because of the different Jewish adaptations to the denominational society. A Catholic who marries a Lutheran, or, for that matter, a Jew, can continue to be a Catholic by maintaining his doctrinal orthodoxy and his church attendance. But since doctrinal orthodoxy is not a powerful requirement to be a Jew in American society, and since a relatively minimum level of church attendance is required for Jewishness, the Jew does not have available the means to reassert his Jewishness once he has married a gentile. So Judaism is less equipped institutionally to cope with intermarriage in the United States. On the other hand, given the generally humane, enlightened, and liberal position which most American Jews take on social issues, it is difficult to mount a case against religious intermarriage which does not sound strongly ethnocentric. For many Jewish families, therefore, religious intermarriage is a far more serious crisis than it is even for a devout Catholic family. While there is no strong evidence that the rate of these marriages is appreciably changing, the very possibility that it might causes some Jewish leaders to wonder whether the available means for maintaining continuity with the past traditions are strong enough to resist the very powerful forces in American society making for assimilation.

The second question is almost the reverse of the first. If one assumes that a vague sense of "peoplehood" combined with certain relatively low levels of religious affiliation and observance is not enough to maintain a sense of continuity with a tradition primarily (if not essentially) a religious tradition, is it necessary or possible for there to be a strong religious and theological revival among American Jews?

There is at present an increase in interest in ceremonial ritual among American Jews. The fact that the study of theology as such is becoming more popular in Jewish seminaries (although there is little in the Jewish tradition to justify speculative theologizing) suggests that a future generation of Jewish leaders, determined to maintain continuity with the past traditions and dissatisfied with the available means of maintaining such continuity, might strive for a much broader religious revival. It is impossible, of course, to speculate what this revival would look like (particularly for a gentile observer), but it is not out of the realm of possibility that the denominational society could lead American Jews in this direction.

A final and as yet unanswered question remains: To what extent does the existence of the beleaguered state of Israel, its present difficulties with the Arab nations, its demands on American Jews both financial and political, intensify the Jewish sense of peoplehood, affiliation, and observation?

Summary

The United States was originally a Protestant nation even though from the very beginning there were small groups of Catholics and Jews. The waves of Catholic immigrants, particularly during the time of the famine in Ireland and the economic depressions in eastern and southern Europe at the turn of the century, made the nation one quarter Catholic. To a very considerable extent, the religious history of the nation between 1840 and the present has involved the working out of the relationship between Protestants and Catholics. The Protestants at first reacted hostilely to the new immigrants (with obvious exceptions, of course). Later on, as they acquired political power and then economic and social resources, Catholics fought for and in many ways won the full, if junior, partnership in the American enterprise. American Protestantism has in considerable part been shaped by the fact that it was the first religion on the shores of this country, and American Catholicism has been shaped by the fact that it was the second. The Jews, for their part, are the smallest of the three denominational groups and also the most successful, playing a major role in government, higher education, scholarship, and the mass media. Both their relatively small size and the fact that they had a long history of persecution behind them have made the Jewish place in the American tripartite partnership unique.

For all their diversities among the three denominations, both in their history and their relative posture in American society, they are still fully American with great similarities in their organizational structure and in the behavior of their religious functionaries. One wonders, for example, how many congregations of the three major denominational groups do not have activities for teen-agers. Certainly not very many. On the other hand, it seems fair to guess that in the European counterparts of the three respective denominational groups, social activities for people in the teen years are neither very frequent nor very successful when they are attempted. American culture is not making the three religious groups indistinguishable one from the other; they have different histories, different traditions and different experiences in this country; and yet, they have also had many common experiences. Above all, the three major denominational groups are committed to living in relative peace and harmony with each other and, given the long and bloody history of religious warfare and persecution, that is no small accomplishment.

Chapter 9

Religion, Prejudice, and Conflict

The world's history is full of violent incidents of religious fighting, and religion and prejudice have often gone hand in hand. This whole problem of intolerance has been enlightened by the work of Gordon Allport, whose studies indicated that people who were the most religious, as well as people who were the least religious, showed the least amount of prejudice. Allport's distinction between intrinsic and extrinsic has laid out more specifically the whole correlation between prejudice and religion. In trying to eliminate prejudice, these patterns bring under question the traditional programs which try to encourage tolerance; now it seems that the changes are not so simply achieved.

The very checkered history of religious toleration in this country dates back to the colonial period when only Pennsylvania had religious freedom in spite of the fact that most of the earliest settlers had left their European homes for that very reason. The Protestants held a majority in the United States, but the waves of Catholic and Jewish immigrants in the nineteenth and twentieth centuries changed the religious balance of the country, particularly in the cities.

In such a background of diverse religious beliefs, certain characteristics and problems of religion make it particularly vulnerable to conflict. The existence of the parochial school system, the attitude of the Catholic Church in the areas of sex (birth control, divorce, and abortion), the separation of church and state, the corruption of supposedly religious politicians, the influence of the Catholic Church on political leaders of that faith, and the tensions created by the state of Israel are all contemporary areas of conflict that impinge on the religious scene. Solutions to these questions are complicated by changes in the attitudes of Jews and toward Catholics.

Religious Attitudes Correlate with Prejudice

That there is a connection between religion and fanaticism scarcely needs historical documentation. The most serious of all wars are religious wars, and the most merciless of conquerors are those who triumph in religious wars. Eric Hoffer's true believer is primarily a man with a religious faith which convinces him of his own profound goodness and of his opponents' malice and bad faith. There are other kinds of fanatics, particularly in the modern world, but religion seems peculiarly suited to the needs of the fanatical personality. It gives him a conviction of his own absolute righteousness and of the chasteness of any activity that he undertakes against the unbeliever.

Religious fanaticism as such is particularly associated with some of the world religions; in these faiths the *individual* is perceived as the responsible recipient of salvation and hence justified if he accepts salvation and unjustified if he rejects it. In the nature religions an enemy society could be an infidel society but the good or bad will of individuals was hardly an issue. However, after the rise of the world religions the individual infidel was presumed to have bad will; hence he was the legitimate object of fanatical hatred.

So, for two thousand years or more Christians have persecuted Jews, and Muslims and Christians have persecuted each other. Christians have exploited pagans in virtually every country they have occupied during the growth of Western imperialism; and finally, Christians have battled each other whenever the opportunity arose. The irony that this killing, persecution, imprisonment, and injustice was done in the name of religions which exalt peace and charity seems not to have occurred to too many of the practitioners of religious fanaticism. For Christians in particular, who were adjured by the founders of their religion to love their neighbor, two millennia of persecution of Jews, Muslims, pagans, and other Christians is hardly a pretty picture. While most overt violence has come to an end, discrimination against some religious groups continues in many Western countries, and religious prejudice and bigotry has by no means vanished from the scene.

At first it seems obvious that there is a connection between religion and prejudice, for the prejudiced person has the conviction of salvation which does not admit the possibility that a member of another group may be in good faith, whether the other group be a religious, racial, or an ethnic group. However, as Gordon Allport, on whom we will rely heavily in this chapter, has observed on a number of occasions, the relationship between religion and prejudice seems to be paradoxical, for some religious people seem to be remarkably unprejudiced while some saints have been fanatics. And while some fervent church members are violent opponents of racial integration, some church leaders have been among its strongest advocates.

The research findings on the connection between religion and prejudice are overwhelming. Those who have no religious affiliation arc less likely to be anti-Negro than those who have. Regular church attenders have higher scores on measures of ethnocentrism than those who go to church infrequently. Religious people are more punitive toward criminals, delinquents, prostitutes, homosexuals, and those

Table 19   Church Attendance and Prejudice Among Faculty Members of a Midwestern University

Frequency of attendance (times per mo.)	N	Prejudice score
0	261	14.7
1	143	25.0
2	103	26.0
3	84	23.8
4	157	22.0
5–7	94	19.9
8–10	26	16.3
11 or more	21	11.7

who need psychiatric treatment than the nonreligious. Nonbelievers are consistently less dogmatic and authoritarian than believers. On internalized measures of intolerance, church attenders are much less sympathetic to nonconformists of any variety than are those who do not go to church. Furthermore, in none of the research findings does the somewhat lower educational level of those who are regular church attenders suffice to explain their higher scores on measures of prejudice.

However, as Allport has pointed out, the relationship between church attendance and religiousness on the one hand and bigotry on the other is curvilinear—that is to say, the least prejudiced respondents are the most devout and the least devout; the most prejudiced are those with middle levels of religious devotion. The accompanying table taken from an article by Allport shows that the highest prejudice scores among faculty members of a midwestern university are to be found among those who go to church once or twice a month, while the very lowest scores are to be found among those who go to church eleven or more times a month and the second lowest among those who do

not go to church at all. Allport points out that this finding of the curvilinear relationship is almost unanimous in any of the studies of prejudice where attempts have been made to sort out levels of religious
devotion.[1]

Allport was then led to hypothesize two kinds of religion—extrinsic and intrinsic:

> Extrinsic religion. *For many people, religion is a dull habit, or
> a tribal investment to be used for occasional ceremony, for family
> convenience, or for personal comfort. It is something to use, but
> not to live. And it may be used in a variety of ways: to improve
> one's status, to bolster one's self-confidence, to enhance one's
> income, to win friends, power, or influence. It may be used as a
> defense against reality and, most importantly, to provide a super-
> sanction for one's own formula for living. Such a sentiment as-
> sures me that God sees things my way, that righteousness is iden-
> tical with His. I see the nature of being as conforming to the facts
> of my particular being.*[2]

Intrinsic religion, on the other hand

> *is not an instrumental formation. That is to say, it is not primarily
> a means of handling fear, or a mode of conformity, or an at-
> tempted sublimation of sex, or a wish-fulfillment. Earlier in life
> it may have been all these things. But now these specific needs
> are not so much served by, as they are subordinated to, an over-
> arching motive. Quandaries, predicaments, cross-purposes, guilt,
> and ultimate mysteries are handled under the comprehensive
> commitment. This commitment is partly intellectual, but more
> fundamentally motivated. It is integral, covering everything in
> experience and everything beyond experience; it makes room for
> scientific fact and emotional fact. It is a hunger for, and a com-
> mitment to, an ideal unification of one's life, but always under a
> unifying conception of the nature of all existence.*[3]

A number of studies have made use of distinctions similar to this.
Gerhard Lenski's study of the Detroit metropolitan area distinguished

---

[1] Gordon Allport and Michael Ross, "Personal Religious Orientation and
Prejudice," *Journal of Personality and Social Psychology*, 5 (April 1967) 433.
Reprinted by permission of the author and the American Psychological As-
sociation.

[2] Gordon W. Allport, "Behavioral Science, Religion, and Mental Health,"
Journal of Religion and Health, 2, No. 3 (April 1963) 193. Reprinted by per-
mission of the Academy of Religion and Mental Health from the *Journal of
Religion and Health*.

[3] *Ibid.*, p. 194.

between church members whose involvement was communal and associational with the former belonging to the church essentially for reasons of sociability and the latter essentially for reasons of religious commitment. Of the Catholics in Detroit, only 27 percent of the communal groups were in favor of school desegregation, while 59 percent of the associational group were in favor of it.[4] In other words, those who are most likely to use religion for their own goals are far more prejudiced than those who view religion as a commitment of faith. Similarly, Joseph Fichter in his study on a Catholic parish in New Orleans reported that the most devout Catholics were the least racially prejudiced.[5]

It is instructive to consider in some detail the Allport study on religious orientation and prejudice [6] (see Table 20). The dependent

Table 20 Prejudice and Religious Orientation

	Mean prejudice score		
Target of prejudice	*Intrinsic type* N–108	*Extrinsic type* N–106	*Inconsistent type* N–95
Anti-Negro	28.7	33.0	36.0
Anti-Jewish	22.6	24.6	28.9
Anti-Other	20.4	23.3	26.1
Jungle	7.9	8.7	9.6
CMI	10.2	11.8	13.4

variables were measured by a social problem questionnaire consisting of items involving anti-Negro, anti-Jewish, and anti-other (Orientals, Mexicans, and Puerto Ricans) attitudes. There were also items from the Custodial Mental Illness (CMI) scale,[7] and four items which suggested a generalized suspiciousness and distrust (jungle).[8] Then there were forty items to measure religious orientation, half of them tapping the intrinsic dimension and half the extrinsic dimension.[9]

[4] Gerhard Lenski, *The Religious Factor* (New York: Doubleday & Company, Inc., 1961).

[5] Joseph Fichter, *Southern Parish* (Chicago: The University of Chicago Press, 1951).

[6] Allport and Ross, op. cit.

[7] For example, "We should be sympathetic with mental patients though we cannot expect to understand their odd behavior."

[8] For example, "The world is a hazardous place in which men are basically evil and dangerous."

[9] A sample from the intrinsic dimension: "My religious beliefs are what really lie behind my whole approach to life." And from the extrinsic: "What religion offers me most is comfort when sorrow and misfortune strike."

In analyzing the patterns of response to religious orientation, Allport and his colleagues discovered that there were actually three patterns of response: First, those who agreed with intrinsic items and disagreed with the extrinsic items were defined as consistently intrinsic. Second, those who agreed consistently with the extrinsic items and disagreed consistently with the intrinsic items were described as consistently extrinsic. Third, there was also a group which agreed with both the intrinsic and extrinsic items; they were termed indiscriminately proreligious. (Since Allport's sample was made up of churchgoers, the indiscriminately antireligious did not appear in his study.) The accompanying table shows both that the extrinsic type is more prejudiced than the intrinsic type and that the indiscriminate type is more prejudiced than either of the two consistent types. In further analysis Allport discovered that the more indiscriminate a person was in his religious attitudes, the higher his prejudice; and he concluded, "It can only mean that some functional relationship obtains between religious muddleheadedness (for that is what indiscriminate scores imply) and antagonism towards ethnic groups." [10]

Summarizing his argument, Allport contends that the person with an extrinsic religious orientation is using religion for his own needs; that someone who needs to be propped up by religion is also likely to need the support of prejudice. On the other hand, one who is able to make an overarching religious commitment is not likely to have the need for prejudice as a support for an insecure personality.

> . . . *a person with an extrinsic religious orientation is using his religious views to provide security, comfort, status, or social support for himself—religion is not a value in its own right, it serves other needs, and it is a purely utilitarian formation. Now prejudice too is a "useful" formation: it too provides security, comfort, status, and social support. A life that is dependent on the supports of extrinsic religion is likely to be dependent on the supports of prejudice, hence our positive correlations between the extrinsic orientation and intolerance. Contrariwise, the intrinsic religious orientation is not an instrumental device. It is not a mere mode of conformity, nor a crutch, nor a tranquilizer, nor a bid for status. All needs are subordinated to an overarching religious commitment. In internalizing the total creed of his religion the individual necessarily internalizes its values of humility, compassion, and love of neighbor. In such a life (where religion is an intrinsic and dominant value) there is no place for rejection, contempt, or condescension toward one's fellow man. Such is our*

10 Allport and Ross, op. cit., p. 439.

explanation for the relationship between extrinsic religion and prejudice, and between intrinsic religion and tolerance.[11]

There remains, then, the problem of the third category, the indiscriminately proreligious—those who are for both intrinsic and extrinsic religion—who think that "religious belief really lies behind their whole life" and that "there are many other important things in life besides religion" and that "religion is also an important place to formulate good social relationships." Allport suggests that the basic theme running through the response patterns of the indiscriminately proreligious is that "religion is O.K." He goes on: "It seems probable that people with undifferentiated styles of thinking (and feeling) are not entirely secure in a world that for the most part demands fine and accurate distinctions. The resulting diffuse anxiety may well dispose them to grapple onto religion and to distrust strange ethnic groups."[12] Thus the indiscriminately proreligious are given to undifferentiated thinking which leads readily to stereotyped overgeneralization, a failure to distinguish members of a minority group as individuals. "Thus, religion as a whole is good, a minority group as a whole is bad." Prejudice, according to the Allport approach, like tolerance is something that is deeply embedded in the personality structure and reflects a consistent cognitive style:

Both states of mind are enmeshed with the individual's religious orientation; one definable style marks the individual who is bigoted in ethnic matters and extrinsic in his religious orientation. Equally apparent is the style of those who are bigoted and at the same time indiscriminately proreligious. A relatively small number of people [about one third of the Allport sample] show an equally consistent cognitive style in their simultaneous commitment to religion as a dominant intrinsic value and to ethnic tolerance.[13]

Allport concludes his article with a word of warning:

Our research argues strongly that social scientists who employ the variable "religion" or "religiosity" in the future will do well to keep in mind the crucial distinction between religious attitudes that are intrinsic, extrinsic, *and* indiscriminately pro. *To know that a person is in some sense "religious" is not as important as to know the role religion plays in the economy of his life.*[14]

[11] Ibid., p. 441.
[12] Ibid., p. 441.
[13] Ibid., p. 442.
[14] Ibid., p. 442.

Not all analysts have kept this caution in mind. For example, Glock and Stark in their book *Religious Belief and Anti-Semitism* [15] make no use at all of the Allport distinction. Their book was published before the Allport article cited here, so they did not have available his explicit warning. Nonetheless, his earlier research ought to have persuaded them that (1) it is very easy to establish a relationship between religiousness and bigotry, and (2) the relationship is not between religion as such and bigotry as such but rather between a particular religious style and bigotry, both of which are related to an antecedent cognitive style.

The matter is not one merely of social scientific import. At a meeting convened to mark the publication of the Glock and Stark book, the present writer along with a number of other sociologists attempted to introduce the Allport distinction between intrinsic and extrinsic religion into a discussion which was made up for the most part of religious leaders and social actionists; however, this distinction was swept aside by many of those participating in the discussion on the grounds that the religious denominations had to assume responsibility for all of their members. A number of Catholic publications took the present writer to task as trying to provide religion with an escape from its responsibility for anti-Semitism by means of a "cop-out" justified by sociological jargon.

But in truth, religion cannot be held to responsibility for the cognitive styles of its members. The prejudiced personality does not result from religious teaching, though it may find reinforcement for its prejudice in some dimensions of religious teaching; its cognitive style is such that it can very easily tune out anything that the churches have to say about religious prejudice. A strong campaign against prejudice is very likely to have its major impact not on those who need religion as a social prop (and who, indeed, will not give it up as a social prop) but rather on those who are already intrinsically religious and hence least likely to be prejudiced. A campaign by the churches, therefore, against religious, racial, or ethnic prejudice is most likely to be successful precisely among those who don't need it and least likely to be successful among those who do. This is not to say that such a campaign should not be attempted, just that our expectations for its success should be moderate. Furthermore, no one would deny that religious denominations ought to examine their own consciences to see to what extent they are providing reinforcement for the bigoted personality. Surely, the behavior of the Christian churches in the past has been grist for the mill of anti-Semitism. On the other hand, a cor-

[15] Charles Y. Glock and R. Stark, *Religious Belief and Anti-Semitism* (New York: Harper & Row Publishers, 1966).

relation is not a cause nor is it a reinforcement, and it is something less than responsible to suggest that religion causes prejudice, particularly when those who make the kind of authentic religious commitment that their faith demands of them are, in fact, the least prejudiced. Nor does it seem reasonable to hold the church responsible for those of its members who refuse to or are incapable of taking religion seriously. The bigoted personality certainly tends to be religious in some sense, but he has a cognitive style which prevents him from being religious in the sense that is demanded by the high ideals of the world religions. And at the present stage of our understanding of the human personality, it does not seem possible for the religious denominations to do very much about changing that cognitive style inherited from his parents rather than from his religion.

It is well to remember, therefore, in considering both religious prejudice and religious conflict, that the conflict is most likely to occur among those who have strong personality needs for simple, unambiguous answers and for clear-cut distinctions between good and evil. Since these personality types are often driven by their own needs to become explicit spokesmen for their own respective religious denominations, they are the ones who in an age of religious controversy are most likely to dominate the public scene. What often passes as religious conflict is, in fact, merely a public battle between two extrinsically religious personalities—between two people who have strong personality needs for seeing the other as being bad and representing a bad group. One of the great advantages of interreligious dialogue as opposed to controversy is that it gives the intrinsically religious a chance to see how much they have in common, and takes the public discussion of religion out of the hands of those whose emotional disturbance leads precisely to a need for public disturbance.

Sources of Friction

Religious toleration in the United States has had a checkered career. Although the early colonists frequently fled from religious persecution in their home country, they were hardly inclined to concede religious freedom to dissenters in the new world. Congregationalism became the established church in most New England colonies as did Anglicanism in the southern colonies. Only in Maryland, for a time, and Pennsylvania was some semblance of religious freedom maintained. In Maryland the Act of Toleration was Catholic in origin, based on the practical need for the Catholic minority in the colony, sponsored by the Catholic Calvert family in England, to maintain freedom for itself. The Act was later repealed when Protestants gained political control of the State. Only in Quaker Pennsylvania did authentic toleration persist. The disestablishment of the Puritan churches in New England was completed only in the nineteenth century. In fact, as late as the 1870's the public schools in Boston remained open on Christmas on the grounds that it was a Popish feast.

The revivalist voluntarism of the Great Awakening, the Unitarian schism in New England, and the general good feeling toward minority religious groups because of their participation in the Revolutionary War led to a decline in discrimination at the end of the eighteenth and beginning of the nineteenth century. Catholics under the leadership of the Carroll family in Maryland came to be accepted as relatively harmless.

However, the tremendous influx of Catholic immigrants in the nineteenth century and the Jewish immigrants at the end of the nineteenth and beginning of the twentieth century changed the picture completely. Anti-Catholic bigotry flourished through successive nativist waves throughout the nineteenth century (occasionally reinforced by mistaken decisions by Catholic leadership) and persisted into the twentieth century. Jewish immigration turned the conflict situation into a three-cornered race, with Jewish-Catholic animosity probably becoming more serious, because Jews and Catholics were concentrated in the same urban population centers and because Jews brought from Europe fear of and resentment toward traditional anti-Jewish attitudes of Catholics, particularly in the countries of common origin such as Poland.

The situation became even more complicated in the middle of the twentieth century as Protestants became aware that the United States was no longer in any sense a Protestant country; and that indeed in some of the major population centers Protestants were distinctly a minority group with little political power, although still with considerable financial resources. In smaller towns and rural areas fundamentalist Protestantism frequently combined antiurbanism, anti-Catholicism, and anti-Semitism with distrust of Wall Street, intellectuals, and Communists; the result being a powerful radical right-wing fundamentalism which is still an important element of American culture and not without influence in both political parties.

Catholics, on the other hand, became fully conscious of their own political and increasing economic power. They frequently were accused of using that power to further the cause of their church against the rules of the American game of pluralism. Finally, the Jewish group, though numerically small (only 3 percent of the population), had become so successful in American society and occupied such key positions in important industries that it was able to insist not merely on toleration but on rights as a full-fledged partner in the American enterprise and to push its claims with increasing militancy and success. The combination of fear of the return of anti-Semitism and a new pride in Jewishness (both, in part at least, influenced by the horrors of the Second World War) reinforced the new Jewish militancy.

James S. Coleman, one of the most astute of the contemporary analysts of social conflict, summarizes the five attributes peculiar to religion which make it a potential source of the social conflict:

(a) *A major source of cleavage within religious groups is the private, personal nature of religion. Since any man can communicate with his own God or interpret the scriptures anew, a diverse array of beliefs can spring up, inhibited only by the fact that religious belief needs the company of at least a few if it is to survive.*

(b) *A second source of cleavage within religious groups, closely tied to the first, is the status and power rewards available to a leader by successfully establishing a new cult or sect. Given the private revelations which constitute the basis of religion, an ambitious leader has the possibility of breaking away and has much to gain from a successful break with the parent church (though, to be sure, much to lose if he fails).*

(c) *Religion's function of providing an* alternative *set of values creates a potential for conflict between religion and secular society. These values elevate in one's own eyes his religious group above its social position. Thus like a political ideology they provide the ferment for conflict by releasing members from the dominant values in society and providing an alternative set of values, and a group identity to go with them.*

(d) *Closely related to feelings of group identity is a pattern of* association. *Both induced by feelings of identity, and acting in turn to reinforce these feelings, the in-group associations of religion determine lines of social interaction to a degree surpassed only by a few other groupings, such as race. Lack of association with other groups generates the familiar feelings of distrust, fear, and hostility between groups, and these are the steppingstones to social conflict.*

(e) *A final source of religious diversity, cleavage, and conflict is the generational transmission of religious values and of personality derivative from these values. Thus the cultural heritage which is so much a part of us from early childhood has a high religious component.*[16]

Of these five factors peculiar to religion, four are relevant to American society. American religion is as private and as personal as it can be, but because of its very private nature it is something to which some Americans can be intensely committed and intensely suspicious of those who do not share the commitment. It is also a commitment for which in certain critical matters there are not only alternative sets of values but opposed value systems. But the most important of the factors which Coleman lists are the final ones. The religious groups in the United States are to a considerable extent identity-providing institutions. They constitute within the larger society several in-group associations which in turn generate distrust, fear, and hostility toward members of the out-group, a hostility which is particularly powerful because the felt differences are the result of very early socialization. Growing up religious in America means growing up not only as a member of one religious group but also as someone distinct from and distinctly in opposition to members of other religious groups. The fact that American religious groups are also ethnic groups and rooted in the ethnic origins of the various nationalities within the republic intensifies the potential for religious conflict. All things considered, what is surprising is not that there is religious conflict in American society but that for most of the history of the republic it has been kept within limits by the rules of the game—that is to say, the broad consensus existing among the members of all religious groups as to the nature of the operations of the American political process.

It is possible to outline six principal foci for interreligious conflicts in the United States. Perhaps the most critical area of division has to do with education, with the Catholic Church's insistence on maintaining a separate school system being the central issue. For many Protestants a separate school system appears as a symbol of refusal by Catholics to become wholly American. While the nature of opposition to Catholic schools varies greatly among Protestants, there are still some right-wing Protestant groups who suspect that a dangerous foreign doctrine (that is to say, un-American or un-Protestant doctrine) is being propagated within the Catholic schools. The root of such opposition is to be found early in the nineteenth century, and

[16] James S. Coleman, "Social Cleavage and Religious Conflict," *The Journal of Social Issues,* 12, No. 3, 1956, 56.

one need only glance at the nativist literature of that century to see how infuriated the nativists were by the sight of a Catholic school.

The Jewish group is less disturbed by the existence of Catholic schools (particularly since some Jews also may maintain Jewish parochial schools) than it is by the suspicion which it shares with Protestants that Catholics would like to raid the public treasury to support their school system. For many Jews this is viewed as a dangerous breach of the wall of separation between church and state, a wall which they think is essential to their preservation as members of a religious minority group which has always suffered when church and state were identified. Similarly, many American secularists who have great faith in the public school system as a homogenizing force in American society, argue that Catholic schools are divisive and that they separate Catholics from other Americans and hence preserve religious barriers which are a threat to the fabric of the society.

Not all Protestants, Jews, or secularists, of course, hold these positions, though many leaders are officially committed to such positions. Some of them are persuaded of the validity of the arguments; others, one suspects, are motivated more by latent anti-Catholic prejudices which have been rationalized by arguments. It should be pointed out, of course, that a substantial and articulate Catholic minority is as critical of the separate Catholic school system as are Protestants and Jews. However, the overwhelming majority of the Catholic population sees nothing un-American or divisive about its schools (and at the present time can cite empirical data to sustain their position). Further, a large proportion of the Catholic population resents the "double taxation" which is imposed on it to support both public and parochial schools, and wonders why every other major nation in the Western world can support parochial schools while the United States cannot. It is also argued that all Catholics are asking for is a small part of the vast saving to the nation which parochial schools make possible. They point out the staggering increase in school taxes that would be necessary in the large urban centers if there were no Catholic school system. At least some Catholics are fully prepared to use political power to obtain some sort of support for their schools.

While the conflict over the parochial schools seems to be quieting down somewhat, it is still by no means settled with some Protestants and Jews arguing that if Catholics are serious about interreligious dialogue they will abandon their claim for public support for their schools. Some Catholics, on the other hand, respond that if Protestants and Jews are serious about their desire for dialogue they will cease to discriminate against denominational and private schools. A gradual national consensus seems to be emerging in which certain kinds of support will be made available to Catholic (and other) parochial schools under certain sets of circumstances, in return for which Catholics will abandon their claim for more general support. Further, the suspicion and animosity toward Catholic schools seems to be declining. The *New Republic,* for example, some years ago endorsed the idea of federal help to parochial schools, arguing, as do many liberals at the present time, that the Catholic school system must be presumed to be a permanent part of the American educational environment and hence ought to be encouraged to become as good as possible. On the other hand, many Catholic critics of the schools feel that the parochial school system is and ought to be on the way out.

But the impartial observer (and he probably would have to be someone from another planet) would be struck by the irrationality of much of the discussion on the subject of parochial schools from both sides, and would suspect that the subject of the separate Catholic school system touches deep roots of resentment in the souls of many Americans. Education has as its object the passing on of values to the younger generation, and the religious school system is seen as essential by many to the passing on of religious values—values which are terribly important to some people and terribly dangerous to others—not merely because of their substantive content but, more important, because of their symbolic value as self-defining and self-localizing differences. Even if one did not know of the conflict over parochial schools in the United States, one could almost argue to such a conflict on a priori grounds.

Another aspect of the conflict over education is the question of religious instruction in the public schools. The current constitutional practice permits released-time instruction in religion so long as the instruction itself does not occur on the school premises and shared-time instruction in which some classes are taken in the public school and some in a private religious school. It does not permit religious instruction on the school premises and much less does it permit religious instruction, Bible reading, or praying as part of the regular public school curricula. It is still somewhat ambiguous as to the precise limitations on the teaching of religion as part of cultural education. The Catholic and Protestant position on these points have been reversed in the last century, for in the 1840's it was the Catholics who objected to the reading of the Protestant Bible in the public school; today, many Catholics lament the Godlessness in public schools, and many Protestants, Jews, and secularist groups tend to be adamantly opposed to any kind of religious activity in the public school system as a threat to the separation of church and state. Bible reading and praying apparently continue in many public schools in sections of the country where there is no one to bring a case to court in opposition to such practices. The basic axis of conflict on this issue tends to be between certain conservative Protestant groups favoring some sort of religious instruction in the public schools and liberal Protestants, Jews, and secularists opposing it, with many Catholics lending theoretical support to the conservative position, though one suspects that if in practice a form of nondenominational religious instruction or religious prayer were evolved for the public schools, there would be much Catholic opposition to the possibility of Catholic students having to participate in such classes. It is dubious, of course, whether Bible reading and praying and watered-down denominational religious instruction in public school classrooms would have much impact at all on the students, given the fact that even the highly elaborate parochial school system seems only really to have influence on those who are already disposed to the influence by the family environment. But such an argument does not persuade those for whom the question of religious instruction in the public schools is an important symbolic issue; one around which many of their dissatisfactions and suspicions of members of the out-groups can be focused.

A second very sensitive area of religious conflict focuses on the subject of sex, with the official Catholic positions on abortion, birth control, and divorce creating considerable antagonism among Protestants, Jews, and secularists. (Though many Protestants and some Jews would side with Catholics on the question of abortion, and some of each group also on the other two questions.) Catholic opposition to divorce reform, legalizing abortion, and particularly to the use of birth control measures in both foreign aid and domestic welfare programs, has led many non-Catholics to charge the Church with using political power to impose its own moral viewpoint on those who do not accept the viewpoint. Furthermore, the activities of such organizations as the now inactive National Office of Decent Literature and the Legion of Decency (recently renamed the National Catholic Office for Motion Pictures) have also led to the charge that Catholics wish to censor the mass media in order to impose their standards of sexual morality on non-Catholics. Within the Catholic group there are many differences of opinion. The Catholic liberals are highly critical of the Legion (though much less so of its successor) and of the NODL. They argue that at least as far as birth control and divorce go, the Church has no justification for attempting to interfere in the political decision-making process. Other Catholics maintain that the efforts of motion picture, magazine, and book censorship are directed only at the Catholic population and furthermore that Catholics ought not to be expected to pay taxes to support welfare ventures with which they cannot, in conscience, agree. In response, it is objected that both the Legion of Decency and the NODL have brought considerable pressure to bear on the industry not to violate Catholic standards and that birth control and divorce are rights which many non-Catholic Americans think are inalienable.

The issues are clearly complicated and the general tendency has been for the Catholics to become increasingly moderate in their position, realizing that in some matters of sexual morality they may represent a distinct minority of the American population and will only harm themselves by trying to impose their standards on the whole population, especially when some of these standards (such as birth control) themselves are apparently undergoing drastic change. Most recently many Catholic leaders have been in the forefront of opposition to the liberalization of divorce laws, an opposition which has infuriated some Protestants, Jews, and liberal humanists—and a few liberal Catholics. On the other hand, some Catholics are not hesitant to point out that anti-birth control legislation which still exists was enacted not by Catholics but by Protestant fundamentalist groups in the last century.

The conflict between Catholics and non-Catholics over matters of sexual morality is probably more intense in the United States than any place in the world (with the possible exception of Italy). Part of the explanation is that in the United States the Catholic Church's teachings on divorce and birth control have acquired an important symbolic value that it may not have in other nations, an importance that was reinforced by the fact that the early birth control campaign seemed to Catholic immigrants as an attempt to reduce their political power. While the issue is losing some of its intensity with the passage of time and the change in the Church's posture on the questions of sex, it can still be a powerfully disruptive force in the larger society.

Third, there is also considerable controversy on the subject of separation of church and state. Secularists, most Jews, and many liberal Protestants, as well as a handful of liberal Catholics have questioned tax exemption for religious institutions, the religious chaplains in the military, the religious motto for the country, the celebration of Christmas in public schools or on public property, and almost any religious activity that the government might conceivably be imagined as involving itself with. Protestants were particularly upset some time ago at the possibility of a Catholic ambassador to the Vatican, and Jews tend to be incensed at Christmas cribs on public property and Christmas carols and celebrations in public schools. Some Christians, on the other hand, argue that Jews and secularists wish to prevent the overwhelming Christian majority of the population from celebrating the

Christmas feast. Such questions that have far more important symbolic content than they have substantive content. The fierceness with which some of the controversies rage is hardly appropriate to the importance of the issues, either for the commonweal of the whole society or for the religious commitments of its various members. It should really matter very little to Christians whether they can sing Christmas carols in school or not. And as Norman Podhoretz has pointed out, even if Jews succeed in having Christmas carols banished in the schools, they will hardly be able to banish them from the radio or television. We do not intend to argue that the issues are completely without substantive content, but it must be noted that the separation of church and state as well as religious education and sexual morality do not present problems that are insoluble, at least so far as their substance goes in American society. But the symbolic intensity of these issues impedes a practical solution at the present time.

Fourth, the questions of religion and public morality also contribute to interreligious conflict in the United States. Protestants argue that Catholic political leaders are frequently corrupt, permit (if they do not encourage) graft, and are closely allied with gangster elements. It is further argued that these Catholic political leaders who are so devout religiously are also politically and morally corrupt and grow rich by stealing from the public till. There is, at least at the present time, probably little grounds for such suspicions.

Some Protestant groups further resent the fact that Catholics do not support legislation regulating the consumption of alcohol and the prohibition of gambling. Catholics, on the other hand, have replied that the political corruption certain Catholic leaders have permitted was the only way the Catholic population could wrestle some kind of economic power for itself away from the Protestant establishment which does not want Catholics to be successful in American society; and that clean government or good government frequently meant nothing more than government which discriminated against ethnic immigrants. Further, it might be argued that Catholics have had no monopoly on political corruption in the United States. There seems to be an inclination on the part of some Americans to think that Irish corruption is worse than WASP corruption.

They also respond that any gambling legislation, or alcohol prohibition legislation is an attempt to impose private morality on the public far more extensive than any Catholic efforts in matters sexual. Most liberal Protestants would agree with Catholics on this point, although they still harbor an intense dislike for the Catholic practice of "Holy Bingo." Both sides are moving away from attempts to impose particularistic moral principles on the whole society through general legislation, but they are moving, it must be confessed, with some reluctance and with considerable looking-back-over-their-shoulders at the historic and symbolic origins of these controversies.

Fifth, many non-Catholics are particularly suspicious of the influence of the Catholic Church on political leaders who are themselves Catholic. While this suspicion surges to the surface on special issues, such as education or sex, it is also latent beneath the surface on many other matters. Non-Catholics suspect the mayors of many Catholic cities of being in constant communication with the bishops of these cities, just as the aldermen and precinct captains are in cahoots with the local monsignor. Catholic political leaders lean over backward not to be influenced by religious leaders, but the suspicions of the past do not easily die.

Within this same category of criticism it is frequently argued, on occasion by Catholics themselves, that while Catholics tend to be members of the Democratic party, they are also anti-Communist, conservative, and unconcerned about problems of social justice for other disadvantaged groups. Thus one Catholic author (Michael Novak) argued before the 1964 election that a massive Catholic defection to Goldwater was possible because of the conservative and anti-Communist political stance of Catholics. However, statistical data do not support such a contention, and on the vast variety of political issues, American Catholics are, if anything, more likely to be on the liberal side than are American Protestants, though less likely than are American Jews. Catholics, for their part, are frequently inclined to be suspicious of Jews and Protestants, particularly the liberal variety, as being soft on Communism or immoral (which generally means sexually immoral), and likely to contribute to undermining the political structure of the American nation by such "softness." In the classic phrase of Daniel Patrick Moynihan, speaking of the Joseph McCarthy era, "If Harvard men were to be investigated, Fordham men would do the investigating." These issues are all quite diffuse and vague but do not for these reasons lack a substantial emotional intensity. While the intensity may be declining as the immigrant era comes to an end, it has not vanished from the scene completely.

The sixth and final area of tension to be described is that created by the state of Israel. Most American Jews are not Zionists; there is, nonetheless, broad sympathy in American Judaism for the Israeli state. They suspect that gentiles, particularly Catholic gentiles, are not as enthusiastic as they might be about the existence of Israel. Thus, at the time of the most recent Arab-Israeli war, many Jewish leaders were infuriated at the failure of Catholics and Protestants to leap to the defense of the Israeli side, and have, privately if not publicly, suggested that the failure was equivalent to the failure of those leaders who stood by while Hitler exterminated six million Jews. Some gentiles have responded that they fail to see the similarity between the two situations, and that opposition to anti-Semitism and, indeed, even enthusiasm about the Israeli experiment do not necessarily commit Christians to supporting Israeli foreign and military policy decisions. It has also been argued that if support for Israel is a precondition to interreligious dialogue, then so ought to be support for the liberation of Catholic countries in Eastern Europe. However, if the truth be told, there are at least some elements within the Catholic and Protestant populations that have an extreme distaste for Israel and feel that the Arabs are merely fighting for homes from which they were unfairly ejected in 1948. One might be inclined to suspect that the state of Israel is important in the controversy between Jews and gentiles in the United States more for its symbolic than for its real value. Unquestionably, there can be important substantive differences of opinion on American policy toward Israel, but these substantive issues probably pale into insignificance compared to Israel as a focus for the mutual suspicions and hostilities that exist between Jew and gentile in the United States.

Jews Versus Catholics

We have suggested throughout this chapter that the interreligious controversies which rage in the United States are important not so much in their substantive content but rather in their utility as symbols around which the members of a religious group can rally in their loyalties to one another and their animosities to those who are different from them. In view of our discussion of the Allport article we would say that religious controversies are particularly important to those who are indiscriminately proreligious. Even if all Protestants, Catholics, and Jews in the United States were "intrinsic" in their religious orientation, the differences would still exist, but they would hardly consume as much time, energy, and violent emotion as they do. For the personality which has tendencies toward rigidity (and most of us have some such tendencies) religious controversy is a strong temptation, and in a society where religious differences are extremely important as a means of self-definition, the temptation becomes exceedingly powerful. The alternative to the controversy, however, is not no controversy but dialogue. Controversy intends either to make converts or at least to win arguments in the public forum while dialogue seeks only to understand the other and to enable the other to understand oneself. The social structure of the United States, based as it is on an official commitment to pluralism and to the political process, tends to favor dialogue. But the paranoid style of much American political discussion and the rigid personalities of many American citizens make dialogue difficult. There is a wide tendency to believe, with characteristic American optimism, that "things are getting better," that dialogue is becoming easier. However, as we shall see, progress is not uniform. Antagonism between Protestants and Catholics is declining, as is anti-Semitism among Catholics and Protestants and anti-Protestantism among Jews. However, anti-Catholicism among Jews seems to be increasing, so that between the years of 1952 and 1965 Jews and Catholics passed each other on measures of antipathy toward the other, with Jews going up and Catholics coming down (see Table 21).

In 1965, Jews were far more likely than they were in 1952, for example, to say they thought their own group was prejudiced against Catholics and that Catholics were prejudiced against Jews. They were also far more likely to express the feeling that Catholics do not respect Jewish beliefs, that Catholics do not want to intermarry, that Catholic priests are not intelligent and do not promote understanding or civic cooperation, and that Catholic magazines are not fair. On five of these seven subjects, the Catholics' attitude toward Jews had become more favorable. Altogether the responses suggest that the two groups have switched places. In 1952, Catholics had a more negative attitude toward Jews than Jews did toward Catholics; by 1965, the reverse seemed to be true.

What is even more troubling is that this apparent increase in anti-Catholic feeling appeared to be concentrated among the younger and the more religious Jews. Moreover, the negative feelings occurred most often among the college-educated; they evidently did not stem from ignorance or lack of sophistication, and could not be counted on to go away in time.

Let me stress that we must be very cautious in interpreting this apparent change in Jewish attitudes toward Catholics. The Jewish sample of the 1952 survey was quite small, and though the size of the 1965 survey was large enough to permit some confidence in the accuracy of the data, the findings are nonetheless highly tentative and must be viewed with considerable reservation.

If, however, our sample is representative of the Jewish population, and *if* it continues to be representative when the Jews are divided into educational and age subgroups, then not only is there an increase in anti-Catholic feeling among American Jews, but this increase is

Table 21   Attitudes of Jews and Catholics Toward Each Other, 1952 and 1965

| | Changes in attitudes of | | | |
| | Catholics toward Jews | | Jews toward Catholics | |
	Favorable	*Unfavorable*	*Favorable*	*Unfavorable*
Think "we" are prejudiced against "them"	7%	—	—	15%
Think "they" are prejudiced against "us"	6	—	—	14
They interfere with our liberties	1	—	—	6
They are unfair in business	8	—	2%	—
They are dishonest in public office	5	—	—	8
They don't respect our belief	—	5%	—	10
Would vote for one of them as President	26	—	27	—
They would not want to intermarry with us	17	—	—	17
Employers in their group would discriminate against us	6	—	—	17
They stick together too much	5	—	—	6
They are getting too much power	21	—	6	3
Their clergymen are not intelligent	0	0	—	—
Their clergymen don't promote understanding	3	—	—	17
Their clergymen don't promote civic cooperation	4	—	—	13
Their clergymen don't set a good personal example	1	—	—	5
They try to influence the press	5	—	—	7
Their magazines are not fair	2	—	—	12
Have had unpleasant experience, causing dislike, with one of them	1	—	—	4

The figures in column 1 represent an increase in favorable attitudes held by Catholics towards Jews. Figures in column 2 indicate an increase in unfavorable attitudes of Catholics held towards Jews. The figures in column 3 indicate an increase in favorable attitudes held by Jews towards Catholics and figures in column 4 indicate an increase in unfavorable attitudes held by Jews towards Catholics.

From Marty, Rosenberg, Greeley, op. cit.

most marked among college graduates and younger Jews and therefore seems likely to grow worse instead of better.

Indeed, if these phenomena are valid representations of reality, a very notable problem in Catholic-Jewish relationships may be facing us in years to come—particularly when Catholics, whose attitudes toward Jews appear to have improved substantially in the last ten years, discover that the reverse has happened among Jews. Such a discovery might lead to a resurgence of anti-Jewish feeling among Catholics; and the widespread optimism that an era of religious goodwill in the United States is about to begin may prove unjustified. A minimal conclusion from these findings is that considerably more research is necessary on the subject of Catholic-Jewish relationships. Perhaps it also would not be inappropriate to suggest that Catholic and Jewish agencies join together to study the relationships between their two groups.

Summary

Whatever one makes of the changes for the past fifteen years, it must still be observed that no American religious denomination has a monopoly on either fanaticism or open-mindedness, and all have been guilty to some extent of ethnocentric behavior. What else could be expected in a society where religions also "double in brass" as ethnic groups? Some of the controversies are subsiding because the issues on which they were based are no longer real issues, even symbolically. Others are subsiding because it becomes obvious that compromise solutions have to be found—obvious to all save the most bigoted. Still others are declining in intensity because men of goodwill (Allport's intrinsically religious men) are striving for evermore adequate understanding of one another. Nevertheless, new issues for controversy are arising as the major partners of the American pluralistic experiment readjust positions one to another. In the final analysis, one can be hopeful of a long-range decline in interreligious antagonism, but it is idle to suppose that religious controversy will ever vanish, given the fact that ours is a denominational society, that is to say, a society where the meaning function of religion is strongly reinforced by and even to some considerable extent shaped by the belonging function. It is important for sophisticated Americans at least to realize the ethnic and ethnocentric origins of much of the arguing in which they engage. They also should understand that, while a symbol can be terribly important, content is more important in the long run, and that there is much common content among all the major religioethnic groups in American society.

Chapter 10

Growing Up Religious

In this chapter we propose to summarize much of what we said in previous chapters of the book by describing in broad outline how a young American acquires the system of core values around which he organizes his life. In this way we will see how the general religious values of the whole culture as well as the specific values of his own denomination mesh with one another into a reasonably coherent system. Furthermore, we will come to understand that since these values, both general and peculiar to his own denomination, are part of the very early socialization process and extremely important to his self-definition, they become so much a part of him that he is unlikely to change his religious denomination as his life goes on.

A Pattern of Values

The basic ethical values that a child learns in American society do not differ greatly among the various denominations. The young American is expected to be committed to honesty, fairness, diligence, sobriety, personal kindness, curiosity, optimism, and respect for the American political system. He is also, as Thomas Luckmann points out, expected to honor autonomy, self-expression, self-realization, mobility, sexuality, and family. He is expected to be competitive, risk-taking, eager to learn, but also cooperative, careful, and eager not to learn too much, for, after all, while young America is expected to be intelligent, it might be risky for him to become too much of an egghead. Within the various denominations there are certain areas of special emphasis. Catholics may be taught the need for obedience to the Church and also certain special attitudes toward sex. Some young Protestants will undergo a socialization experience which puts extra emphasis on the evils of smoking, drinking, and gambling, and on the obligations of civic responsibility. And most Jews will learn the need for personal generosity and the obligation to be Jewish. However, it ought to be emphasized that these and other variations among denominations, while they do produce personality types that are in many respects different, they also produce a general population which has far more in common in the way of ethical values than it has differences.

There are also certain basic doctrinal values that all Americans learn. They learn first of all the benefits of the American way, political and economic. They may be told that there are many things wrong with American society, but nonetheless the tremendous physical and economic benefits of American society are so obvious that parents hardly need to observe that children ought to be grateful for the greatest affluence that the world has ever known. Central to this cult of the American way of life is the civil religion which represents the sacred element in the general value commitment which most Americans share. As we noted in a previous chapter, this religion is constructed around the office of the presidency and the ceremonial attached to the office—the Declaration of Independence, the Constitution, the Supreme Court, the national monuments in Washington, and to some extent, Congress. It has its great heroes—Washington, Lincoln, and Jefferson; and its great myths—the Revolutionary and Civil wars; and its feast days—Memorial Day, Independence Day, Labor Day, Armistice Day (or, as it is now called, Veterans Day), and Christmas thrown in as a partially national, partially familial feast. This civil religion provides the ritual and the sense of sacredness that is required around which the commitments of most of the population can be arranged.

Secondly, the young American learns that he must be grateful to God for the American way, both on the special Thanksgiving feast and at other times in the year, particularly when he says grace before meals. Even though he says it rarely, it's still an important ritual reserved for symbolic occasions, either public or private. In all likelihood, most young Americans learn of God for the first time as the object of gratitude for the American way. It might be remarked that gratitude is not an undignified stance for a human being to take so long as it is authentic gratitude and not self-justifying by assuming that God has given us only what we deserve and that the abundance we have is a reward for merit. Unfortunately, it seems fair to assume that there may be just a little *hubris* in the American posture of gratitude to the Divinity.

Thirdly, the young American learns that religion is part of the American way; that God, church, and piety are essential to being a respectable and responsible citizen. While not everyone goes to church and not everyone belongs to church, nevertheless, going to and belonging to the church of one's choice is the valued, responsible, and respectable way to behave, particularly if one takes seriously the ethical commitments to diligence and to upward mobility. Religion does not guarantee respectability, and yet it is hard to be respectable if one does not have a religion, at least in most segments of American society.

Religion is also advanced to the young American as a means of explaining ultimate questions and responding to crises that produce a challenge to the stable order and operation of the world and of his life. Birth, growth, marriage, death, sickness, suffering, success, and joy are all clothed in a religious orientation so that they may be seen as part of a general pattern of events. It should be noted that the American's view of religion tends to be rather optimistic and that the American believes in progress, both for himself and for the society, so long as the progress is not too rapid.

The young American further is informed that religion is a basis on which to root his ethical commitments, and it is almost indispensable as a means for passing on his ethical commitments to his own children. He cannot, therefore, be honest or diligent, or open or optimistic, or self-fulfilled or a dedicated member of the family without having all these riches rooted in a commitment to God, to church, and to piety. He who is not a believing man has no guarantee that he or his children will be moral men.

It will be seen that the values, both ethical and doctrinal, described in the previous paragraphs, are a rather high level of generality and tend to be vaguely Protestant in their orientation. The young Frenchman or Spaniard or Italian would have the Western value traditions filtered through to him in a manner rather different from that to be found operative in the United States. Furthermore, an American Catholic would be likely to have much more in common with his Protestant counterpart in this early value socialization experience than he would his religious counterpart from Spain or Italy.

But there is more to the early value socialization experience. For the young American also learns that he is one of the "we" who stands over against the "they." There are many different kinds of "we's" just as there are many different kinds of "they's." One "we" group is social class (though he may not learn the words until he gets to college); another "we" is the region of the country or even the region of the city in which he lives; still another may be his political party or his ethnic group. But an extremely important "we" is his religious denomination. The denominational "we" is experienced by the young American as a subgroup within American society that has its own traditions, its own culture, its own shared experiences of the past, and its own values, all of which it is highly important to preserve. Because "we" are all Americans, "we" trust "them," at least up to a point, even though "we" have certain suspicions about "their" leadership and think that some of "their" ideas are pernicious. "We" may associate with "them" and on occasion do so enthusiastically, but "we" also realize that "we" must be cautious in our associations with "them" and that it is much better, most of the time at least, to associate with "our own kind."

"We" can remember what "they" did to us in the past; "we" are aware of the strange things that "they" do now, which seem to us to be pagan or barbaric; and "we" are just a bit suspicious of some of the goals of the leadership and certain of the business or political or social practices of most of "their" membership. Even though "we" work with "them" and have "them" into our house, still "we" are more comfortable with our own kind because "we" believe in the same things and "they" don't share our values.

Furthermore, we must be especially wary of getting involved in romantic entanglements or, God save us, marrying them. If this should happen we can adjust to it, of course, either by maintaining our own religious commitment despite the marriage, or, if our commitment is weak, modifying it to harmonize with the other's commitment. But if we do this we are nonetheless not being true to our own tradition and at least in some instances actually betraying the tradition.

We ought to be active in our own groups, both as a means of being loyal to the tradition, of keeping the tradition going, and also of being a loyal American, because our particular tradition is seen as one of the patterns, and probably the best pattern, for being American. In practice, therefore, we are active in our churches both as a means of associating with our own kind and also avoiding too intimate association with others. We reinforce those symbolic differences between us and others that happen to be important in our society at the time we are alive. These symbolic differences are important not so much because of their doctrinal content but because they differentiate those who are committed to our traditions from those who are committed to another tradition. Before the changes of the Vatican Council, abstaining from meat on Friday was a highly important distinction between Catholic and non-Catholic, not because the prohibition was near the core of the Catholic tradition (which it surely was not) but because it was an excellent differentiation between Catholics and other Christians who represented a tradition with which Catholics as a matter of self-definition did not wish to be identified. Similarly, the Latin language, which has recently shown itself to be all too dispensable, was important for a long time and maintained a differentiation between Catholics and Protestants. The Jewish Feast of Hanukkah, of relatively minor importance in the elite Jewish tradition, nonetheless acquires considerable importance in the American environment as the Jewish response to the Christian feast of Christmas. There is nothing in Catholic doctrine which would incline Catholic graduates to overchoose specialization in English or history or political science or law in college, but there is much in the history of Irish American Catholicism that would explain this tendency. There is little in the way of religious difference that would explain why Protestants overchoose the biological sciences while Catholics and Jews underchoose them, but there is a great deal in the historical experience and geographical location of the three religious groups which would explain it. A larger proportion of the Protestants, for example, live on farms than do the more urban Jews and Catholics. Nor are the differences in sexual morality between Catholics and non-Catholics as important in Europe as they are in the United States, but they assume importance in the American environment precisely because they serve to define the "we" over against the "they."

Identifying One's Place in Society

We are arguing in this chapter that the differences—doctrinal, ethical, and cultic—which are emphasized among the various American denominations are to a considerable extent shaped by the fact that the denominations are superethnic groups providing means of identification and location within the larger American social structure. Loyalty to the religioethnic denomination comes first. This loyalty in its turn involves loyalty to the denomination's tradition, and particularly to those elements of the tradition which for reasons of history, geography, culture, or social structure, most sharply differentiate this tradition in the American experience from other traditions. But at the same time the traditions are all perceived, to a greater or lesser extent, as valid patterns of being American, and each in its own way is conceded to be reinforcement for the more general commitments that most if not all Americans accept.

If this description is correct, it means that a young American grows up perceiving his society in terms both of unity and diversity; yet the diversity is organized, and, indeed organized to some considerable extent along the lines of religious denominationalism. In some respects the denominational lines of diversity correspond with the lines of social class, geography, and nationality background, but there is a sufficient overlap to prevent the polarization of society into rigid, religioethnic sectors. Thus Catholics tend to be Democratic but there are many Republican Catholics. Southerners tend to be Baptist, but there are also southern Methodists, southern Episcopalians, and some southern Catholics. Jews tend to live in the Northeast and particularly in New York City, but there are also substantial Jewish settlements in cities such as Cleveland, Chicago, and Minneapolis, and a sprinkling of Jews in the rest of the country. Most Jews are rich, or at least well-to-do; most Negroes are poor; and Baptists have far less money than do Jews, at least on the average. But some Jews drive taxicabs and some Baptists are millionaires.[1] Episcopalians and Congregationalists and Presbyterians are overrepresented in the national government, but an occasional Catholic millionaire can be president.

It is idle to ask whether religion or nationality or social class or geography is the most important component of the American social structure. It would be far more relevant to ask under what circumstances and for which people which of these components become most important. What happens, for example, to a well-to-do Catholic Republican living in southern California when a Catholic Democrat from Boston runs for the presidency? Which one of his various conflicting loyalties becomes operative? It hardly need be asserted that religion is a terribly important loyalty in American society since many previous research publications have established this fact. What we are arguing in the present volume is that religion is a means of social differentiation, and as a modality of participation in a larger American society it is a manifestation of the fact that America is a denominational society—that is to say, a society in which denominational loyalty profoundly affects much of what a young person learns as he grows up, many of the decisions he will make in his life, and the kinds of relationships he will have with other Americans. It also means that loyalty to the religious tradition, particularly to those doctrinal, ethical, and cultic elements which are of major symbolic importance in the context of American society will be extremely important to the young American for his becoming himself and being an American. Devotional practice and doctrinal orthodoxy have persisted in American

[1] One is reminded of the famous joke about the University of Chicago that in the time of Robert Hutchins it was an institution where Baptists' money was paid to agnostic professors to teach Roman Catholic philosophy to Jewish students.

society when they have faltered in other countries precisely because sociologically and psychologically such attitudes and activities are important to being a member of the American society.

Must One Be a Martyr to Be Religious?

As we have noted in previous chapters, some religious leaders, both lay and clerical, are considerably upset about the phenomenon we have described in the previous paragraph. From their point of view it is somehow wrong for religion to be part of being an American and for religious orthodoxy and devotionalism to be in part attributable to the workings of social forces. For such religionists to discover that Emile Durkheim was right seems to be sufficient grounds to dismiss American religion as cultural religion, implying that if religion is part of the culture, it somehow ceases to be authentic religion.

But it seems to us that such critics miss the point entirely. No society could possibly be neutral on the subject of religion, civil libertarian organizations to the contrary notwithstanding. For reasons of history, geography, culture, and social structure, American society happens to be favorably disposed toward religion. It makes it easier for Americans to be religious. One would think that most religionists would rejoice at this fact, but many of the more liberal ones apparently do not, for if it is easier to be religious, somehow religion seems to lose its authenticity. Apparently, then, religion is only authentic when it exists in the face of the most violent kind of opposition from culture and society. One is not honest or authentic in one's religion, apparently, unless one is a martyr.

But there may be an alternative view. The cultural and social structure of American society does make possible, perhaps, more religious hypocrisy than would be found in other countries. It also may encourage a great deal of religious mediocrity and saddle the churches with apathetic, conservative members who have no interest in important religious issues; but at the same time, the fact that there are strong religious denominations with elaborate institutional systems has, as we have noted before in this book, made possible a great deal more enthusiasm, zeal, and scholarship in matters religious than one can find in almost any Western society at the present time. The choice for the religious groups in the Western world seems to be between a society that is committed to religion but is relatively mediocre religiously and one which is apathetic and indifferent to any and all religious activity. Some religionists apparently would prefer the latter, arguing that in such situations the church's activity becomes authentically missionary. But it must be acknowledged that in the so-called missionary countries of the West, the imaginative and vigorous missionary movements have been largely unsuccessful, because most of those at whom the movements have been directed have not been particularly interested in listening.

Prophecy, witness, zeal, charity are terribly difficult to measure, but it is at least tenable to suggest that the denominational society for all its weaknesses and failings seems to produce more of these phenomena than does the indifferent society. For all its many weaknesses, religion in the United States is still a more vital and authentic force than it is in England, France, or even Italy.

But in the final analysis such a discussion is largely pointless. Cultural religion, at least if the assumptions in this book are correct, does not seem likely to waste away. It is rooted deep in the American past and in the historical, social, and cultural experiences of those who belong to the various religious traditions. However authentic or unauthentic it may be, it has been around for a long time, and there is no statistical data which we have been able to uncover to suggest that it will not be around for a long time to come.

Summary

A young American acquires his religious perspectives in a way not unlike the manner in which he learns his language. His fundamental belief system is absorbed from his parents not so much by listening to what they say as by imitating what they do. In all likelihood he acquires a good deal of his religious perspective at the same time and in the same set of experiences as he acquires his sexual identity—that is to say, as part of working out the complex set of relationships in the primordial triad of mother, father, and child. Not only does he learn a fundamental world view, certain basic doctrinal formulations and political perspectives and cultic practices which are part of his religious tradition, he also acquires certain attitudes and habits which, while they are not necessarily linked with his tradition, have become linked in the historical and social circumstances of American life. (There is no basic reason why Catholics should be more likely to be Democrats than Protestants, and Jews more likely than Catholics, but the American social experience does create this linkage which, to some extent, is passed on as part of the religious socialization process, however unconscious the linkage may be.) For a wide variety of reasons, it is relatively easy to grow up as a moderately religious person in American society and relatively difficult to be totally unreligious. That is not to say, that a young person cannot be raised an atheist or become an atheist during his formative years. But religion is so much a part of both the self-definition and the social location of most Americans that the strain and the thrust is toward some kind of conscious and explicit religious affiliation. This affiliation may or may not lead to the kind of authentic religious faith and practice which would please those whose job it is to preach the ideals of religion, but at least in most sectors of American society there is little pressure to be irreligious.

Chapter 11

Theories and Predictions

The present volume has been an exercise in sociological theorizing in the sense that the author has tried to use the tools of the theories of the sociology of religion to explain the state of religion in American society. It has not been very high-level theorizing, certainly not comparable to that of Professor Parsons or Professor Luckmann; nor has it been even in the middle range of Professor Merton or Peter Blau. At best, it has been an attempt to use the theories of other men to understand a little better the complexities of American religious phenomena. It is not our intention, however, to apologize for such low-level theorizing, because the lower the level the more likely it is to lead to hypotheses that can be tested. That, one assumes, is what sociology is all about. One whole set of hypotheses are listed in the concluding section (ten of them, in fact), and only the course of history will enable them to be adequately tested. One could be much more precise, however, and say that if the 1952–1965 time series study we referred to in Chapter 6 were to be financed once again by the *Catholic Digest* in, let us say, 1975, the trends reported there and more completely in *What Do We Believe?* [1] would not be appreciably changed. We are inclined to think that such a prediction is a braver one than most sociological theorists would make, especially since it is very likely that the *Catholic Digest* or some similar journal *will* repeat the 1965 study in 1975 when, hopefully, there will still be some people reading the present volume.

However, the 1952–1965 trends were more the sources for the theorizing in the present volume than the results of that theorizing, so it would be appropriate before concluding this book to list some

---

[1] Andrew M. Greeley, Martin Marty, and Stuart Rosenberg, *What Do We Believe?* Des Moines, Ia.: Meredith Corporation, 1967).

other hypotheses derived—more or less rigorously—from our theorizing that have been tested or at least can be tested in the future. We will, then, attempt to evolve four different sets of hypotheses—two which are readily testable against data that is already available and two more which could be tested without too much difficulty in future research.

Apostasy

One would predict that in a denominational society, apostasy levels would be low, and that there would be little in the way of change over time in such rates. One would further predict that apostasy would represent a profound act of alienation, because it would involve breaking out of the social structure into which one had been socialized. It would therefore be in the denominational society a highly individualistic act of revolt, rooted more in personality variables than in social structural or cultural variables.

To some extent this prediction was not made completely independent of the data, since the material reported on graduate students' religious behavior in Chapter 6 of the present volume would lead us to believe that apostasy rates would be comparatively low. However, three different bodies of research done after the speculations in this volume were begun confirm our predictions about apostasy, particularly the predictions about social and personal alienation.

With the aid of a grant from the Carnegie Commission on the Future of Higher Education, the National Opinion Research Center in 1968 made a new study of its sample of June 1961 college graduates. Three different studies were made of this group, one in 1961, another in 1964, and most recently one in 1968. Although the main concern of the research was the attitudes of the alumni toward their higher educational experience, a secondary analysis of the data enabled additional information to be obtained about religious behavior among the young people who are now for the most part approaching their thirtieth birthday. We asked what patterns of apostasy and/or return to religion have taken place since 1964.

We can summarize the net gains and losses of the three major religious groupings (shown on Table 22). Twenty-nine percent of those who were born Protestant relinquished their Protestant affiliation some time between their childhood and 1968, a figure arrived at by totaling the leavers in all three studies. Seven percent, however, had returned by 1968, and Protestantism acquired 5 percent addi-

Table 22   Net and Gross Loss for Major American Religious Groupings

| | Original Denomination | | |
	Protestant	Catholic	Jew
Stayers	71%	85%	81%
Gross loss	29	15	19
	100	100	100
	(4,800)	(1,780)	(509)
Returners	7	2	10
Net loss after returners	22	13	9
Converts *	5	10	2
Net loss after returners and converts	17	3	7

* Number of converts from other groups as a proportion of size of original group.

tional membership through conversions, reducing the net loss to 17 percent. The Catholics with a gross loss of 15 percent recouped rather little (2 percent) through returners, but offset most of the loss through a 10 percent gain because of conversions, while Jews reduced their gross loss of 19 percent to 7 percent, mostly through a substantial return of those who at one point had relinquished Jewish affiliation.

Protestants, the largest religious group in the society, suffered the heaviest losses. Catholics and Jews, perhaps because of their minority group status, had a greater retentiveness, with Catholics replenishing most of their losses by conversions and Jews by the return of those who at one time had not thought of themselves as Jews.

As one might expect, the major gains of the two gentile religious groups involve very few conversions from Judaism (Table 23). Three-

Table 23   Sources of Conversions for Protestants and Catholics

| Original Denomination | New Denomination | |
	Protestant	Catholic
Protestant	—	83%
Catholic	28%	—
Jew	1	4
Other	47	3
None	24	10
Total	100	100
	(166)	(129)

quarters of those who now are Protestants were either "others" or "none." In both these instances, the "converts" were in all likelihood young people affiliated with small religious groups in the Protestant tradition who were not willing to describe themselves as Protestants until they joined a major Protestant denomination; or they were people who came from a vaguely Protestant but nondenominational background and hence listed themselves in their earlier affiliations as "none." Catholics, on the other hand, attract most of their converts from among the Protestants.

Protestant leavers (Table 24) were more likely to be male in 1961 though not in 1968. They were somewhat younger than the general Protestant group, and in 1961 were also somewhat more likely

Table 24   Character of Protestant Leavers (1961 and 1968) and Returners (1968)

| | Leavers | | Returners | Protestant Graduates |
	1961	1968	1968	As a Whole
Male	73	55	60	54
Over 31 (in 1968)	24	24	24	29
Father college graduate	38	27	42	31
5 years in graduate school	31	35	10	8
In good health	12	29	9	28
High on rebel index:				
1961	12	13	14	10
1964	10	28	15	9
Very happy	24	35	40	42
Liberal Democrat	17	20	23	14
Quality graduate school	15	26	18	19
N	(240)	(125)	(201)	(4,800)

to come from a college-educated background. They were much more likely (31 and 35 percent as against 8 percent) to have attended graduate school than their Protestant peers, and in 1961 were less than half as likely as the 1968 leavers to say they were in good health. Those who left in 1968 were more likely than Protestant graduates to consider themselves as rebels, and both groups were less likely to consider themselves as "very happy." The 1968 leavers, but not the 1961 leavers, were also somewhat more likely to have attended a high quality graduate school and to describe themselves as liberal Democrats. Thus, those who left Protestant churches between 1964 and

1968 were those who one might have expected to leave—the better educated, the alienated, and the rebellious.

Those who returned in 1968 differ from the main body of Protestants studied here in having more graduate school training, in being more likely to describe themselves as liberal Democrats, in being much less likely to say that they had good health (even less likely than the leavers), and in having a higher score rebelliousness index than the Protestant graduates in general. The returners seem to be a restless lot—well educated, not confident of their health, slightly more likely to be politically liberal, but much more likely to consider themselves happy than the leavers. One would dearly like to know how their poor health, their happiness, and their return to religion relate with one another.

The Catholics (Table 25) who left the Church in 1968 were strikingly different both from the 1961 leavers and from all the Cath-

Table 25   Characteristics of Catholic Leavers

Characteristics	Leavers		Catholic Graduates As a Whole
	1961	1968	
Male	71%	47%	64%
Catholic schools	0	41	46
Father college graduate	20	43	43
Grades A or B	45	30	29
5 Years graduate school	9	12	9
Quality graduate school	25	8	14
Irish	12	32	37
Italian	18	38	20
Good health	41	18	30
High on rebel index:			
1961	23	21	11
1964	11	13	8
Happy	18	31	41
Liberal Democrat	21	12	20
N	(51)	(55)	(1,780)

olics in this survey. The 1968 apostates were more likely to be women, graduates of Catholic schools, to have come from better educated family backgrounds, and to be Irish or Italian than the 1961 leavers. On the other hand, their academic performance tended to be lower than that of the 1961 leavers; they were less likely to report good health, and more likely to score higher on the 1964 rebelliousness index. They were more likely to describe themselves as happy than the 1961 leavers though less likely than the other Catholic graduates and less likely than either group to consider themselves as liberal Democrats. The 1968 apostates, then, among Catholics were not only different from earlier Catholic apostates but from apostates from other denominations. Their grades were not as good; they did not attend high quality graduate schools; they were rebellious but not politically liberal, not confident about their health, and yet happier than the 1961 apostates. We must conclude that they were a mixed group, probably containing a very substantial portion of women graduates of Catholic colleges, who found the years between 1964 and 1968 both personally and religiously disturbing.

The Jewish returners (Table 26) tended to be professional men with substantial graduate school training and fairly low morale. If they returned in 1964, they had much more conservative political

Table 26 Characteristics of Jewish Returners

Characteristics	Returners		Jewish Graduates As a Whole
	1964	1968	
Male	57%	78%	66%
M.D.'s	10	16	7
Law	15	16	6
Father college graduate	32	12	32
Grades A or B	41	49	40
5 years graduate school	30	40	28
Happy	33	20	40
Church 2 or 3 times a year	25	10	55
Church never	50	75	
Liberal Democrat	10	37	34
N	(21)	(32)	(509)

leanings than the typical American Jew. The extent of their return is indicated by the fact that only a quarter of the 1964 returners and a tenth of the 1968 returners went to church at least two or three times a year, and half of the first group and three quarters of the second group never attended church. Their return to Judaism, at least so far, was to reassume a nominal affiliation which they had earlier rejected. They were willing to describe themselves as Jews but not yet willing to be seen at religious services very often. The strong correlation between a professional career and nominal Judaism is striking.

To sum up the five tables: the Protestants are the heaviest losers in the game of changing religious affiliation. The Catholics had the least net losses, largely because of their ability to attract converts. The Jews suffer only moderate losses, mostly because of a tendency of some Jewish apostates to reassume a nominal Jewish affiliation. The 1968 Protestant leavers were substantially what one might expect from one's knowledge of the 1961 leavers. The Protestants who returned in 1968 scored high on "happiness" but low on "good health" —a combination that neither the leavers nor those who remained Protestant indicated. The Catholics who left in 1968 were a deviant group, disproportionately female, Irish or Italian, and graduates of Catholic schools.

A second piece of research confirming our predictions about apostasy was done by John Kotre.[2] He explored in detail the psychological and personality correlates of apostasy among Roman Catholics. In a sample of graduate students in secular universities, all of whom had attended Catholic schools for sixteen years previous to attending graduate school, Kotre interviewed fifty who still defined themselves as "in" the Catholic Church and fifty who defined themselves as "out." The major predictor whether one was "in" or "out" was not a cultural variable or a structural variable but rather the existence of religious conflict in one's family background—either a mixed marriage or a nonpracticing parent. In other words, Kotre discovered a strong relationship between the religious atmosphere in which one was socialized and one's later apostasy from Catholicism. As he points out, Catholicism, like all religion, offers a vast variety of stimuli to the young adult, and which stimuli the adult chooses to focus on is largely the result of his own personality experiences. It is precisely those who experienced a religious conflict in their family background who are most likely to break out of the structure the denominational society had created for them.

Finally, David Caplovitz, in the most elaborate analysis of apostasy among the June 1961 NORC graduating class population, concludes: "A central thesis of this report is that apostasy is symptomatic not only of the loss of religious faith, but of rejection of a particular ascriptive community as a basis for identification."[3] In a later passage Caplovitz comments on one of his tables (reproduced opposite):

Instead of parental relations explaining away the impact of the personality attributes on apostasy, we see that both have

[2] John Kotre, *View From the Border* (Chicago: Aldine Publishing Company, 1971).

[3] The author wishes to thank David Caplovitz for making the foregoing material available to him. It is contained in an as yet unpublished book on apostasy.

independent effects and combine to increase apostasy. Among Jews and Protestants it would appear that the personality syndrome has a somewhat stronger effect on apostasy than quality of parental relations (this can be seen by comparing the percentage differences in the rows and columns). Among Catholics, quality of parental relations is about as important as the personality syndrome. In any event, we now know that the personality syndrome is a determinant of apostasy independent of the quality of parental relations. Although poor parental relations may contribute to this personality syndrome, it by no means fully accounts for the syndrome nor does it explain the impact of the personality traits on apostasy.

Emerging from this analysis is a picture of the apostate as a person who is likely to be maladjusted in his social milieu, who is oriented to values that are not widely held in society (intellectuality, culture, and idealism) and who is highly critical of the societal status quo, that is, committed to radical social change. Although these traits seem to have their origin, at least in part, in poor childhood relations with parents, their connection to/with apostasy is largely independent of parental relations. On a higher level of abstraction, these traits would appear to be indicators of alienation, particularly that meaning of alienation which implies

Table 27 The Joint Effects of Parental Relations and the Personality Predisposition Index on Apostasy in Each Religious Group

Predisposition Index	Good		Quality of Parental Relations Fair		Poor		% Difference
Jews							
Low	5%	(671)	6%	(344)	11%	(125)	6
Medium	9	(293)	18	(225)	28	(141)	19
High	21	(84)	36	(98)	57	(75)	36
% Difference	16		30		46		
Protestants							
Low	6	(5349)	11	(2210)	19	(619)	13
Medium	15	(1313)	18	(796)	32	(305)	17
High	30	(186)	44	(166)	56	(108)	26
% Difference	24		33		37		
Catholics							
Low	3	(1937)	5	(842)	16	(289)	13
Medium	6	(566)	10	(329)	17	(165)	11
High	14	(109)	24	(76)	34	(57)	20
% Difference	11		19		18		

rejection of popular values and goals. The alienated in this sense are apt to reject a religious identification on the grounds that religious institutions are part of the societal status quo and furthermore, that religion is more of an ascribed rather than an achieved characteristic, and for this reason, too, is apt to be alien to their more modernistic value-orientations.

We do not wish to argue, of course, that apostasy is purely a matter of personality orientation or of parental relationships. We simply want to assert that in the denominational society religious apostasy is an extraordinarily difficult thing for the individual. The theory of the denominational society would predict this, and the data reported by Caplovitz and Kotre confirm the prediction.

Intermarriage

To some extent, as we noted before, the prediction of apostasy was made after the collection and inspection of certain data, and hence cannot be taken as providing completely creditable support for the theorizing of the present volume. But the data on religious intermarriage reported in this section were completely unavailable until long after the main portion of this book was written. Until very recently we did not have national statistics on religious intermarriage. It was only when the 1957 census of religious data were finally released by act of Congress that one could speak with any degree of precision about exogamy rates among the various American denominations. However, when we heard that such data had become available we hypothesized on the basis of the framework of the present volume that exogamy rates would be fairly low and that they would be roughly similar in all major American denominations.[4]

Secondly, we hypothesized that the rates would not change across time. It was possible to test this in the final phase of our research on the 1961 alumni, and with deliberate intent examine this hypothesis. Questions were included in the final phase which enabled us to compare the religion of the respondent and the religion of his spouse both at the present time and in the past. It must be remembered that the 1957 data were collected from the general population at all age levels, whereas the 1961 alumni interviewed in 1968 were all college graduates seven years after graduation, a class, that is to say, that was

[4] The material in this section is from an article by Andrew M. Greeley, "Religious Intermarriage," *The American Journal of Sociology*, 75, No. 6 (May 1970). © 1970 by The University of Chicago.

younger and far better educated than the general population. Our specific hypothesis was, therefore, that there would be little difference in the exogamy rates among the young alumni in 1968 and those among the general population of 1957.

The first row in Table 28 provides the rather striking information that approximately four fifths of the members of each of the four Protestant denominations are married to people whose present religious affiliation is the same as their own. Not only are Protestants married to other Protestants, as previous studies have shown, but they are married to Protestants who share the same denominational affiliation. And the ratio of mixed marriages *does not vary much across denominational lines.*

Table 28   Denominational Intermarriage

Denominational Intermarriage	Catholic	Baptist	Lutheran	Methodist	Presbyterian	Jew
Proportion of U.S. population married to member of same denomination in 1957	88%	83%	81%	81%	81%	94%
Proportion of 1961 alumni married to member of same denomination in 1968	86 (1,130)	84 (355)	83 (354)	86 (712)	78 (402)	97 (353)
Proportion of alumni in which marriage took place between two people whose original denomination was the same and who currently belong to that denomination	75	35	34	30	15	94
Proportion of alumni whose original denomination has remained unchanged and whose spouse has converted to that denomination	11	14	22	16	15	2

The 1957 census data contained information for the whole population. If there had been some decline in homogeneity of denominational affiliation, one would expect to find evidence of it among the young and the better educated. Furthermore, one would expect that the data gathered after 1957 would show such a change.

In 1968, eleven years after the national census of religion, NORC collected data on original and present religious denominations of both the respondent and spouse, as part of its ongoing study of June 1961 college graduates. The second row in Table 28 shows the proportions of the major denominations who are presently married to spouses who share the same religious affiliation. There is virtually no difference between the endogamy ratios for young college alumni in 1968 and the general population in 1957. The tendency to seek denominational homogeneity in marriage does not seem to have weakened in the slightest.

The first two rows in the table represent data indicating present denominational affiliation of both respondent and spouse, but they do not tell us whether the denominational homogeneity in marriage has been attained by marrying within one's own denomination or by conversion as a result of the marriage. However, the third row in Table 28 shows the proportion of respondents who married a spouse whose original religious denomination was the same as their own, with both now practicing that religion. It becomes clear that denominational homogeneity is maintained by Catholics and Jews through the process of marrying within one's own denominational boundaries, whereas it is maintained by other religious groups largely through considerable shifting of denominational affiliations. For Catholics and Jews it is important that one marry within one's own denomination (and far more important for Jews than for Catholics). When Catholics marry into other denominations, the non-Catholic is likely to convert. Protestants may marry across denominational lines, but then denominational change occurs if religious homogeneity is wanted in the family environment.

It also appears from the fourth row in Table 28 that those of Lutheran background are able to attract a considerable proportion of their non-Lutheran spouses to join their own Lutheran denomination; thus one fifth of the Lutherans have married people who have converted to Lutheranism, but none of the other three major Protestant denominations seems to have any special relative strength in the game of denominational musical chairs that is required to maintain the family religious homogeneity.

We do not know, of course, whether the patterns of denominational change to maintain homogeneity observed in the college population is the same as the pattern in the more general population since the 1957 census did not provide information about original denominational affiliation. However, further research on the subject is clearly indicated.

In summary, then, one may say that America is still very much a denominational society to the extent that denominational homogeneity in marriage exists for at least three quarters of the major religious denominations.[5]

One may speculate that the strain toward denominational homogeneity is rooted in the American belief that religious differences between husband and wife are not good either for the marriage relationship or for the children of the marriage. This belief is probably reinforced by the fact that it is simpler and more convenient for everyone in the family to belong to the same denomination. For example, one need not worry about two sets of contributions to the support of one's church. Whether the maintenance of high levels of denominational homogeneity in marriage has any specifically religious or doctrinal significance may be open to question. Nevertheless, it is still extremely important in American society that one's spouse be of the same religious denomination as oneself.

Ecumenism

We turn now to two sets of hypotheses about which no data exist, but concerning which data could be collected with some ease. First of all, it seems to be a readily observable phenomenon that ecumenism is a bureaucratic and scholarly rather than a grass-roots movement. What would one expect, therefore, the attitudes of the rank and file members of a denomination to be toward church unity, if one is approaching the question from the context of the present volume? One would presume that the more sophisticated members of the denomination would be more open toward ecumenism; so too would those who score on the intrinsic dimension of Allport's scale. We will hypothesize that, holding constant the Allport dimension and educational level, there will

[5] Denominational homogeneity in marriage seems equally important in another denominational society, Canada. In 1967, 69 percent of the marriages which took place in Canada were between members of the same denomination, a slight dip from 71 percent of 1957. It should be noted that this statistic represents homogeneity at time of marriage. Presumably some postmatrimonial conversions would push the Canadian statistic even closer to the one for the United States (*Canada Year Book,* 1968 [Ottawa: Dominion Bureau of Statistics], p. 284.)

be a strong negative relationship between the importance of religion as a means of self-definition and one's openness toward church unity. The hypothesis is clear enough; education in the Allport dimension can be controlled easily enough; and presumably it should not be too difficult to provide operational measures both of openness toward church unity and importance of religion as a means of self-definition. All that remains is for a test to be made.

The Relationship Between Meaning and Belonging

In the final analysis, the most important test of our hypothesis would be based on an examination of the relationship between the two dimensions of religion that we have called the "meaning" and "belonging" dimensions. A general hypothesis is clear: in American society the meaning function of religion takes on added importance—at least in terms of propositional orthodoxy—precisely because of the strong belonging function that a denominational society makes possible for religion. One would have to hold constant both education and Allport's intrinsic-extrinsic dimension, as described in the previous paragraph, as well as using various careful measures of the importance of religion for self-definition. The difficult variable to operationalize, however, would be the meaning variable, because meaning indicates not merely propositional orthodoxy but adherence to religion as an "interpretive scheme"; and none of the research done thus far, in the judgment of the present author, comes even close to elaborating measures on religion as an interpretive scheme. Simply to ask a respondent whether he believes in God, or in the divinity of Christ, or in an afterlife, or in the inspiration of the Scripture does not get at the root questions of graciousness of being, of life, of death, of resurrection, and of the general orientation toward reality which might properly be subsumed under religion as a cultural system or interpretive scheme. If the speculations in this book have any merit, however, they would suggest that one of the first items on the agenda of sociologists of religion would be the fashioning of operational measures of the relevance of religion as an interpretive scheme to individuals in the religious population.

   To summarize: We advanced four hypotheses. Two were tested, one is testable, and one is difficult to test. Stated briefly, they are:

1. Apostasy levels are low with little change over time.
2. Exogamy rates across denominational lines are low and relatively constant over time.

3. Acceptance of church unity will be high among those for whom religion is an important means of self-definition (Allport's intrinsically religious) and low for those who view religion primarily for social location (extrinsic).
4. The meaning and belonging functions of religions are more strongly related in a pluralistic society.

The Future of Religion

In another volume [6] this writer addressed himself to the question of what the future of religion is in American society. It ought to be evident, however, even in the context of the present volume, that he is profoundly skeptical of arguments which see American religion losing its influence. The sacred seems to be too deeply engrained in the structure of human existence, and denominationalism too deeply engrained in the structure of American society for there to be any precipitous decline in religious influence in the remaining decades of the present century. One cannot program for the overwhelming impact of an unexpected event, of course. Surely no one in the late 1950's would have anticipated that we could have become involved in another major war in Asia. Political leaders of both parties were against it, the wisest of the military leaders lived in terror of it, and after the Korean War the whole country would be profoundly skeptical of another such involvement. Thus, projections of the America of the 1960's would have put aside the possibility of such a conflict and would have projected a very different society than the one in which we now live. Similarly, in the remaining thirty years of the century there may be a religious disaster like the political disaster of the Vietnam War. Anyone familiar with the workings of the American Catholic hierarchy, for example, would surely not preclude the possibility of their committing some kind of organizational suicide. However, if one excludes the always possible disaster, in the context of the present volume one would arrive at the following conclusions about the future of American religion.

1. Religion will not lose its adherents. In the United States this means that membership, church attendance, and doctrinal orthodoxy will persist at the levels reported in the 1952–1965 surveys. In countries such as England where organizational participation and church attendance levels are much lower, this means minimally that levels are

---

[6] In this section we lean very heavily on material taken from Greeley, *Religion in the Year 2000*, op. cit.

likely to fall no lower than they are, and, even as Professor Martin suggests, they may begin to rise slightly.

2. Nor is religion likely to lose its influence. It will still provide at least a substantial component of the ultimate interpretive scheme or meaning system with the overwhelming majority of the population. It will still have indirect impact on society through the religiously influenced ethical decisions of its members, and it will also have direct influence over society, both because it provides part of the underpinning for general social consensus and because in certain critical situations the direct confrontation between religion and social problems contributes to the amelioration of these problems.

3. The sacred is not being replaced by the secular. Scientific rationalism will not generate a new faith. It will not provide satisfactory alternatives to those modes of coping with problems of interpretability currently popular with the overwhelming majority of the population. The transcendent may no longer be coterminous with all human activity, but the "really real" will still persist where the core problems of interpretability are faced. On the contrary, in fact, the popularity of the current revolt against scientific rationalism suggests that new and deviant forms of the sacred will emerge.[7]

4. Full-time parochial clergy may diminish in relative proportion to part-time specialized or limited-term clergy, but the full-time clergy working with the local congregations will continue to be the majority of religious functionaries.

5. Simple, dignified, Low-Church Appolonian ritual will not replace all other forms of liturgy. Rather, on the contrary, Dionysian and ecstatic ritual may be at least as common as the Low-Church liturgy of the underground.

6. Religious institutions will no more wither away than will the Marxist state. On the contrary, they will become more elaborate and

---

[7] The resurgence of the sacred we see emerging among the young (and not so young) centering around the occult has gone on quite independently of the religious denominations. Indeed, to some very considerable extent it is a reaction against the organized structure of denominationalism. Whether the generally high level of conventional religious concern which the denominational society sustains does in fact facilitate the present outburst of neosacralism must remain open to question for the moment. One would have to determine, for example, whether the new cult of the occult is going on only in religiously pluralistic countries or can be found in countries where levels of religious practice are much lower than they are in the United States. Our inclination is, on rather a priori grounds, to suspect that in a denominational society there is likely to be more of the current resurgence of the sacred if only because the organized denominations have served to keep the religious question somewhat more open than it would be in nations where religious behavior was at a lower level.

more sophisticated and more dependent on academic experts than they are at the present time.

7. Neither will denominations cease to be characteristic of the Western religious scene. Whatever ecumenism is likely to exist at the end of the present century and the beginning of the next century will, in all probability, continue to be denominational ecumenism.

8. Doctrinal orthodoxy has not breathed its last, and there probably lurks in a divinity school even now some *fin de siècle* Karl Barth ready to rise up and bear prophetic witness for orthodox traditions.

9. The local congregation will not perish. They may become smaller and more diversified, but the tendency for man to worship where he lives with his wife and family will not be eliminated—not, at least, as long as there are suburbs.

10. The crusade for social and secular relevance will not sweep away either the passivity of the religious masses or drive them out of the churches. Neither will the this-worldly religious concerns currently so popular eliminate the other-worldly residue which survives even in American religion. On the contrary, it is possible, perhaps toward the end of the present century, that the other-worldly and the monastic will undergo a notable resurgence in American religion. The monastic element within deviant social movements (and especially the rural communes) might even lead us to expect that this resurgence could occur much sooner.

Summary

The principal theme of this book is that America is a denominational society, that is to say, a society in which denominational affiliation is an important component of the social structure. The roots of denominationalism go back even before the emergence of the American nation, so that the society was religiously pluralistic before it became politically pluralistic. Furthermore, to some considerable extent, it became politically pluralistic because of its religious pluralism. Religious pluralism in the United States and in most western European societies seems to enhance rather than weaken the strength of organized religion precisely because it provides the members of the society with a collectivity standing somewhere between the family and the larger society, which can play a quasi-ethnic role in providing identity and social location to the members of the denominations. In some Western countries nationalism reinforces organized religion (as in Ireland or Poland); in other countries social class weakens religious affiliation (as in Britain and France); in still other countries religious pluralism plays its role in reinforcing religious activity.

What we are arguing, then, is that there is a long-run drift toward sustained religious affiliation because religious identification is very much a part of the early socialization process. The drift is diverted away from religion when social and cultural forces militate against it (as in England, France, and the Scandinavian countries); and the vigor of religion is enhanced when social and cultural forces militate in favor of it (as in Holland, the United States, and Ireland). The French and English working classes tend not to be religious because it is hard to be a member of the working class and still accept the essentially upper middle-class and upper-class shape which religion takes in their countries. In Ireland, on the other hand, it is easy to be religious because religion is reinforced by Irish patriotism. Church affiliation and activity in the United States are high because religion plays a quasi-ethnic role in America, as it does in most other religiously pluralistic countries in the West. Whether a given Western country, then, is a "religious" country or not is not a function of how scientifically or technologically advanced it is but rather of its history and its cultural and social structure.

We are not arguing, however, that religion is just a "belonging" affair. We are saying, rather, that the precise nature of the relationship between the meaning and belonging functions is shaped to a considerable extent by the history and social structure of a given country and, in the United States in particular, by denominational pluralism. American Christians score higher on measures of doctrinal orthodoxy because these measures are in some way connected with the social location function that religion plays in American society. Nevertheless, this does not mean that religious faith is just a function of social location but rather that orthodox doctrinal values are substantially reinforced by the social location function. In fact we have noted that it is precisely the elaborate institutional structure that denominational pluralism makes possible which in its turn generates a considerable amount of prophetic self-criticism which is not to be found in countries where organizational indifference is commonplace.

The critics of American religion argue that it is a cultural religion which consoles and comforts but does not challenge. Perhaps they are correct, but it still must be noted that this is a value judgment based on the Judeo-Christian tradition. We have argued in this book that the cultural religion, or religion of comfort, in a curious paradox generates its own countervailing criticism. But even if it did not, an anthropologist studying American religion would have to admit that even if it were not authentic or prophetic religion, it was religious in the sense that primitive religions are religious—that is to say, it underpins the structure of society to provide meaning and belonging for society's members.

One of the weaknesses of much of the criticism of American religion, however, seems to be that it sees human behavior in dichotomies. Religion either comforts *or* challenges; it is either cultural *or* prophetic; it is either authentic *or* complacent. In fact, most people's religious motivations are probably a combination of the prophetic and the complacent, of the authentic and the inauthentic, of comfort and challenge. Historical and social circumstances have combined to produce a denominational society in the United States in which the very structure of the nation reinforces religious observance, religious affiliation, and religious orthodoxy. It is a truism to say that if America were not a denominational society, Americans probably would not be such a religious people. It does not follow from this that because there are increments in the levels of religious practice, denominationalism produces in the United States inauthentic religion. An appropriate test would be to determine whether American religions produce a higher level of Gordon Allport's intrinsic religious orientation than is to be found in comparable societies where denominationalism is not strong. If such a test does indicate that there is a higher intrinsic score in American society, then one has to say that denominationalism has, through the medium of its social location function, actually produced a higher level of authentic religious behavior, that is to say, a higher level of authentic religious meaning than is to be found in a society where the social location function of religion is not important. Until such a test is tried, the sociologist will be skeptical of any attempt to write off the denominational increment in religious behavior in American society as simply inaccurate.

We have also expressed considerable skepticism in this volume about the alleged secularization of American society. The relationship between the religious and the secular is changing constantly in any society and changing rapidly in a society as dynamic and complex as ours. But this process of change ought not to be conceived as a simple pilgrimage from superstition to enlightenment, from faith to skepticism, from the sacred to the profane. Rather an endless process of adjustment and readjustment goes on; and while much changes, much remains constant—particularly religion's important contribution to answering the question of who one is and where one stands. It is precisely this ethnic role of religion that gives American religion its unique flavor and its unique combination of sacrality and profanity. America has always been a nation in which the sacred and the profane, the comfort and the challenge have existed more or less amicably side by side. Denominationalism helps to maintain and to reinforce the remarkable stability of the society and culture of the United States, so diverse in origin and infusion that one marvels at its survival.

Bibliography

Allport, Gordon W. "Behavioral Science, Religion, and Mental Health." *Journal of Religion and Health* 2 (April 1963): 187–197.
———. "The Religious Context of Prejudice." *Journal for the Scientific Study of Religion* 5 (Fall 1966): 447–457.
———, and Michael Ross. "Personal Religious Orientation and Prejudice." *Journal of Personality and Social Psychology* (April 1967): 432–442.

Bellah, Robert N. "Civil Religion in America." *Daedalus* 96 (Winter 1967): 1–21.
———. "Religious Evolution." *American Sociological Review* 29 (June 1964): 358–374.

Bendix, Reinhard. "Max Weber's Interpretation of Conduct and History." *American Journal of Sociology* 51 (May 1946): 518–526.

Cohn, Norman. "Medieval Millenarism: Its Bearing on the Comparative Study of Millenarian Movements." In *Religion, Culture and Society*, edited by Louis Schneider, pp. 168–177. New York: John Wiley & Sons, Inc., 1964.
———. *The Pursuit of the Millennium*. New York: Oxford University Press, Inc., 1957.

Coleman, James S. "Social Cleavage and Religious Conflict." *The Journal of Social Issues* 12 (Summer 1956): 44–66.

Durkheim, Emile. *The Elementary Forms of Religious Life*. Translated by Joseph Ward Swain. London: Geo. Allen & Unwin, Ltd., 1957.
———. "Search for a Positive Definition." In *Religion, Culture and Society*, edited by Louis Schneider, pp. 27–35. New York: John Wiley & Sons, Inc., 1964.

Eckardt, A. Roy. *The Surge of Piety in America*. New York: Association Press, 1958.

Eister, Allan W. "Toward a Radical Critique of Church-Sect Typologizing." *Journal for the Scientific Study of Religion* 6 (April 1967): 85–90.

256   *Bibliography*

Eliade, Mircea. *The Sacred and the Profane.* New York: Harcourt Brace Jovanovich, Inc., 1959.

Ennis, Philip. "Ecstasy and Everyday Life." *Journal for the Scientific Study of Religion* 6 (April 1967): 40–49.

Fichter, Joseph. *Southern Parish.* Chicago: The University of Chicago Press, 1951.

Francis, E. K. "The Russian Mennonites: From Religion to Ethnic Group." *American Journal of Sociology* 54 (September 1948): 101–107.

Frazer, James G. *New Golden Bough.* Edited by Theodor Gaster. Abridged. New York: S. G. Phillips, Inc., 1959.

Freud, Sigmund. *The Future of an Illusion.* Translated by W. D. Robeson Scott. New York: Doubleday & Company, Inc., 1957.

Geertz, Clifford. "Religion as a Cultural System." In *Anthropological Approaches to the Study of Religion,* edited by Michael Bonton, pp. 1–46. New York: Praeger Publishers, Inc., 1966.

Glazer, Nathan. *American Judaism.* Chicago: The University of Chicago Press, 1957.

————, and Daniel Patrick Moynihan. *Beyond the Melting Pot.* 2nd ed. Cambridge, Mass.: The MIT Press, 1970.

Glock, Charles Y., and Rodney Stark. *Religion and Society in Tension.* Chicago: Rand McNally & Co., 1965.

————. *Religious Belief and Anti-Semitism.* New York: Harper & Row, Publishers, 1966.

Goode, Erich. "Some Critical Observations of the Church-Sect Dimension." *Journal for the Scientific Study of Religion* 6 (April 1967): 69–77.

Greeley, Andrew M. *Religion in the Year 2000.* New York: Sheed & Ward, Inc., 1969.

————. "The Religious Behavior of Graduate Students." *Journal for the Scientific Study of Religion* 5 (Fall 1965): 34–40.

————. "Religious Intermarriage in a Denominational Society." *The American Journal of Sociology* 75 (May 1970): 949–951.

————. *Why Can't They Be Like Us?* New York: Institute of Human Relations Press, The American Jewish Committee, 1969.

————, Martin Marty, and Stuart Rosenberg. *What Do We Believe?* New York: Meredith Corporation, 1967.

Harrison, Paul M. *Authority and Power in the Free Church Tradition.* Princeton, N.J.: Princeton University Press, 1959.

Herberg, Will. *Protestant, Catholic, Jew.* Rev. ed. New York: Doubleday & Company, Inc., 1955.

James, William. *The Varieties of Religious Experience.* New York: The New American Library, Inc., 1961.

Kotre, John. *View From the Border: A Social Psychological Study of Current Catholicism.* Chicago: Aldine Publishing Company, 1971.

Lenski, Gerhard. *The Religious Factor.* New York: Doubleday & Company, Inc., 1961.

Levy-Bruhl, Lucien. *Primitive Mentality*. Translated by Lillian A. Clare. Boston: Beacon Press, 1923.

Lipset, Seymour Martin. Chapter entitled "Extremism, Political and Religious," in *Political Man*, pp. 107–108. New York: Doubleday & Company, Inc., 1960.

———. *The First New Nation*. New York: Basic Books Inc., Publishers, 1963.

Littell, Franklin Hamlin. *From State Church to Pluralism: A Protestant Interpretation of Religion in American History*. New York: Doubleday & Company, Inc., 1962.

Luckmann, Thomas. *The Invisible Religion*. New York: The Macmillan Company, 1967.

Malinowski, Bronislaw. "Social and Individual Sources of Primitive Religion." In *Religion, Society, and the Individual*, edited by J. Milton Yinger, pp. 380–385. New York: The Macmillan Company, 1965.

Marty, Martin. *The New Shape of American Religion*. New York: Harper & Row, Publishers, 1959.

Merton, Robert K. *Social Theory and Social Structure*. New York: The Macmillan Company, 1949.

Niebuhr, Richard R. "The Churches of the Disinherited." In *Religion, Culture and Society*, edited by Louis Schneider, pp. 466–471. New York: John Wiley & Sons, Inc., 1964.

Nisbet, Robert N. *The Sociological Tradition*. New York: Basic Books, Inc., Publishers, 1966.

O'Dea, Thomas. "Dilemmas in Institutionalization." In *Religion, Culture and Society*, edited by Louis Schneider, pp. 580–588. New York: John Wiley & Sons, Inc., 1964.

Otto, Rudolf. *Idea of the Holy*. Translated by John Harvey, 2nd ed. New York: Oxford University Press, Inc., 1958.

Parsons, Talcott. "Christianity and Modern Industrial Society." In *Religion, Culture and Society*, edited by Louis Schneider, pp. 273–298. New York: John Wiley & Sons, Inc., 1964.

———. "Motivations of Religious Belief and Behavior." In *Religion, Society, and the Individual*, edited by J. Milton Yinger, pp. 350–359. New York: The Macmillan Company, 1965.

Schneider, Louis, ed. *Religion, Culture and Society*. New York: John Wiley & Sons, Inc., 1964.

Sklare, Marshall, and Joseph Greenblum. *Jewish Identity on the Suburban Frontier, A Study of Group Survival in the Open Society*. New York: Basic Books, Inc., Publishers, 1967.

Smelser, Neil S. *Theory of Collective Behavior*. New York: The Macmillan Company, 1962.

Sperry, Willard L. *Religion in America*. Boston: Beacon Press, 1963.

Warner, W. Lloyd, ed. *Yankee City*. New Haven: Yale University Press, 1963.

Weber, Max. *From Max Weber: Essays in Sociology*. Translated by C.

Wright Mills and H. H. Gerth. New York: Oxford University Press, 1958.

X ———. *The Protestant Ethic and the Spirit of Capitalism.* Translated by Talcott Parsons. New York: Charles Scribner's Sons, 1930.

———. *The Religion of China.* Translated by H. H. Gerth. New York: The Macmillan Company, 1951.

———. *The Religion of India.* Translated by H. H. Gerth and Don Martindale. New York: The Macmillan Company, 1958.

X Williams, J. Paul. "The Nature of Religion." *Journal for the Scientific Study of Religion* 2 (Fall 1962): 3–14.

X Wilson, Bryan. "An Analysis of Sect Development." In *Religion, Culture and Society,* edited by Louis Schneider, pp. 482–497. New York: John Wiley & Sons, Inc., 1964.

X Yinger, J. Milton. *Religion, Society, and the Individual.* New York: The Macmillan Company, 1965.

Index

Abolition movement, 103–104, 181
Abortion, 219
Abramson, Harold, 114
Academia, attitudes toward, 148, 149
Act of Toleration, 213–214
Adultery, 27
Alcohol, 12, 221
Allport, Gordon W., 20, 65, 205, 206, 207, 208, 209, 210, 211, 247, 248, 253
Altizer, Thomas J., 130
American Baptists, 97–101
American Lutherans, 97–101
American Way of Life, The, 158–162, 165–166, 167
Americanism, the religion of, 156–167
Anabaptists, 67, 68
Andaman Islanders, 37
Anglicanism, 176
Anglo-Catholics, 182, 183
Animism, 31
Anthropology, 38
Anti-Catholicism, 181, 214, 217, 224
Anti-negro attitudes, 124, 207, 209
Anti-Protestantism, 224
Anti-Semitism, 124, 181, 195–196, 209, 212, 214, 223, 224
Apostasy, 145–146, 198–200, 237–244
Apollonian liturgy, 23
Archaic religions, 56
Ascetism, 42, 43–44, 47
Ashkenazim, 196

Baird, Robert, 151
Baptists,
  beliefs of Southern Baptists, 97–101

Baptists (cont.)
  capitalism, 43
  church attendance, 89
  history, 177, 182
  intermarriage, 245
  statistics, 89, 90, 91
  subgroups, 90
Barth, Karl, 22
Baxter, Richard, 43
Becker, Howard, 74
Belief-attitude, 6
Beliefs, 94–102, 137–141, 143
Bellah, Robert N., 8, 17, 55–58, 60, 61, 135, 136, 156, 167–174
Bendix, Reinhard, 49
Bible,
  belief in inspiration of, 138, 139, 143
  reading, 139
  reading, in schools, 218–219
Birth, symbolism of water, 15
Birth control,
  attitudes of young people, 143
  Catholic attitudes, 140, 141, 192, 193, 219, 220
Blau, Peter, 80, 236
Bockelson, Jan, 67, 68
Buddhism, 47, 72–73
Bultmann, Rudolf, 22
Bureaucracy, 105

Callahan, Daniel, 132, 153
Calvinism, 42–43, 49, 179, 180, 182
Campbell, Thomas, 178
Camus, Albert, 18
Cane Ridge Revival, 177
Canon Law Association of America, 192
Capitalism, 39, 41–49, 50
Caplovitz, David, 242
Cargo Cults, 67

Carroll, Charles, 186
Carroll, Daniel, 186
Carroll, John, 119, 186, 187, 189, 194
Catholics,
    apostasy, 238, 239, 240, 241, 242, 243
    attitudes of young people, 143–144
    attitudes toward clergy, 140, 192, 193
    attitudes toward Jews, 214, 223–226
    beliefs and behavior, 95, 96, 97–101, 131, 137–141
    changing attitudes, 140, 141
    church attendance, 89, 95, 131, 139, 146, 147
    clergy, 25–26
    ethics, 27
    ethnic groups, 90–91, 108–109, 114, 116, 119–126, 187–188, 190–191
    history, 108–109, 119–123, 186–194, 203
    intellectualism, 191
    intermarriage, 114, 224, 245, 246
    liturgy, 24, 81, 193
    political leaders, 120, 221, 222
    prejudice, 209
    Saints, 19
    school system, 71–72, 124, 205, 216–218
    social class, 91, 93
    statistics, 89, 91
    students, 148–149
    theology, 22–23, 103, 183
Charisma, 76, 79
Celibacy, 26
Charity, 134
Childbirth, magic rituals, 37
Chinese religions, 45–47
Christ, belief in divinity of, 95, 96, 100–101, 137
"Christian Century," 130, 149
Christian Scientists, 75, 182
Christmas, 157, 221, 228

Church, defined, 71–79
Church attendance, 89, 131, 139, 146, 147
Church membership, 44–45, 95, 137, 151
Civil Religion, The, 156–174
Civil War, 17, 172, 182
Clergy,
    attitudes of young people, 143, 144
    Catholic attitudes, 140, 192, 193
    future of, 250
Cohn, Norman, 21, 65, 67, 68
Coleman, James S., 215
Collective unconsciousness, 15
College education, percentage by denomination, 89
Comfort theory, 63–70
Communism, 9
Confucianism, 45–47
Congregationalists,
    beliefs, 96, 97–101
    history, 176, 179, 180, 182
    liturgy, 24
Conservatism, 65
Conservative Judaism, 196, 197
Contemplation, 102–103
Cox, Harvey, 130, 132, 153, 154
Cults, 74

Darwin, Charles, 106
Death, 15, 35, 38
Death-of-God, 22, 137
Democrats, 89, 91, 92, 93, 121, 123, 124, 222, 232, 234
Deprivation, 31, 65, 68, 69
Dietz, Peter, 121
Dionysian liturgy, 23
Disciples of Christ,
    beliefs, 97–101
    history, 177–178, 182
Divorce,
    attitudes of young people, 143, 144
    Catholic attitudes, 140, 141, 192, 219, 220

Doctrine, 22, 23
Drugs, 12, 13
Durkheim, Emile, 13–14, 17, 30, 31, 32–34, 63, 118, 163, 233
Dutch Jews, 196
Dutch Reform denominations, 182

East, Religions of the, 45–49
Eastern Rite Catholics, 123
Eckhardt, A. Roy, 153, 163, 164, 165, 166, 174
Ecstasy, 11, 12
Ecumenism, 104, 184, 193, 247–248
Edwards, Jonathan, 176, 177
Eisenhower, Dwight, 160, 162
Eister, Allan W., 73, 77, 78
Eliade, Mircea, 14–15, 16
Ellington, Duke, 11
Encounter groups, 25
England, John, 105, 187, 189, 194
Ennis, Philip, 11–12
Episcopalians,
    beliefs, 97–101
    church attendance, 89
    history, 182–183
    statistics, 89, 92
Established church, 84
Ethnicity, 108–126, 127, 190
    Catholic ethnic groups, 91, 108–109, 114, 116, 119–126, 187, 190–191
    defined, 109–115
    Jewish ethnic groups, 109, 196, 197, 199–200
    role of the churches, 115–119
Evangelism, 177, 178
Evolution, 106
Extrinsic religion, 20, 208–212

Faith healing, 106
Fanatacism, 206
Fertility rites, 16
Fichter, Joseph, 209
Fisher, Dorothy Canfield, 160

Folk religion, 19, 106, 164, 165, 166, 173
Fourth of July, 17, 157, 173
Francis, E. K., 109
Franklin, Benjamin, 41
Frazer, James G., 31
French Catholics, 121, 124
Freud, Sigmund, 12, 30, 64
Freylinghausen, Domine, 177
Freylinghausen, Theodore, 176
Functionalism, 31–38
Fundamentalism, 104–105, 176, 214
Funerals, Javanese, 38

Gallup Polls, 130, 131
Gambling, 221
Geertz, Clifford, 9, 15–16, 18, 38, 54–55, 58, 60
Gemeinschaft society, 2, 3, 80, 125
German Catholics, 108, 120–121, 124, 125, 187, 190
German Jews, 196, 197, 200, 201
Gerth, H. H., 40
Gesellschaft society, 2, 80
Ghost dance, 67
Gibbons, James, 189
Glazer, Nathan, 110, 114, 197, 198
Glock, Charles Y., 7–8, 64, 65, 95, 96, 97, 151, 212
God,
    belief in, 95, 96, 98–99, 137, 143, 144
    gratitude to, 228
    referred to in inaugural addresses, 168–170
Goode, Erich, 77–78
Graham, Billy, 103, 164, 165, 177
Great Awakening, 103, 176, 177, 185, 214
Greeley, Andrew M., 137, 139, 140, 146

Hanukkah, 231
Harrison, Paul M., 78, 105

Hasidism, 199
Heaven, belief in, 95, 137, 143, 144
Hell, belief in, 143, 144
Herberg, Will, 110–112, 115–116, 118, 153, 156, 158–162, 163, 165, 166, 174
High Church liturgy and ritual, 23
High Islam, 19
Hinduism, 47
Hippies, 27
Hoffer, Eric, 206
Hughes, John, 187–188
Huxley, Aldous Leonard, 16

Immigrants, 110–112, 186, 187, 189, 190, 191, 194–198, 214
Inauguration addresses, 168–170
Independence Day, 228
Indian religions, 47–48
Institutional religion, 79–85
Intermarriage, 113, 114, 143, 144, 202, 224, 230, 244–247
Intrinsic religion, 20, 208–212
Ireland, John, 189, 194
Irish Catholics, 108, 109, 114, 116, 119–120, 121, 124, 125, 187, 190–191
Irish Revolution, 110
Islam, 19, 72–73
Israel, 203, 222, 223
Italian Catholics, 109, 121, 122–123, 124, 125, 190

James, William, 11
Javanese funeral rites, 38
Jefferson, Thomas, 153, 170
Jehovah's Witnesses, 75
Jesus, belief in divinity of, 95, 96, 100–101, 137
Jews,
apostasy, 198–200, 238, 241, 242, 243
attitudes toward Catholic schools, 217

Jews (*cont.*)
attitudes toward Catholics, 214, 223–226
attitudes toward religious activity in public schools, 218–219
beliefs and behavior, 95, 137, 138, 139
Conservative, 196, 197
ethnicity, 109, 196, 197, 199–200
Hanukkah, 231
history, 48, 194–203
intermarriage, 202, 245, 246
Orthodox, 197
persecution of, 206
Reform, 196, 197
statistics, 89, 92
synagogue attendance, 89, 131, 139, 146, 147, 199, 200, 201
synagogue membership, 95
theology, 202
youth, 228
John xxiii, Pope, 191
Johnson, Lyndon B., 171, 173
Jung, 15

Kallen, Horace, 6
Keane, John, 189
Kenkel, Frederick, 121
Kennedy, Eugene, 25
Kennedy, John,
funeral of, 10, 16, 166
inaugural address, 168–169, 170
inauguration, 191
Kennedy, Ruby Jo Reeves, 113
Kierkegaard, Søren, 58
Kotre, John, 242

Labor Day, 228
Laity, Catholic, 192, 193
Latin Mass, 24
Lazerwitz, Bernard, 89, 94
Legion of Decency, 219–220
Lenski, Gerhard, 208
Lévy-Bruhl, Lucien, 31

Liberalism, 22
Life after death, belief in, 95, 137, 143, 144
Lincoln, Abraham, 172
Lipset, Seymour Martin, 65–66, 68, 128, 136, 151–153, 154, 166
Littell, Franklin Hamlin, 176, 177, 178, 180–181
Liturgy,
  Catholic, 24, 81, 193
  Protestant, 23–24
Low Church Anglicans, liturgy, 24
Lowell, Robert, 172
Luckmann, Thomas, 6, 8, 17, 58–63, 72, 133, 134, 227, 236
Luther, Martin, 132
Lutherans,
  beliefs of Missouri Synod Lutherans, 97–101
  branches of the Lutheran Church, 90
  capitalism, 42
  church attendance, 89
  history, 182
  intermarriage, 245, 246
  statistics, 89, 92
Lying, 27

Magic, 31, 36–37, 45
Malinowski, Bronislaw, 34–37, 63, 166
Martineau, Harriet, 151, 152
Marty, Martin E., 138, 139, 140, 153, 163, 165, 166, 174
Marx, Karl, 30, 38–39, 69
Marxism, 19
Maurice, Morris, 83, 84
Meaning and belonging, 184–185, 248–249
Memorial Day, 17, 157, 172–173, 228
Mensching, Gustav, 18, 19
Merton, Robert K., 38, 65, 156, 236
Methodists,
  beliefs, 97–101
  church attendance, 89

Methodists (*cont.*)
  conservatism, 66–67
  history, 176, 177, 181, 182
  intermarriage, 245
  liturgy, 24
  statistics, 89, 91–92
  subgroups, 90
Michel, Virgil, 121
Michels, Roberto, 79, 80
Middle Ages, 129
Millenarian religious movement, 67–69
Mills, C. Wright, 40
Ministers, 25–26
Miracle working, 106
Missouri Synod Lutherans, 90, 97–101, 182
Modernism, 22
Money, church too concerned about, 140, 143, 144
Mormonism, 182
Morse, Jedidiah, 179
Moynihan, Daniel Patrick, 114, 222
Muntzer, Thomas, 67
Murder, 27
Mysticism, 26

Naïve functionalism, 38
National Council of Churches, 97, 105, 183
National Office of Decent Literature, 219–220
National Opinion Research Center, 145
"New Side" Presbyterians, 177
Newman, John Henry, 21
Niebuhr, H. Richard, 73
Niebuhr, Reinhold, 184
Niebuhr, Richard R., 66
Novak, Michael, 222

O'Daniel, Daniel, 83, 84
O'Dea, Thomas, 80–81
Orthodox Jews, 197
Otto, Rudolf, 13

Parochial school education, 71–72, 124, 205, 216–218
Parsons, Talcott, 6, 30, 50–54, 55, 58, 60, 61, 62, 63, 69, 72, 118, 129, 132–133, 134, 135, 136, 151, 153, 154, 236
Paul, Saint, 86, 158
Paul vi, Pope, 10
Peace, 181
Peale, Norman Vincent, 162, 165
Pentecostal sects, 181
Pentecostalism, 23
Pietism, 43, 176
Piety, 26
Pluralism, 104, 115, 116, 186, 251, 252
Pluralistic causation, 50
Podhoretz, Norman, 221
Polish Catholics, 109, 122, 124, 125, 190
Polish Jews, 197
Polish National Catholic Church, 91
Portuguese Jews, 196
Prayer,
belief in, 95, 137, 143, 144
in public schools, 218–219
Predestination, 42
Prejudice, 195, 205–213, 214, 217, 223, 224
Presbyterians,
beliefs, 97–101
church attendance, 89
divisions of the Presbyterian denomination, 90
history, 176, 182
intermarriage, 245
liturgy, 24
statistics, 89, 92
Primitive religion, 56
Primitive societies, 32, 35–38
Prohibitionism, 181
"Protestant Ethic and the Spirit of Capitalism, The" (Max Weber), 41, 42, 43–44, 45, 48
Protestants,
abolition movement, 103–104

Protestants (*cont.*)
apostasy, 237, 238, 239, 240, 241–242, 243
attitudes of young people, 143, 144–145
attitudes toward Catholic schools, 216–217
attitudes toward religious activity in public schools, 218–219
beliefs and behavior, 95, 97–101, 137–139
capitalism, 41–49
church attendance, 95, 131, 139, 146, 147
ecumenism, 184
history, 175–186, 203
meaning and belonging, 184–185
politics, 184
social class, 93
theology, 22–23, 183
youth, 228, 231
See also Baptists, Congregationalists, Lutherans, Presbyterians, etc.
Psychology, of religious beliefs, 96–97
Public schools, religious instruction in, 218
Puritans, 43, 46–47, 180–181, 214

Quakers, 182

Racial integration, 207
Racial prejudice, 124, 207, 209
Radcliffe-Brown, A. R., 37
Radicalism, 64–69
Rais, Sabatamo, 196
Rationalism, 48
Reform Judaism, 196, 197
Reformation, 57, 81
Religion,
as an organization, 71–85
beliefs, 94–102, 137–141, 143
defined, 5–10
dimensions of, 21–28

Religion (*cont.*)
  ethnic phenomenon, 108–126
  future of, 236–254
  institutional, 79–85
  nature of, 5–29
  origin and functions of, 30–44
  prejudice and conflict, 205–226
  present condition of, 86–107
  and social class, 93–94
  sociology of, 49–70
  styles of, 18–21
Religious freedom, 205, 213–214
Religious revival, after World War
  II, 130–131, 151, 165
Revival churches, 177
Revivalism, 103, 177, 180, 181
Revivalistic fundamentalism, 183
Rites of passage, 17
Ritual, 23–24, 35, 37, 81
Roman Catholics. *See* Catholics
Rosenberg, Stuart E., 139
Rossi, Peter H., ii, 124–125
Russian Jews, 197

Sacred cosmos, 59, 61
Sacred space, 14, 15
Sacredness, 10–18, 28, 33, 81, 130,
  153, 154, 250
Sartre, Jean Paul, 18
School desegregation, 209
Science, and religion, 106, 128,
  146–147
Second Great Awakening, 177
Sects, 24–25, 74–75, 76, 80
  defined, 71–79
Secularization, 127–155, 200–201,
  220–221, 253
Sephardim, 196
Sexual morality, 140, 141, 143–
  144, 189, 192, 219–220
Simple Church liturgy, 23
Sklare, Marshall, 200, 201
Smelser, Neil S., 78
Social class, 91–94, 113, 229
Social consciousness, 134
Sociology of religion, 49–70

Solemn High Mass, 24
Sorokin, Pitirim, 132
Southern Baptists, 90, 97–101
Space, sacred, 14, 15
Spanish Catholics, 123
Spanish Jews, 196
Spaulding, Lancaster, 189, 194
Sperry, Willard L., 179–180
Stark, Rodney, 64, 65, 95, 96, 97,
  151, 212
Story, Justice, 175
Students,
  church attendance, 147
Students, graduate,
  church attendance, 146
  religious affiliation, 145
Synagogue attendance, 89, 131,
  139, 146, 147, 199, 200, 201

Taoism, 45
Teilhard de Chardin, Pierre, 28
Tennent, Gilbert, 176
Tennent, William, 176
T-groups, 25
Thanksgiving, 17, 157, 172, 228
Theology, 22–23, 183, 202
Thomas Aquinas, Saint, 22
Tillich, Paul, 22
Tocqueville, Alexis de, 151, 152,
  158, 167
Tonnies, Ferdinand, 80
Trappists, 102
Trinitarians, 179, 180
Trinity, belief in, 95, 137
Trobriand Islanders, 37
Troeltsch, Ernst, 73, 80
Twain, Mark, 22
Tylor, E. B., 31

Underground church, 25, 83–84
Unitarians, 179–180, 182, 183, 185,
  214

Value systems, 133–136, 142, 151,
  153, 216

Vatican Council, Second, 22, 141, 189, 191, 194
Veterans Day, 228
Voluntaryism, 178, 181, 184

Washington, George, 170, 186
Weber, Max, 17, 18, 30, 31, 39–45, 46, 48, 49, 50, 73, 76, 77, 79, 80, 84, 102, 109, 116
Weigel, Gustave, 27
Wesley, John, 66, 92, 176, 181
Whitefield, George, 92, 176, 177

Williams, J. Paul, 5–6
Williams, Roger, 177
Wilson, Bryan R., 75
Wilson, Woodrow, 160
Wise, Isaac Mayer, 196

Yinger, J. Milton, 6, 74–75
Youth, and religion, 142–150, 227–235

Zionists, 197, 198, 199, 222